Existence, Faith and Responsibility

Contemporary Existentialism

Howard Slaatte
General Editor

Vol. 2

PETER LANG
New York • Bern • Frankfurt am Main • Paris

Samuel R. Roberts III

Existence, Faith and Responsibility

Carl Michalson's Christian Ethics

PETER LANG
New York • Bern • Frankfurt am Main • Paris

Library of Congress Cataloging-in-Publication Data

Roberts, Samuel R.
  Existence, faith, and responsibility : Carl
Michalson's Christian ethics / Samuel R. Roberts.
    p. cm. — (Contemporary existentialism ; vol. 2)
  Bibliography: p.
  1. Christian ethics—History—20th century.
  2. Michalson, Carl—Ethics. I. Title. II. Series.
BJ1231.R63   1989   241'.047632'0924—dc19   88-8208
ISBN 0-8204-0875-1   CIP
ISSN 0895-0520

CIP-Titelaufnahme der Deutschen Bibliothek

Roberts, Samuel R.:
Existence, faith and responsibility : Carl Michalson's Christian ethics / Samuel R. Roberts III. – New York; Bern; Frankfurt am Main; Paris: Lang, 1989.
  (Contemporary Existentialism; Vol. 2)
  ISBN 0-8204-0875-1

NE: GT

© Peter Lang Publishing, Inc., New York 1989

All rights reserved.
Reprint or reproduction, even partially, in all forms such as microfilm, xerography, microfiche, microcard, offset strictly prohibited.

Printed by Weihert-Druck GmbH, Darmstadt, West Germany

To Stella

Hearer and Doer of the Word

ACKNOWLEDGMENTS

Grateful acknowledgment is made to the following publishers for permission to reprint material from the books or periodicals indicated:

Abingdon Press
 for material from A Handbook of Christian Theologians edited by Martin Marty and Dean Peerman. Copyright c 1965 assigned to Abingdon Press. Used by permission.

Augsburg Fortress Press
 for material from Doing Theology in a Revolutionary Situation and Toward a Christian Political Ethics both by Jose Miguez Bonino. Copyrights c 1975 and 1983, respectively, by Fortress Press. Used by permission.

Beacon Press
 for material from Sexism and God-Talk by Rosemary Ruether. Copyright c 1983 by Rosemary Radford Ruether. Reprinted by permission of Beacon Press.

Discipleship Resources
 for material from The Witness of Radical Faith by Carl Michalson. Copyright c 1974 by Tidings. Used by permission of Discipleship Resources, 1908 Grand Ave., P.O. Box 840, Nashville, TN 37202.

William B. Eerdmans Publishing Company
 for material from A Private and Public Faith by William Stringfellow. Copyright c 1965 by William B. Eerdmans Publishing Co. Used by permission.

Graded Press
 for material from "New Testament Teaching for Modern Living" Carl Michalson, in Christian Action, Vol. 10 #40: October/December, 1955. Copyright c 1955 by Pierce and Washbaugh (The United Methodist Publishing House). Used by permission.

Harper & Row Publishers
 for material from Christ and Culture by H. Richard Niebuhr. Copyright c 1951 by Harper & Row, Publishers, Inc. Reprinted by permission of the publisher.

Katallagete
 for material from "The Good News from God in Jesus is Freedom to the Prisoners" and "Can There Be a Crusade for Christ?" by Will D. Campbell and James Holloway. Copyrights 1972 and 1973, respectively.

 for material from "Repentance and Politics I: Milestones into Millstones" by Will D. Campbell. Copyright 1966-67.

Katallagete
   for material from "Vocation as Grace" by Will D. Campbell. Copyright 1972.

   for material from "The World of the Redneck" by Will D. Campbell. Copyright 1974.

Macmillan Publishing Company
   for material from Faith for Personal Crises by Carl Michalson. Reprinted with permission of Charles Scribner's Sons, an imprint of Macmillan Publishing Company. Copyright c 1958 Southwestern University; copyright renewed 1986.

   for material from The Hinge of History by Carl Michalson. Reprinted with permission of Charles Scribner's Sons, an imprint of Macmillan Publishing Company. Copyright c 1959 Carl Michalson; copyright renewed 1987.

   for material from The Rationality of Faith by Carl Michalson. Reprinted with permission of Charles Scribner's Sons, an imprint of Macmillan Publishing Company. Copyright c 1963 The University of Virginia.

   for material from Worldly Theology by Carl Michalson. Reprinted with permission of Charles Scribner's Sons, an imprint of Macmillan Publishing Company. Copyright c 1967 by Janet M. Michalson.

   for material from The Meaning of Revelation, by H. Richard Niebuhr. Copyright c 1941 The Macmillan Company. Reprinted with permission of Macmillan Publishing Company.

Paulist Press
   for material from Up to Our Steeples in Politics, by Will D. Campbell and James Y. Holloway. Copyright c 1970 by Paulist Press, Reprinted by permission.

Trinity University Press
   for material from Character and the Christian Life: A Study in Theological Ethics, by Stanley Hauerwas. Copyright c 1975, 1985 by Trinity University Press. Reprinted by permission.

University of Chicago Press
   for material from Can Ethics Be Christian?, by James Gustafson. Copyright c 1975 by The University of Chicago Press. Permission granted for use.

Word Incorporated
   for material from An Ethics for Christians and Other Aliens in a Strange Land and Conscience and Obedience: The Politics of Romans 13 and Revelation 13 in Light of the Second

Coming, both by William Stringfellow. Copyrights 1976 and 1977, respectively by Word Publishing Company. Used by permission.

World Council of Churches Press
for material from <u>Room to be People: An Introduction of the Bible for Today's World</u> by Jose Miguez Bonino. Copyright c 1979 by World Council of Churches Press. Used by permission.

Mention should also be made and acknowledgment given to the following:

University Press of America
received a request for permission to reprint from <u>The Implications of Carl Michalson's Theological Method for Christian Education</u>, by Edward J. Wynne, edited by Henry O. Thompson (1983). Though this text is not quoted directly, its bibliographical information proved invaluable, thus the request for permission to reprint. The publisher, had "no record of the title" and failed to respond to further inquiry.

Ryerson Press
was sent a request for permission to reprint from <u>Christian Humanism and The Modern World</u>, by Lynn Harold Hough (1948). The request was returned "address unknown", and no recent address of the publisher could be found.

The United Methodist Publishing House
initially granted permission to reprint from "Carl Michalson's Contribution to Theology," by Larry Shiner, in <u>Religion in Life</u>, XXXVI, No. 2 (Spring, 1967). The United Methodist Publishing House then stated "Records for this article were destroyed several years ago so [we] cannot supply the author's address [though] the author retained all rights. . ." The author, Mr. Shiner, could not otherwise be located.

University Microfilms
received a request for permission to reprint from "The Concept of the Holy Spirit in the Thought of Carl Michalson" by Olin Marion Ivey, Ph.D. dissertation, Claremont Graduate School, Claremont, California, 1974. University Microfilms indicated that rights were retained by the author, whose whereabouts are unknown.

The Drew Gateway
received requests for permission to reprint from each of the <u>Gateway</u> articles cited herein. No response was tendered and the author's whereabouts are unknown.

Other sources though gratefully acknowledged here and correctly cited throughout the book were utilized to a limited extent (350 words or less), and permission to reprint was not deemed necessary.

TABLE OF CONTENTS

Preface	xiii
Introduction: Michalson Research	1
Chapter One: Michalson's Life and Work	17
Historical Setting	17
Systematic Principle:	40
Michalson's Nature/History Distinction and its Importance to his Understanding of Responsibility in the World	
Chapter Two: Responsibility in the Thought of Carl Michalson	53
The Prominence of Responsibility in Michalson's Thought	53
Responsibility in the Context of Michalson's Historical and Theological Development	58
Responsibility in a Soteriological Context	93
Ethical Implications of Responsibility in Michalson's Thought	105
Chapter Three: Ethics in Carl Michalson: Theory, Substance and Application	111
Ethics of Responsibility: Theory and Substance	111
Ethics of Responsibility: Application	139
Chapter Four: Ethics in Carl Michalson: Evaluation	145
Character of Michalson's Ethics	145
Adequacy of Michalson's Ethics	151
Chapter Five: Ethics in Carl Michalson: Summary (A Michalsonian Model for Theological Ethics)	163
Michalson's Understanding of Good and Evil: (The Object of Faith)	166
The Means for Bringing About the Good and Combatting Evil: (The Faith in Action Through Preaching)	169
The Good that is Realized by Responsible Faith: (The Telos of Preaching)	173
Chapter Six: The Implications of Carl Michalson's Ethics for More Recent Christian Ethics	179
Ethics of Responsibility and Liberation Theology as a Source of Ethics	180
Ethics of Responsibility and Rejection of Accomodation to the World (Evangelical Perfectionism)	204
Ethics of Responsiblity and Ethics of Character and Virtue	220

Chapter Seven: Conclusion 237
    Michalson's Concept of Responsibility:
        The Influence of H. Richard Niebuhr and
        Friedric Gogarten 237
    Michalson's Ethics: Preaching Engaging the World 241
    Michalson's Ethics: Command and Context;
        Character and Virtue 242
    Michalson's Contribution: The Possibility of
        Ethics in a New Key 243

Appendix A: Focus on a Revolution 253

Bibliography 257

PREFACE

Carl Michalson was a Minnesota-born Methodist who took his B.A. degree from John Fletcher College (1936), his B.D. and M.A. degrees from Drew Theological Seminary (1939, 1940), and his Ph.D. degree from Yale University (1945). While completing his Ph.D., Michalson returned to Drew and taught in the theological and graduate schools from the fall of 1943 until his untimely death in an airplane crash on November 8, 1965.[1] During this time, Michalson wrote six books, edited a volume entitled <u>Christianity and the Existentialists</u>, and translated Friedrich Gogarten's <u>The Reality of Faith: The Problem of Subjectivism in Theology</u>. Michalson also published a dozen articles, and wrote numerous book reviews, sermons, lectures, etc.[2] He was revered by his students, respected by his colleagues and the academic community at large, and known by both secular and faithful audiences across the United States and the world.[3] The Methodist Church (now the

---

[1] For additional biographical information, see Edward J. Wynne, Jr., <u>The Implications of Carl Michalson's Theological Method for Christian Education</u>. (Lanham, Md.: University Press of America, 1983), pp 13-35.

[2] For a complete bibliography of Michalson's writings, see Ibid., pp 329ff. (Appendix -- Part A). This bibliography is an updated and enlarged version of the one compiled by Lawrence O. Kline for the <u>Drew Gateway</u>, Vol XXXVI #3, Spring-Summer, 1966.

[3] For students' comments about Carl Michalson, see Dow Kirkpatrick, "Carl D. Michalson '39: 1915-1965," Alumni Notes, Theological School and Graduate School, <u>Drew University Magazine</u> (Winter, 1966), n.p. See also Robert T. Osborn, "Carl Michalson as Teacher," <u>Drew Gateway</u> XXXVI, No. 3 (Spring-Summer,1966): 101-108. See also Olin Marion Ivey, "The Concept of the Holy Spirit in the Thought of Carl Michalson" (Ph.D. dissertation, Claremont Graduate School, 1974). p. iv-viii.

United Methodist Church), in which Michalson was an ordained clergy person, was especially appreciative of his theologizing.[4]

As will be seen, Michalson was a scholar and teacher who sought to make the Christian faith relevant and meaningful in a secular age. His theology, though confessional in nature, performed an "apologetic" function[5] and was aimed finally at procla-

---

For colleagues' comments about Michalson, see Will Herberg, "Some Comments on the Theological Scene at Drew," Drew Gateway XXXI, No. 2 (Winter, 1961):82. See also "Minutes of the Faculty Meeting, The Theological School, Drew University, Madison, N. J., Dec. 10, 1965. (Mimeographed.)
For Carl Michalson's reputation throughout academia, see the following obituaries: Janichi Asono, The Journal of Christian Studies 12 (May, 1966):1-2; Ben Kempel, American Philosophical Association XL (October, 1967):125; Yoshio Noro, The Journal of Christian Studies 12 (May, 1966):3-6; Charles W. Stewart, The Journal of Pastoral Care XX, No. 1 (March, 1966):34-35.

[4]Methodism's appreciation of Carl Michalson, besides being expressed through numerous invitations to speak at denominational gatherings, can be seen in his being asked to write a faith question and answer column from October, 1952 to April, 1958 for Together Magazine, a denominational publication. Michalson also served as the Methodist Church's spokesman in a November 15, 1965 article for Concern magazine, entitled "The Maturity of Sonship--The Methodist Church and Alcohol."

[5]To call Carl Michalson an apologetic theologian is both dangerous and necessary. Michalson is totally opposed to apologetics where Christianity has to rationally justify itself. On the other hand, he says,
"The Christian man has the privilege of living within a church which is constantly developing 'an honest theology of cultural high standing,' to use Paul Tillich's phrase. This is no longer apologetics in the sense of establishing a bridgehead on enemy territory. It is the consolidation of gains. . . .It is a frankly bifocal enterprise which, while informed by the substance of Christianity, is patterned by the dominant issues in the culture of the time." (Carl Michalson, Worldly Theology: The Hermeneutical Focus of an Historical Faith. [New York: Charles Scribner's Sons, 1967], p. 68.

mation of the Gospel through preaching. Writes Michalson:

> A Christian is one who acknowledges that God has turned to man in Jesus and who takes upon himself the responsibility of turning to the world with that report. Hence, to be a Christian is to be involved in the responsibility of the communication of the gospel.[6]

Michalson employed Bultmann's existentialist methodology in his theology and preaching, and was indebted to Friedrich Gogarten and the post-Bultmann new hermeneutic for much of his mature thought.[7]

---

[6] Carl Michalson, The Hinge of History: An Existential Approach to the Christian Faith. (New York: Charles Scribner's Sons, 1959), p. 214. See also David J. Randolph, "Carl Michalson's Theology of Preaching," in Hermeneutics and the Worldliness of Faith: A Festschrift in Memory of Carl Michalson, eds. Charles Courtney, Olin M. Ivey, Gordon E. Michalson. Drew Gateway XLV, Nos. 1,2,3 (1974-5):68-87. See also Lawrence E. Toombs, "The Foolishness of Preaching," Drew Gateway LII, No. 1 (Fall, 1981):14-20.

[7] According to his brother, Gordon, Carl Michalson moved "from Lewis to Heim to Barth to existentialism and Kierkegaard to Husserl and phenomenology to Heidegger and hermeneutics." (Gordon Michalson, Introduction to Hermeneutics and the Worldliness of Faith, p. xiii). John Godsey, while agreeing with Gordon Michalson "chronologically speaking", writes:
"From the standpoint of his mature theological position, however, his lineage might better run from Kierkegaard (subjectivity is truth) and H. Richard Niebuhr (revelation occurs in inner history) to Bultmann (existentialist interpretation) to Gogarten (theology as history) to Fuchs (Jesus' words interpret his conduct) and Ebeling (revelation as word event)." (John Godsey, "The Maturity of Faith in Carl Michalson's Theology," Drew Gateway XLIX, No. 3 [Spring, 1979]:5).
Godsey thus chronicles his claim that Michalson decided "to adopt Bultmann's perspective." (ibid.) Olin Ivey, in seeing Michalson's thought as having "three distinct but intertwining chronological periods" (Olin Ivey, "The Concept of the Holy Spirit in the Thought of Carl Michalson" p.i) concurs with Godsey's assessment. The truth of Godsey's assertions and Ivey's schema regarding influence is evident upon examining Michalson's thought. See Chapter I, B below for a brief overview of Michalson's theology. See also John D. Godsey, "Thinking the Faith Historically: The Legacy of Carl Michalson" and Theodore Runyon, "Carl Michalson as

In addition to being an "apologetic" theologian with an existential orientation, Michalson was a dedicated churchman. The faith he sought to make relevant and meaningful was a communal faith, a faith that found life in dialogue with others and was sustained and strengthened through fellowship.[8] His seeking to address the world from a necessarily communal context made Michalson a valuable resource to his denomination and one of its foremost spokespersons.

Michalson, then, sought to proclaim the viability of the Christian faith and affirmed the church as necessary to the Christian life. This relevant faith, to which the church was central, culminated in responsibility for the world. Responsibility for the world was, in Michalson's theology, the end to which a person's faith was directed. In Worldly Theology he wrote: "The implication of faith is not preoccupation with the absolute but, in faithful relationship to the absolute, preoccupation with the relativities of the world."[9]

The salient features of Michalson's theology are his seeking to make the faith viable, his recognizing its communal nature, and his conviction that Christianity enables responsibility for the world. Herein lies Michalson's attractiveness as a theolo-

---

a Radical Theologian" Drew Gateway XXXVI, No. 3 (Spring-Summer, 1966):76-100; and Larry Shiner, "Carl Michalson's Contribution to Theology," Religion in Life XXXVI, No. 2 (Spring, 1967):80-91.

[8]See Michalson, Hinge of History, p. 237.

[9]Michalson, Worldly Theology, pp. 125-126.

gian and his contribution to Christian theology. In a day when many view the Christian faith as completely invalid, when the importance of the church as the communuity of faith is in many ways declining, and when, for many, personal piety is at odds with social responsibility, Michalson studies can and should bear fruit.

The substance of this work was presented as part of a dissertation at Drew University. To Professor Arthur B. Holmes of West Virginia Wesleyan College, who first taught me theology and was responsible for my enrollment at Drew, I am deeply indebted. I am in great debt, as well, to three members of the Drew faculty: Edward L. Long, Jr., Michael Ryan, and Kenneth Rowe, who taught me ethics, Michalson, and Methodism and served on my dissertation committee. I must also mention the great help I received from Howard Slaatte and the folk at Peter Lang Publishing, Inc. who somehow found room for my work in their series on "Contemporary Existentialism."

It is well recognized that Michalson's theology reflected and evolved out of an existential point of departure. The implications of Michalson's theology for ethics, and the possibility of existentialist ethics, generally, are not so widely seen. These associations, though not my primary concerns, are expressed here and I think are significant. I am thankful for a forum that calls attention to my, albeit underlying, concerns.

Finally, I want to thank the library staff at Drew and the congregation of St. James United Methodist Church in Elizabeth, New Jersey for assistance with and support of my graduate work. And I want to thank my wife, the Reverend Stella Millett Roberts, partner in life, love, and faith, without whom this would not have been possible. It is to Stella that the book is dedicated.

INTRODUCTION

Michalson Research

A. Michalson Study to Date

Since Carl Michalson's untimely death on November 8, 1965, there has been continued interest in his theology. Admittedly, most of this interest has been stimulated by former students and colleagues, outside of whom Michalson has not found a particularly large audience. Michalson studies have thus centered in the Carl Michalson Society and The Drew Gateway Magazine.

Michalson studies are not confined to the Drew community, however. In addition to Society publications, Gateway articles, three Michalson theses written by former students, and other Drew related articles and books, there have been two theses written at Boston University that, as far as I can tell, are independent of direct influence. Michalson has also been independently recognized as contributing to discussions in theological method, and he has been recognized as an important United Methodist theologian. Michalson's thought then, while not attracting large numbers, is recognized as important and has an established place in at least a segment of the theological community--a segment comprised of Michalson's students, colleagues, and others as well.

There were eight articles about Michalson published soon after his death. Four of these appeared in a memorial issue of

The Drew Gateway;[1] four appeared elsewhere.[2] All of these articles were influenced by close personal association with Michalson, and the shock of his death. Nonetheless, they provide helpful introductory material for this study.

In 1974, Tidings published The Witness of Radical Faith,[3] edited by Gordon E. Michalson and Olin M. Ivey, containing seven lectures/sermons delivered by Carl Michalson in the years and months just prior to his death. Ivey's introduction to the volume contains a concise summary of Michalson's theological concerns. Also, in 1974, The Drew Gateway published a Michalson Festschrift entitled, Hermeneutics and the Worldliness of Faith.[4] Part one deals with Michalson's theology per se. Part two deals with hermeneutical themes common to his theology.

---

[1] See "Carl Michalson: An Appreciation" Drew Gateway XXXVI No. 3 (Spring-Summer, 1966). John Godsey's article, "Thinking the Faith Historically: The Legacy of Carl Michalson" and Theodore Runyon's article, "Carl Michalson as a Radical Theologian" are especially helpful.

[2] See Bernhard W. Anderson, "Carl Michalson's Vision: The Power of the Interpreted Word," Christian Advocate X, No. 12 (June 16, 1966):7-8. See also Dow Kirkpatrick, "Carl D. Michalson '39", Drew University Magazine (Winter, 1966); Larry Shiner, "Carl Michalson's Contribution to Theology," Religion in Life XXXVI, No. 2 (Spring, 1967):80-91; and J. Edward Maddox, "Carl Michalson, Author, Teacher, Churchman," Methodist History VIII, No. 4 (July, 1970):30-40. Shiner's article is excellent and is especially recommended.

[3] Carl Michalson, The Witness of Radical Faith, ed. Gordon E. Michalson and Olin M. Ivey (Nashville: Tidings, 1974).

[4] "Hermeneutics and the Worldliness of Faith: A Festschrift in Memory of Carl Michalson," ed. Charles Courtney, Olin Ivey, and Gordon E. Michalson. Drew Gateway XLV, No. 1-3(1974-1975).

Several addresses to the Carl Michalson Society that were subsequently published in The Drew Gateway should also be cited. At the April 28, 1978 meeting a former colleague, John D. Godsey, delivered an address entitled, "The Maturity of Faith in Carl Michalson's Theology."[5] At the April 27, 1979 meeting, a former student, Theodore Runyon, spoke on the theme, "Carl Michalson as a Wesleyan Theologian."[6] At the May 5, 1981 meeting, a former colleague, Lawrence E. Toombs, presented "The Foolishness of Preaching."[7] The Michalson Society also sponsored, in 1982, the publication of Prayer for Today's People,[8] a collection of sermons and lectures written by Michalson on the subject "Prayer."

The following academic theses have been written about Michalson's theology. James D'Angelo, a former Drew student, wrote a 1968 Masters thesis at Princeton Theological Seminary, entitled "The Historical and Hermeneutical Focus of Theology: Carl Michalson's Contributions to the Problem of Theological Language." Ellis Blane Johnson submitted a 1969 doctoral dissertation to the Boston University Graduate School, entitled "Carl Michalson's Concept of History as a Theological Method." Richard

---

[5]John Godsey, "The Maturity of Faith in Carl Michalson's Theology," The Drew Gateway XLIX, No. 3 (Spring, 1979):1-9.

[6]Theodore Runyon, Jr., "Carl Michalson as a Wesleyan Theologian," Drew Gateway LI, No. 2 (Winter, 1980): 1-13.

[7]Lawrence E. Toombs, "The Foolishness of Preaching," Drew Gateway LII, No. 1 (Fall, 1981):14-20.

[8]Carl Michalson, Prayer for Today's People (Washington, D.C.: University Press of America, 1982).

Laurence Eslinger submitted a 1970 dissertation to the Boston University Graduate School, entitled "Historicity and Historicality: A Comparison of Carl Michalson and Oscar Cullman." Edward James Wynne, Jr. submitted a 1971 dissertation to New York University, entitled "The Implications of Carl Michalson's Theological Method for Christian Education." In 1983, The Carl Michalson Society sponsored the publication of this dissertation by University Press of America, under the same title. Olin Marion Ivey submitted a 1974 dissertation to the Claremont Graduate School, Claremont, California, entitled "The Concept of the Holy Spirit in the Thought of Carl Michalson."[9]

The articles, books, addresses, and theses cited above comprise the corpus of Michalson study thus far produced. The articles introduce Michalson's person and work, and help define his primary concerns. The theses by Eslinger and Johnson explore Michalson's nature/history distinction, his theologizing within the category of history alone, and his developing a theological method commensurate with this understanding of theology *as* history. Ivey's and Wynne's theses are similar in that they trace Michalson's developing theology from seminary days until his death, and then seek to apply it. Ivey explores Michalson's thought in search of "an adequate contemporary framework by which

---

[9] I am indebted to Edward J. Wynne, Jr., <u>The Implications of Carl Michalson's Theological Method</u>, Appendix, Part A" for the above bibliographical information.

to speak of the Holy Spirit.[10] Wynne examines the implications of Michalson's theological method for Christian Education. James de Angelo focuses on Michalson's understanding of language and hermeneutics as the key to and the major contribution of his theology of history.

In addition to the articles and theses devoted solely to Carl Michalson and cited above, Michalson is mentioned elsewhere too. Langdon Gilkey cites him as contributing to discussions about theological method[11] and Thomas Langford notes his contributions as a United Methodist theologian.[12]

The secondary literature introduces Michalson well (although it is certainly no substitute for the primary material), develops fundamental points of his theology, and demonstrates ways that Michalson's theology is important and can contribute to current theological discussion. However, while this literature is an indispensible tool to understanding Michalson, his thought and its importance, it in no way exhausts the subject matter. In fact, I will maintain here that the secondary literature to date

---

[10] Ivey, "The Concept of the Holy Spirit," p.i.

[11] See Langdon Gilkey, Reaping the Whirlwind: A Christian Interpretation of History. (New York: Seabury Press, 1981), p. 336.

[12] Thomas Langford, Practical Divinity (Nashville: Abingdon Press, 1983), pp. 220-222.

has largely neglected a crucial and significant aspect of Michalson's thought--his ethics.[13]

B. Statement of Thesis and Method

This study will examine and evaluate the importance of the concept of responsibility in the thought of Carl Michalson. It will demonstrate that responsibility is a key concept for Michalson, and will treat, characterize, and evaluate Michalson's ethics as an integral part of his theology. It will also point to ways that Michalson's ethics might contribute to contemporary studies in theological ethics. The manner in which responsibility informs Michalson's theology and ethics will be investigated and criticized, and the importance of his theology and ethics will be explored.

The methodology that will be employed to develop the study follows from the above. The concept of responsibility will serve as the focal point, and allow for an analysis, an evaluation, and a summary, of Michalson's ethics. Then, by establishing a dialogue between Michalson's ethics and important trends in recent

---

[13]Though the secondary literature about Michalson has largely neglected his ethics, John Godsey writes that this is precisely the point where "those who would carry Michalson's banner today must advance his cause. . . ." ("The Maturity of Faith," p.7) Though Godsey is skeptical about the possibilities in this regard, Theodore Runyon, in his essay "Carl Michalson as a Wesleyan Theologian," responds to Godsey's challenge by "extending the vectors of Michalson's theology to the present" and favorably comparing him with Latin American liberation theology (p.11). These articles, by raising the question about Michalson's ethics and by making a preliminary assessment of his ethical importance, serve as a point of departure for the present study.

Christian ethics, conclusions will be drawn from this study as to how Michalson's ethics might be viewed and utilized.

I do not have a model study by which this study will be developed. However, Olin Ivey's thesis, "The Concept of the Holy Spirit in the Thought of Carl Michalson," and Edward Wynne's thesis, The Implications of Carl Michalson's Theological Method for Christian Education," will provide guidance in certain areas. Ivey's analysis of Michalson's theological development as first neo-orthodox, then existentialist, then hermeneutical and phenomenological[14] will be utilized, especially when I structure the historical and theological contexts of Michalson's concept of responsibility. Since Edward Wynne's dissertation deals with implications of Michalson's thought, it should also prove helpful[15]. The Drew Gateway articles by John Godsey ("The Maturity of Faith in Carl Michalson's Theology") and Theodore Runyon (Carl Michalson as a Wesleyan Theologian") will serve as points of departure for my study, since both raise the issue of Michalson's ethical viability and contribution.

C. The Need for the Present Study

By exploring Michalson's ethics, an aspect of his thought that has received little attention, this study should prove use-

---

[14] Ivey, "The Concept of the Holy Spirit," p. i-iii.

[15] Wynne, The Implications of Michalson's Theological Method for Christian Education.

ful to Michalson students and fill a need in Michalson studies. And by detailing Michalson's integrally relating faith and works (i.e. theology and ethics), it should be useful to students of Christian ethics as well.

It is true that Carl Michalson's writings contain few explicit references to ethics.[16] Michalson's writings do, however, have a great deal of ethical import. In *The Rationality of Faith*, Michalson maintains that there is no separation of the religious and the moral:

> Traditionally, historical interpretation was made in three successive stages: understanding, exegesis and application. In contemporary hermeneutics, understanding and exegesis are merged. One does not first understand, then explain. The understanding must be self-explaining. Thereafter, what becomes of the responsibility for applying what is understood? If historical understanding is an act of decisiveness, meaning ought not be looked upon as an intellectual preface to action. Meaning is itself a kind of action; meaning is realized in action. Theologians endorse this method of interpretation when they refuse to separate theology and ethics: faith *is* what a man does that is meaningful. . . .Faith is *not* what a man does *with* the claims of the gospel. Faith is the act of being claimed by the gospel in such a way as to have one's life illuminated. In matters of faith, one does not understand, then decide. Nor does one decide, then understand. Understanding is itself decision and decision is itself the form of understanding.[17]

---

[16]The term "ethics" is indexed only twice in Michalson's published works. These citations are: *The Rationality of Faith: An Historical Critique of the Theological Reason* (New York: Charles Scribner's Sons, 1963), p. 80ff.; and *Worldly Theology*, pp. 32-34 (Reprinted from John Macquarrie, ed. *Dictionary of Christian Ethics*, s.v. "Existential Ethics" [Philadelphia: Westminster Press, 1967], pp. 124-125). Both references are discussed below. Michalson also contributed to Paul Ramsey, ed. *Faith and Ethics: The Theology of H. Richard Niebuhr* (New York: Harper and Row, 1957), "The Real Presence of the Hidden God," pp. 245-267.

[17]Michalson, *Rationality of Faith*, p. 80.

This refusal to separate theology and ethics is not to disregard ethics. Instead, insofar as ethics and theology are inseparable, ethics is a primary concern. Repeated references to responsibility in the world,[18] the church's mission in the world,[19] faith as historical maturity,[20] and Christian worldliness[21] are all ethical constructs. These references offer evidence of the importance of ethics for Michalson, and allow for an examination of his ethical thought. His citing, in Worldly Theology, the possibility for ethics in the existentialist position is a crucial reference to ethics,[22] as are references to the relationship between prayer and ethics in Prayer for Today's People.[23]

---

[18] Carl Michalson, Faith for Personal Crises (New York: Charles Scribner's Sons, 1958), p.8.

[19] Michalson, Hinge of History, pp. 235-246.

[20] Michalson, Rationality of Faith, pp.107-153.

[21] Michalson, Worldly Theology, esp. pp. 127-158.

[22] Ibid. pp. 32-34. As stated above, Michalson's thought--theological and ethical--clearly evolves out of and reflects an existential posture. An understanding of this point of departure can be gained by reference to Chapter one of Michalson's Christianity and the Existentialists, (New York: Charles Scribner's Sons, 1956). See also: George W. Davis, Existentialism and Theology, (New York: Philosophical Library, Inc., 1957) and Howard Slaatte, The Pertinence of the Paradox: A Study of the Dialectics of Reason-in-Existence, (Washington D. C.: University Press of America, 1982). The relationship of Michalson's thought to existentialism is explored below, p. 49ff, 58ff (63-65 especially) and 151ff.

[23] Michalson, Prayer for Today's People. See esp. pp. 34-35 and pp. 60-61.

By taking seriously and seeking to explicate the Christian's living responsibly in the world, Carl Michalson had a discernible ethic with implications for theological ethics today. In fact, for Michalson, the Christian faith leads, finally, to a reorientation toward the world, wherein "man come of age" in holiness and the maturity of faith, acts responsibly in the world.[24] Ethics, then, in the sense of responsible living in the world, is of crucial importance to Michalson. Here is his "ethics integral to theology," the ethics he referred to later in Worldly Theology, and Prayer for Today's People; and here, is a formulation that could prove useful to ethicists today.

Recent Christian ethics has been incredibly diverse, giving attention to liberation theology as a source of ethics,[25] the rejection of accommodation to the world,[26] and virtue and character[27] among other concerns. It is my contention that these ethical concerns, especially, can and should be impacted by Michalson's ethics of responsibility.

Theodore Runyon, in writing of "Carl Michalson as a Wesleyan Theologian" has asked,

> Would it be too bold to suggest that if the vectors which we have drawn from Michalson's existentialist period through his last developments were extended down to the

---

[24]See Michalson, Worldly Theology, pp. 114-183, 201-217.

[25]Edward LeRoy Long, Jr., A Survey of Recent Christian Ethics, (New York: Oxford University Press, 1982), pp. 156-174.

[26]Ibid. pp. 83-97.

[27]Ibid. pp. 101-111.

present they would bear surprising resemblance to what is now emerging in Latin American liberation theology?"[28]

In support of this suggestion Runyon says:

> . . . The Latin Americans have decried the dependence of North Atlantic theologians, both Protestant and Catholic, on Reformation views which equate salvation with personal faith. On the basis of Marxist analysis the Latin Americans are calling instead for an understanding of salvation which is world-transforming. Where in church history, we might ask, has such a transformationist theology come to the fore: It would be difficult to find a better historical precedent than Wesley's doctrine of sanctification [which is adopted by the later Michalson]. . .
>
> Though it may be true that on a continuum running from Luther to Marx. . .Wesley and Michalson would be only about half-way, this is no reason to consign them to pietism and existentialism respectively and assume that they have little to contribute to the current theological debate. . . .I am convinced that theologies of liberation could themselves benefit from the insights and correctives they have to offer. Indeed, this cross-fertilization ought to be high on our theological agendas during the next decade. . .[29]

Though my suspicion is that Runyon overstates the case, his point is well taken. Michalson, as was Wesley before him, is more than a (purely individualistic) pietist or existentialist (narrowly defined), and he does understand salvation as world transforming.[30] Worldly responsibility is at the forefront of his later writings. At the same time Michalson urges us to assume responsibility for the world, however, he cautions us

---

[28]Runyon, "Michalson as a Wesleyan Theologian," p. 11.

[29]Ibid. pp. 11-12.

[30]For a complete discussion and further clarification of Runyon's views, see below, p. 58ff. See especially pp. 62-65.

against turning the world into "a new object of devotion;"[31] he cautions us against worldliness and thus losing our souls. For Michalson, responsibility for the world is necessary, but possible only if our worldliness is tempered by an historical/meaningful God relationship that separates us from the world as surely as we live in it. Michalson thus provides both insight and correction to the liberation theologies of our day, such as those presented by Jose Miguez Bonino, Rosemary Ruether, and James Cone.

In much the same way that Michalson provides input to liberation theology, I think he also provides input to those ethicists, like William Stringfellow and Will D. Campbell, who "radically challenge the accommodation to principalities and powers that began when Constantine recognized the church and Augustine worked out the theory of the two cities."[32] These authors, while seeking as surely as the liberationists to transform the world, reject contextual input as a source of ethical guidance.

> Central to Stringfellow's thesis [for example] is the contention that 'biblical faith. . .possesses an essentially empirical orientation,' which means that it judges the realities of a particular and existing order rather than search for an idealized conception of a perfected society. He accuses Platonism, Marxism, and Buddhism of projecting an idealistic or mythological idea which is either extra-,

---

[31]Michalson, Worldly Theology, p. 158. See also Michalson, Worldly Theology, pp. 127-158, 171. See also Runyon, "Michalson as a Wesleyan Theologian, p. 11.

[32]Long, Survey of Recent Christian Ethics, p. 82.

pseudo-, or post-historical in locating the social enterprise.[33]

With regard to these intentional ethicists, Michalson again provides both insight and correction. Michalson's ethics of responsibility recognizes that God continues to reign.[34] And yet, Michalson's ethics of responsibility is worldly too, to the extent that it utilizes worldly expressions in its coming to be. Michalson's thought, with its emphasis on existentialism (even existential atheism) as a source for theology and ethics[35], is an exemplary synthesis of word and world. The divine command, so crucial to intentionalists, is central. At the same time, Michalson gleans from the world, or context, that which can assist in bringing his ethics of responsibility to fruition.

Finally, I would maintain that Carl Michalson's thought provides useful and necessary input to those ethicists who give attention to virtue and character.

> There is an increasing interest among Christian ethicists in the significance of the character of the moral agent and in the question as to how the kind of person one is bears upon the kind of decisions one makes. Attention to virtues, certainly not new in Christian ethics, has again become an important focus of attention.[36]

---

[33]Ibid. p. 87. See also William Stringfellow, <u>An Ethic for Christians and Other Aliens in a Strange Land</u>. (Waco: Word, 1973).

[34]Michalson, <u>Worldly Theology</u>, p. 215.

[35]Ibid. pp. 32-34.

[36]Long, <u>Survey of Recent Christian Ethics</u>, p. 101.

James Gustafson is a primary exponent of the ethics of virtue and character.

In his book *Can Ethics Be Christian?*, Gustafson asks how "the 'sort of person' one is" affects morality. Edward L. Long, Jr. succinctly summarizes Gustafson's explication and argument.

> Factors such as character type, life-style, motivation, and the quality of personhood that shape predictably consistent responses, become central to ethical inquiry. It is not enough to arrive at conceptual clarity concerning norms. We must inquire how we can come to be certain kinds of persons.
>
> . . .Gustafson is modest concerning the extent to which a Christian commitment results in a transformation of the self. . .He recognizes that is is often difficult to pinpoint the formative influences which shape people's values and outlooks, and particularly difficult to trace the extent to which religious influences are determinative in their lives. . ." It is plausible to claim, however, not only that religious communities tend to form persons with certain preferences for values, including moral values, but also that a conscious awareness of the reality of God, a living of a life of faith, can alter the values that persons have come to hold."[37]

Because his ethics of responsibility emphasizes the transformation of the individual (by God in Christ), Michalson shares the concern of the ethics of virtue and character. Carl Michalson's task is not only similar to Gustafson's; in fact, Michalson might be viewed as an ethicist of virtue and character, and as such he makes a direct contribution to theological ethics today. His ethics of responsibility is an attempt to think through the

---

[37]Ibid., pp. 101-102. See also James Gustafson, *Can Ethics Be Christian?* (Chicago: University of Chicago Press, 1975) and Stanley Hauerwas, *Character and the Christian Life: A Study in Theological Ethics*, (San Antonio: Trinity University Press, 1975) and Hauerwas, *Vision and Virtue: Essays in Christian Ethical Reflection*, (Notre Dame, Ind.: Fides, 1974).

transformation that occurs in faithful response to the Gospel, and to think through the implications of such a transformation. Therefore, Michalson's ethics of responsibiity deal precisely with how a "conscious awareness of God can alter the values that persons have come to hold."[38]

---

[38] Long, Survey of Recent Christian Ethics, p. 102.

CHAPTER ONE

Michalson's Life and Work

A. Historical Setting

1. Development During Childhood and College

Carl Donald Michalson, Jr. was born June 29, 1915 in Waverly, Minnesota. He was one of four children. Gordon Elliot and Edna preceded him, and Eva was born after him. Shortly after his birth, his family moved to Minneapolis and joined Park Avenue Methodist Episcopal Church. Until his death, on November 8, 1965, Michalson maintained his Quarterly Conference membership as a Methodist minister in his home church. Throughout his life, Michalson quoted from the King James Version of the Bible, the version he learned from the Park Avenue Church. These are testimonies to how important the Park Avenue Church was to Michalson, and indicate its influence on his life. Writing in 1966 on "Carl Michalson as Churchman", Chester Pennington stated:

> The ministry of Park Avenue Methodist Church is sharply and clearly defined. It remains a bastion of characteristically conservative Wesleyan theology, with fervently personal experience. It is precisely the sort of pietistic community which gave a whole generation--and perhaps several generations--of Methodist ministers their propulsion into the ministry.[1]

Michalson's association with the church began during Dr. George Vallentyne's thirty-eight year pastorate at Park Avenue.

---

[1] Chester Pennington, "Carl Michalson as Churchman." Drew Gateway XXXVI, 3 (Spring-Summer, 1966):112.

In fact, it was Dr. Vallentyne who challenged Michalson to enter the ministry and saw to it that he went to college.

> One day he met Dr. Vallentyne on the street--or perhaps in the drug store. Carl had just finished high school. And Dr. Vallentyne asked him what he planned to do. Carl was not sure. Dr. Vallentyne challenged him to consider the ministry. But there was no money for college--these were depression days. Dr. Vallentyne promised to see that that was cared for.
> So Carl went to John Fletcher College in University Park, Iowa[2]

John Fletcher College was ". . .a Wesleyan oriented school--an unendowed Asbury College. . ." according to Carl's older brother, Gordon Michalson. And though the faith may have been "narrowly interpreted" at Fletcher, it was "fervently expressed". An "education at Fletcher was a serious junction of piety and learning."[3]

Between his freshman and sophomore years at Fletcher, Michalson had a conversion experience that "left a maturing mark on [his] already sincere Christian life."[4] The revival at Park Avenue had begun in 1930. In the year 1931-1932 a Welsh evangelist, Dr. John Thomas, came to Minneapolis and "set the church on fire."[5] From then on Michalson was a different person.

> He was a "no nonsense" Mike now. Mike the student. Mike the recluse. He was to eschew all worldly pleasures--almost.

---

[2]Ibid. pp. 112-113.

[3]Gordon Michalson, Introduction to <u>Hermeneutics and the Worldliness of Faith</u>, p.x.

[4]Ibid. p. xi.

[5]Edna Lund, Personal letter to Olin M. Ivey, January 3, 1973. Quoted in Ivey, "The Concept of the Holy Spirit," p. 13.

He gave up girls, breaking a couple of hearts in the process. He dropped his flamboyance. . . .He was no longer Carl D. Michalson, Jr., but simply Carl Michalson--without flourish. . . .He read, he studied, he wrote copious themes. He analyzed and argued. He frequently argued for causes he did not believe in and posed as a revolutionary of some sort. He was learning, making use of every avenue at his disposal. . . .Sometimes his role would continue for days, with the result that his name would come up in small prayer groups! I will never know just how much of this was mere flexing of his dramatic muscles or a real seeking after answers.[6]

From all indications, Michalson's home and family life fostered the pietism that came to expression at Park Avenue Church and John Fletcher College. Michalson and his father were especially close, and according to Michalson, his father nurtured his faith and gave impetus to his theologizing. It was from his father that he realized the importance of a relationship with God, and it was in his relationship with his father that he came to understand Christian sonship and maturity.

When my father was dying, how remorseful I felt that I had never candidly expressed to him my gratitude for his magnificence as a parent. So under those rather difficult circumstances, I expressed it in just one sentence so he could understand it. I said, "Dad, the thing I have always appreciated about you is, you never came between your children and God." This is what, I think, I meant when I said that. Every time I had a serious issue in my life I would take it to my father. But he would persistently refuse to tell me what to do. Instead, he would simply say, "Well, Carl, have you prayed about it."[7]

---

[6]James P. Davies, Personal letter to Olin M. Ivey, September 4, 1973. Quoted in Ivey, "The Concept of the Holy Spirit," p. 13.

[7]Carl Michalson, "What Christian Faith Means." <u>The Witness of Radical Faith</u>. Quoted in Ivey, "The Concept of the Holy Spirit," p. 15.

Music was an important part of Michalson's family life, and it too served to express his faith. While a student at Drew, Michalson was a member of the Drew Quartet. He also played the recorder. When he died he was working on a cantata with his sister, Edna, and "had great plans for it as a background for his lectures and seminars when he visited colleges and seminaries."[8]

Carl Michalson then, was born and raised in a devout Wesleyan atmosphere. His home life, church life, and college life enabled and supported a pietistic faith that was never completely abandoned. He tried, throughout his life, to make that evangelical faith "relevant, vital, sophisticated, and intellectually honest for his time."[9]

2. Sources of Influence During Seminary and Graduate School

By all accounts, and as will be seen, there were four dominant figures in Michalson's seminary and graduate school days. Edwin Lewis and Lynn Harold Hough of Drew, and H. Richard Niebuhr and Robert Calhoun of Yale "shaped the body of his thought as it

---

[8] Edna Lund, Personal letter to Olin M. Ivey. Quoted in Ivey, "The Concept of the Holy Spirit," p. 17.

[9] Ivey, "The Concept of the Holy Spirit," p. 19. Especially interesting is Ivey's linking Michalson's pietism to existentialism. Existentialism is said to retain pietism's vitality while being intellectually honest.

grew. . . ."[10] The influence of Lewis, Hough and Niebuhr is immediately apparent in Michalson's theology. Calhoun's influence is less tangible.

a. Lynn Harold Hough

Lynn Harold Hough graduated from Drew Theological Seminary in 1905. During the teens and twenties he became internationally known and recognized as a formidable preacher, occupied several of North America's more prestigious pulpits (most notably Central Methodist Episcopal, Detroit[11] and American Presbyterian, Montreal), and was renowned as a lecturer both here and abroad. In 1930, Hough joined Drew's Theological School faculty, and served as Dean of the Theological School from 1934 to 1947.[12] During his tenure at Drew, Hough's tremendous intellect was directed not only to preaching[13] and the study of homiletics, but also to

---

[10] John Godsey, "Thinking the Faith Historically: The Legacy of Carl Michalson," Drew Gateway XXXVI, #3 (Spring-Summer, 1966):78-79. See also Ivey, "The Concept of the Holy Spirit," pp. 20ff; and Wynne, The Implications of Carl Michalson's Theological Method for Christian Education, pp. 14ff.

[11] See Reinhold Niebuhr, "Lynn Harold Hough in Detroit," Drew Gateway XVIII, #3 (Spring, 1947):37.

[12] Lynn Harold Hough, "Then and Now" Drew Gateway XXVIII, #1 (Autumn, 1957):5-10.

[13] Arlo Brown, in "Lynn Harold Hough--Student and Dean" (Drew Gateway XVIII, #3 [Spring, 1947]:33) writes that upon returning to Drew, Hough was Special Preacher for the Madison Methodist Church, preaching three Sundays out of every month during the school year. This assignment lasted for four years, until he became dean and began preaching away from campus on behalf of the seminary.

theological studies, literary studies, and biblical studies as well.[14]

In 1925, Hough delivered the Fernley Lectures at Lincoln, England on *Evangelical Humanism*. Thereafter, this theme became the center of his thought and the focus of his academic endeavors. In 1941, while Michalson was studying at Drew, Hough published *The Christian Criticism of Life*, generally recognized as his principle work on evangelical humanism. In 1945, when Michalson returned to Drew to teach, Hough published *The Meaning of Human Experience*, an extension of his argument in *The Christian Criticism of Life*. According to Hough,

> The two books from my pen, *The Christian Criticism of Life* and *The Meaning of Human Experience* (both religious book club selections), gave ample expression to the whole point of view.[15]

In the fall of 1947, immediately following his retirement from Drew, Hough delivered the Chancellor's Lectures at Queens University, Kingston, Ontario. These lectures were published as *Christian Humanism and the Modern World* and (again, according to Hough) "gave clear and brief expression"[16] to his position.

Hough's evangelical humanism is a highly structured synthesis of humanistic thought and Christian Theology (a selective

---

[14]Ibid. p. 34. Brown notes that Hough "has won distinction in all the fields indicated and more."

[15]Hough, "Then and Now" p.6.

[16]Ibid.

eclecticism[17]), that seeks to affirm the potentiality in humankind, while maintaining humanity's need for God. Hough denies that humanity is "foredoomed by [it's] very essential quality to a course of disintegrating and chaotic evil"[18] He argues instead, for humanity's "addressability, relative freedom and inherent nobility," wherein "the movement from the human to the divine becomes natural and inevitable." This position, Hough says, stands over against "the unethical pessimism of. . .psychopathic theology" (Karl Barth) and seeks finally to allow for humanity's living a responsible moral life in the sight of God.

> It is not that man can become God. It is that by the very necessities of his nature he cannot get along without God. . . .
> . . .If man cannot get along without God, in the very nature of the case he cannot produce the divine revelation or the divine grace. But he can recognize God's voice when it speaks. And he can recognize the incarnation. So the human cry and the divine response meet. So in the profoundest possible way man's very nature prepares him for the Incarnation.[19]

Hough's basic premise is that "the Good Story is possible because there is something in man which calls for good."[20] For Hough, the Gospel exists to be preached. It is preached to elicit a response. And a response (ethical and otherwise) is possible because humanity is redeemable.

---

[17]Ivey, "The Concept of the Holy Spirit" p. 408.

[18]Lynn Harold Hough. *Christian Humanism and the Modern World*. (Toronto: Ryerson Press, 1948), p. 3.

[19]Ibid. pp. 6-7, 9, 8, 9.

[20]Ibid. p. 9.

Hough does not deny the reality of human sinfulness. But in his seeing a structural soundness in human nature, that, coupled with the incarnation, can overcome "man's terrible betrayal," he denies that sin is essential to human nature. Writes Hough,

> You must judge the essential qualities of human nature, not by the lowest depths to which man has sunk, but by the bright and shining achievement of Jesus within human life. So all unholy pessimisms about man are struck lifeless. So all high hopes are given security. You can only judge human nature aright when you consider what Jesus Christ has made of it.[21]

The incarnation, for Hough, represents what Jesus Christ has made of human nature and recalls humanity to its "essential dignity."[22]

> And, like the glory of a sunrise in the Alps comes that great and good moment when a man hears God in Jesus Christ recalling him to that true manhood which he has betrayed and repudiated. The hour when he returns to God is the hour when he returns to his true self.
> That this understanding of man's true dignity, as revealed in the Incarnation, is sorely needed in our age of cynicism and disillusionment and frustration and treachery, it ought not to be hard to see. Man has sunk very low. But he does not belong in the depths to which he has sunk. This is not his true life. From within humanity, God in Christ calls to men to dare to be human in the precise sense of making humanity what God meant it to be.
> The Incarnation is not only a great revelation of God. It is a great revelation of man. It reveals the true genius of human nature. It reveals the true goal of human nature. It reveals a dignity which shines with a strange light of promise even in this bitter and cruel world.
> Thus Christian humanism, sealed and authenticated by the Incarnation, produces a rich and glowing sense of the human inheritance even in this world.[23]

---

[21]Ibid. p. 11.

[22]Ibid.

[23]Ibid. pp. 11-12.

Given this understanding of humanity's essential dignity and the incarnation's being an affirmation of same, it is easy to see how Hough can say,

> . . .The study of man in all the good qualities of his mind and life prepares one to be ready for the Incarnation. . . . In this sense the study of man is the first feature of the study of theology. The study of the man made for God prepares us for the study of the God who became man.[24]

It is also easy to see how Hough can say that Christian humanism "sealed and authenticated by the Incarnation, produces a rich and glowing sense of the human inheritance even in this world."[25]

Lynn Harold Hough's influence on Michalson was more general than that of Lewis and Niebuhr, but tremendous in its impact. Godsey writes that "Hough taught him a love for literature and exposed him to the great treasures of the Christian humanist tradition."[26] But it is Ivey who characterizes Hough's impact (on Michalson and others) most clearly.

> In addition to the substance that flowed influentially from Hough to Carl Michalson, there seems to have been a structural one as well. Sub-human, human, Divine; Nontheistic humanism, Theistic humanism, Christian humanism, Evangelical humanism. This careful distinction of levels of existence and planes of philosophical structure can be seen in Michalson's basic dichotomy of nature and history and in his four-dimensional structure of history: existential history, world history, biblical history, and eschatological history. Throughout Hough's works flowing references are made to a vast arry of literature. His literary style, while pedantic at times, becomes eloquent and poetic at many places. Both this love and effective employment of literature and the flair for a vibrant literary mode of communication were held in common between the two men.

---

[24]Ibid. p. 10.

[25]Ibid. p. 12.

[26]Godsey, "The Legacy of Carl Michalson," p. 78.

>. . .Finally, the centrality of Jesus runs throughout the theological career of Michalson. While the roots of this have. . .been traced back to his youth, Hough surely reinforces this major concern by his Christocentric thought.[27]

b. Edwin Lewis

Edwin Lewis taught at Drew for thirty-five years (1916-1951), and during that time came to be recognized as "perhaps the most significant of the systematic theologians of Methodism."[28] Lewis is credited with being "one of the first to introduce the 'neo-orthodox' revolution into [America] through his Christian Manifesto published in 1934."[29] A Philosophy of the Christian Revelation (1940) and The Creator and the Adversary (1948) are recognized (by Carl Michalson in "The Edwin Lewis Myth"[30] as his greatest and next greatest books.

Lewis' work is generally thought to encompass three fairly distinct phases.[31] His earliest thought, set forth in his first

---

[27] Ivey, "Concept of the Holy Spirit," pp. 48-49.

[28] Charley D. Hardwick, "Edwin Lewis: Introductory and Critical Remarks," Drew Gateway XXXIII (Winter, 1963):91.

[29] Ibid. See also Carl Michalson, "The Edwin Lewis Myth," Drew Gateway XXX,2 (Winter, 1960):104. Also published under the same title in The Christian Century, LXVII, 8 (February 24, 1960).

[30] Carl Michalson, "The Edwin Lewis Myth," p. 106.

[31] See Hardwick, "Edwin Lewis," p. 91. See also Marvin Green, "Contemporary Theories of Evil. An Ethical View: Reinhold Niebuhr; A Philosophical View: E. S. Brightman; A Theological View: Edwin Lewis," (Ph.D. dissertation, Drew University, 1945). See also Stephen Arnett Seamands, "The Christology of Edwin Lewis: A Study in Transition," (Ph.D. dissertation, Drew University, 1983), pp. 77ff, 191ff. Carl Michalson, in "The Edwin Lewis Myth," cautions that this development in Lewis'

major work, Jesus Christ and the Human Quest (1924), reflects a liberal stance. Lewis' later writings, from the publication of A Christian Manifesto, represent a sharp departure from the liberalism of Jesus Christ and the Human Quest.

> The central theme of all Lewis' remaining thought is to expound Christianity in terms of its own integrity as stated in the New Testament without any accommodation to the supposed difficulties of belief inherent in the modern outlook.[32]

The final development in Lewis' theology, is represented by his book The Creator and the Adversary, where he put forth a radical reinterpretation of the problem of evil.

Just as there is general agreement with regard to the development of Lewis' thought, so too certain books and articles are commonly recognized and are lifted up as representative of his work. Jesus Christ and the Human Quest was an expansion of a previously published article entitled "The Problem of the Person of Christ".

> In this book he shows himself as a participant in the American form of the last phase of liberalism. In accordance with this liberal strain, his purpose is "to preserve Christianity's evangelical emphases on a philosophical foundation arrived at on the basis of presuppositions having no particular reference to Christianity itself." As with so much modern theology, the presupposition is that if Christianity is to be saved from irrelevance, then the advances in science and culture demand some kind of adjustment of traditional, orthodox Christian dogma to the world view of modern man. The most obvious way of achieving this adjustment is to presuppose a philosophical position in terms of which Christian affirmations are interpreted or restated. This Lewis does in this book with the typical effect of this kind

---

thought is not a conversion. (See pp. 103-104.)

[32]Hardwick, "Edwin Lewis," p. 93.

of thought that "Christ is glorified as the highest manifestation of God in human history."[33]

Lewis' second period/stage was marked by the 1933 article "The Fatal Apostasy of the Modern Church" and, of course, by *The Christian Manifesto* (which, again, was an expansion of the prior article[34]). While recognizing that "liberalism . . . rendered the church an important service", Lewis maintains that "we lost sight of the fact that the church is the creation of 'the divine Christ,' or at least of faith in Christ as divine."[35]

Commenting on how his mind had changed in a *Christian Century* article entitled "From Philosophy to Revelation", Lewis quotes this extract from "The Fatal Apostasy of the Modern Church" as typical of his "break with the futilities of Modernism".[36]

> What then is the object of Christian faith? Not a man who once lived and died, but a contemporary reality, a God whose awful holiness is 'covered' by one who is both our representative and his, so that it is 'our flesh that we see in the godhead,' that 'flesh' which was historically Jesus of Nazareth, but is eternally the divine Christ whose disclosure and apprehension Jesus lived and died to make possible.

Says Lewis,

> Its main difference from *Jesus Christ and the Human Quest* is that whereas the former book was an attempt to graft the gospel on a philosophy, a procedure which called for the gospel to be mutilated at many crucial points, the latter was an attempt to take the gospel "as is," to compound its

---

[33] Ibid. p. 92.

[34] Edwin Lewis, "From Philosophy to Revelation," *The Christian Century*, LVI, 24 (June 14, 1939):764.

[35] Edwin Lewis, "The Fatal Apostasy of the Modern Church," *Religion in Life* (Autumn, 1933):483.

[36] Edwin Lewis, "From Philosophy to Revelation," p. 764.

29

amazing and overwhelming content, especially as concerns the
personal cost to God of redeeming from the blight of sin the
world which of his own sovereign will he had created, this
gospel being primarily a faith to be accepted or rejected,
but a faith which proves itself by its works.[37]

Having seen Lewis the liberal and having witnessed how his mind changed to "neo-orthodoxy," consideration now needs to be given to that phase of his thought represented by <u>The Creator and the Adversary</u>, where he put forth a radical reinterpretation of evil.

> In <u>The Creator and the Adversary</u> Lewis deals with the
> problem of evil. He notes that . . . orthodox Christian
> views of God have led almost without exception to an onto-
> logical monism. Some form of monism has been felt to be
> necessary in order to preserve the Christian understanding
> of the utter and absolute sovereignty of God. . . It has,
> thus, been felt utterly necessary to conceive of God as the
> absolute ontological ground of all reality. . . .This con-
> ception, of course, immediately gives rise to the question
> of the metaphysical status of evil, and the classical answer
> has been to regard evil as without ontological status at all
> but rather as the negation of being which because it is
> derived from Pure Being must in itself be good. . . .
> To this tradition, which is almost totally inclusive of
> Christian theology. . . Lewis simply raises the question of
> why the theologian should be so anxious to preserve a mo-
> nism. . .especially if both expreience <u>and revelation</u> con-
> strain him to posit something else. . . .He thinks it ob-
> vious that everyday experience constrains us to see evil as
> some kind of positive force in reality. In accordance with
> this. . .he argues that the only way to account for this
> evil metaphysically is in terms of a metaphysical dualism in
> which evil is posited as having irreducible ontological
> status alongside the divine. And he argues that far from
> contradicting revelation, only a dualism can adequately
> account for the total Christian revelation as it appears in
> the Scriptures.[38]

---

[37]Ibid.

[38]Hardwick, "Edwin Lewis," pp. 98-99.

That Lewis would publish a book of such a philosophical and metaphysical nature, after supposedly breaking with these concerns illustrates something fundamental to his theology, and something crucial to his influence on Carl Michalson as well. Lewis' thought was not simply transformed by Barthianism. In fact, and as Hardwick notes:

> Lewis departed from liberalism far less than might be thought and. . . .the defining characteristic of his thought continues to be argued in the context of a basic sympathy with the themes of liberalism.[39]

To be sure, after "The Fatal Apostasy of the Modern Church" and *The Christian Manifesto* his thought is centered in "the strange new world of the Bible"[40] but

> . . .his theological reflections that emanate from this center continue to carry the basic concerns of liberalism although these concerns are necessarily radicalized. . . . He continues to carry on an intimate and rational dialogue with modern humanism in its naturalistic form. . . .Lewis argues that even though God speaks to man in an absolutely original manner, that he *does* speak to man must mean that he has created man as a creature who in some sense continues to have a power to hear. . . .Lewis will have a much higher opinion of reason, philosophy, metaphysics, and the humanist dilemma than one will ever find in Barth. . .[and maintains that] while God may be Wholly Other, . . .He is not therefore Wholly Different. . . .Revelation can be made rational [even though] this does not mean that revelation can be *rationalized*.[41]

In short, as Michalson later points out,

> Lewis, theological development was not a series of zig-zag movements but a dialectical pattern in which philosophical structure and Biblical faith are never really separate. The philosophy of *Jesus Christ and the Human Quest* and the

---

[39]Ibid. p. 95.

[40]Edwin Lewis, quoted by Hardwick, "Edwin Lewis," p. 95.

[41]Hardwick, "Edwin Lewis," p. 96.

Bibliocentrism of <u>A Christian Manifesto</u> were transcended in <u>A Philosophy of the Christian Revelation</u>, but transcended in the sense he learned from the British Hegelians: not repudiated, but enfolded at a higher level, a level which changes previous levels without losing them.[42]

One cannot doubt that Edwin Lewis had a tremendous influence on Carl Michalson. The deep affection which Michalson had for Lewis, and Lewis' lasting influence on Michalson is evident in Michalson's writing about "The Edwin Lewis Myth". Michalson calls Lewis "the rarest spirit most of us eill ever know" and in an oft quoted passage, discloses his (Michalson's) "secret compact to keep pace with him."[43]

John Godsey credits Lewis with having introduced Michalson to the Neo-Orthodox theology of Barth and Brunner, and having impressed upon him the centrality of revelation.[44] This is certainly true, but more needs to be said regarding Lewis' influence. Lewis was, in fact, responsible for Michalson's basic orientation. (This is indirectly substantiated by Michalson himself, in "The Edwin Lewis Myth." Here Lewis' thought is presented as a model that, <u>clearly</u>, reflects the overall schema of Michalson's life and work.) Edwin Lewis bequeathed to Michalson a theological orientation that recognized the dialectical relationship of philosophy to revelation. From his encounter

---

[42]Carl Michalson, "The Edwin Lewis Myth," p. 105.

[43]Ibid. p. 103.

[44]John Godsey, "The Legacy of Carl Michalson," p. 78.

with Lewis until the time of his death, Carl Michalson sought to understand and treat this dialectic.

Michalson's recognition of the dialectical relationship of philosophy and revelation is crucial to understanding his entire life's work. His work with H. Richard Niebuhr and Carl Heim's apologetics focused on this dialectic. His study of Kierkegaard, Bultmann, and the New Hermeneutic, and his acceptance of the truth of subjectivity also reflects his concern for the dialectic of reason and faith. Finally, his "thinking subjectively" culminated in worldly theology and more importantly, in worldly responsibility. In these formulations the dialectical relationship of reason and faith is accounted for and expresses itself concretely as worldly faith. All of this effort represents the fruit of Michalson's laboring in Edwin Lewis' field.[45]

---

[45] Michalson's concern for the dialectical relationship of reason to faith and his flirtation with apologetics (see footnote #5, p.ii) represents his inheriting a Drew concern that can be traced through Lewis back to Olin Curtis. "In his systematic theology, Curtis breaks the traditional order of treatment and begins not with the doctrine of God but the doctrine of humanity." (Stephen Seamands, "The Christology of Edwin Lewis," p. 63). This underlying apologetic concern is reflected in Lewis' Christology (see Seamands, p. 62ff) and by Lewis' affinities with Emil Brunner, as opposed to Karl Barth. Hough, of course, saw "general revelation" as an even greater factor in the God/person relationship.

Though I say it with reservation, and even timidity, it occurs to me that this preoccupation with the problem of faith and reason, and the general symmetry of Curtis', Lewis' and Michalson's solutions to it, reflect Drew's Methodist heritage and a concern for that heritage. Later, this latent Methodism comes to the fore in Michalson's reappropriation of Wesley's doctrine of perfection and his thus tackling the problem of faith and works in a similar Methodist fashion.

c. H. Richard Niebuhr

In his dissertation entitled "The Concept of the Holy Spirit in the Thought of Carl Michalson," Olin Ivey writes: "No academic mentor had more influence upon Carl Michalson than did H. Richard Niebuhr. The depth of such influence becomes most noticeable when the theological concerns and formulations of the two men are compared."[46] Ivey, I believe, is correct in this assessment. Given the theological orientation bequeathed by Hough and especially Lewis, Michalson's interests and Niebuhr's concerns were an ideal match.

H. Richard Niebuhr completed his Yale doctoral dissertation (entitled "Ernest Troeltsch's Philosophy of Religion") in 1924. After serving as President of Elmhurst College and as a teacher at Eden Theological Seminary (both schools from which he had graduated), he returned to Yale in 1931 and served on the faculty there until shortly before his death in 1962. Niebuhr was one of Michalson's advisors at Yale during the years 1940-43, when Michalson was working on his Ph.D.[47]

From Troeltsch, Niebuhr learned "to accept and to profit by the acceptance of the relativity not only of historical objects

---

[46]Ivey, "The Concept of the Holy Spirit," p. 49.

[47]See Kenneth Cauthen, "An Introduction to the Theology of H. Richard Niebuhr," *Canadian Journal of Theology* X, 1 (1964). See also Olin Ivey, "The Concept of the Holy Spirit," p. 49.

but, more, of the historical subject, the observer and interpreter.[48]" He goes on to say:

> I try to understand this historical relativism in the light of theological and theo-centric relativism. I believe that it is an aberration of faith as well as of reason to absolutize the finite but that all this relative history of finite men and movements is under the governance of the absolute God.[49]

Niebuhr's theology then, is first an attempt to reconcile the relativity of history and the absoluteness of God. Niebuhr sought to develop a theology of historical relativity.

In *The Meaning of Revelation* Niebuhr writes that:

> There does not seem then to be any apparent possibility of escape from the dilemma of historical relativism for any type of theology. The historical point of view of the observer must be taken into consideration in every case since no observer can get out of history into a realm beyond time-space; if reason is to operate at all it must be content to work as an historical reason.[50]

Elsewhere he chronicles this historical relativity. In *The Social Sources of Denominationalism*, social forces are seen as relativizing the existence of the institutional church. and in *The Kingdom of God in America*, Christianity's absolute message is seen as coming to expression in relative ways in the history of the world. Many factors, then, "relativize" the believer's faith conclusions. The believer does not stand in immediate relation-

---

[48] H. Richard Niebuhr, *Christ and Culture* (New York: Harper and Brothers, 1951) p. x. Also quoted in Ivey, "The Concept of the Holy Spirit," p. 50.

[49] Niebuhr, *Christ and Culture*, p. x.

[50] H. Richard Niebuhr, *The Meaning of Revelation* (New York: The Macmillan Company, 1941; Paperback edition, 1960), p. 12.

ship to the absolute; instead, the believer's faith conclusions are affected by historical position, by societal duties and station, etc.

> The conclusions at which we arrive individually in seeking to be Christians in our culture are relative in at least four ways. They depend on the partial, incomplete, fragmentary knowledge of the individual; they are relative to the measure of his faith and his unbelief; they are related to the historical position he occupies and to the duties of his station in society; they are concerned with the relative values of things.[51]

Over against this historical relativity stands the absoluteness of God, and Niebuhr sees the two in relationship.

> The recognition and acknowledgment of our relativity, however, does not mean that we are without an absolute. In the presence of their relativities men seem to have three possibilities: they can become nihilists and consistent skeptics who affirm that nothing can be relied upon; or they can flee to the authority of some relative position, affirming that a church, or a philosophy, or a value, like that of life for the self, is absolute; or they can accept their relativities with faith in the infinite Absolute to whom all their relative views, values and duties are subject. In the last case they can make their confessions and decisions both with confidence and with the humility which accepts completion and correction and even conflict from and with others who stand in the same relation to the Absolute. They will then in their fragmentary knowledge be able to state with conviction what they have seen and heard, the truth for them, but they will not contend that it is the whole truth and nothing but the truth, and they will not become dogmatists unwilling to seek out what other men have seen and heard of that same object they have fragmentarily known.[52]

Niebuhr calls his attempting to bring historical relativity and the absoluteness of God into relationship a "social existentialism".

---

[51]Niebuhr, <u>Christ and Culture</u>, p. 234.

[52]Ibid. p. 238. See also Niebuhr, <u>The Meaning of Revelation</u>, p. 63.

> In...faith we seek to make decisions in our existential present, knowing that the measure of faith is so meager that we are always combining denials with our affirmations of it. Yet in faith in the faith-fulness of God we count on being corrected, forgiven, complemented, by the company of the faithful and by many others to whom He is faithful though they reject Him.
> To make our decisions in faith is to make them in view of the fact...that there is a church of faith in which we do our...work and on which we count. It is to make them in view of the fact that Christ is risen from the dead, and is...the redeemer of the world. It is to make them in view of the fact that the world of culture...exists within the world of grace--God's Kingdom.[53]

George Thomas, in reviewing Niebuhr's *Meaning of Revelation* has summarized his position as follows:

> His acceptance of the truth of "historical relativism"...[led] Niebuhr to a "confessional" rather than an "apologetic"...theology....Christian theology should simply tell "the story of our life" as Christians....This historical relativism does not mean that we must accept subjectivism and skepticism. The fact that what we see is conditioned by our historical situation does not mean that what we see is unreal but that it can be seen only from our situation or a similar one. We must, therefore, develop a new, historically oriented "critical idealism" which will discriminate the essential from the secondary elements of Christian faith, on the realistic assumption that at least the former reveal reality.[54]

In *The Meaning of Revelation*, Niebuhr seeks to set forth, from an historically relative confessional point of view, the "story" of God's revelation which is the starting point for his theology. He insists

> ...that theology must start with the "story" of God's revelation in history rather than with nature, religious experience in general, or even the scriptures. Unless interpreted by the historical revelation, all these speak

---

[53] Niebuhr, *Christ and Culture*, pp. 255-256.

[54] George F. Thomas, critical review of *The Meaning of Revelation*, by H. Richard Niebuhr, in *The Journal of Religion* 21 (Oct., 1941):455.

with different voices in different contexts and to different men.[55]

Niebuhr looks to history then,--and to inner history as opposed to outer history--for the story of God's revelation.

> The differences between the outer history of things and the inner history of selves . . . need to be be analyzed. . . .The data of external history are all impersonal; . . .Internal history, on the other hand, is not a story of things in juxtaposition or succession; it is personal in character. . . .In external history we deal with objects; in internal history our concern is with subjects. . . .
>
> The inspiration of Christianity has been derived. . . not from history as seen by a spectator; the constant reference is to subjective events, that is to events in the lives of subjects. . . .[But] subjectivity here is not equivalent to isolation, non-verifiability and ineffability; our history can be communicated and persons can refresh as well as criticize each other's memories; . . .on the basis of a common past they can think together about the common future.
> Such history, to be sure, can only be confessed by the community, and in this sense it is esoteric. . . .The history of the inner life can only be confessed by selves who speak of what happened to them in the community of other selves.[56]

Niebuhr's theology seeks to bring humanity's historical relativity into relationship with the absoluteness of God. Revelation, which establishes this relationship and provides its content, is understood as inner history, rather than outer history. (Michalson states this dichotomy in terms of historical meaningfulness [history] and past facticity [nature]). Although Niebuhr's schema has a definite rationality, revelation is not verified by reason, but by its being a communal experience. Witnessing to revelation occurs on this basis and takes the form

---

[55]Ibid. p. 457.

[56]Niebuhr, The Meaning of Revelation, pp. 47, 53.

of sharing rather than dogmatizing, of confessing rather than apologizing. Finally, acceptance of revelation by others is on these terms. Niebuhr has thus attempted to give content to his earlier concept of "social existentialism", and in doing so has developed a theological method that seeks to do justice to humanity's historical relativity and the absoluteness of God.

As indicated above, H. Richard Niebuhr's influence on Michalson was considerable. Godsey writes that Niebuhr "intensified his awareness of the existential meaning of revelation and provided him with the important distinction between inner and outer history."[57] Niebuhr's significance though, is seen most clearly when one compares his and Michalson's theologies. Niebuhr's theological task--that of finding an adequate theological method to deal with historical relativity and the Christian faith--was similar to, almost to the point of being identified with, Michalson's concern (from Lewis) to bring reason and faith into relationship. From Niebuhr, Michalson learned to characterize the two arenas as historical relativity and the absoluteness of God, and thus give his concern content and form. In the distinction between inner and outer history, Niebuhr offered an understanding of history that later allowed Michalson to theologize from the standpoint of "history alone," the place where Michalson saw reason and faith coming together.

> . . .No wild imagination will be needed to see how directly dependent Michalson was on the thought of his former professor. Some of his most basic theological themes, and

---

[57]Godsey, "The Legacy of Carl Michalson," p. 78.

distinctions, as well as some of the key hermeneutical insights find direct parallels in the thought of H. Richard Niebuhr.[58]

d. Robert L. Calhoun

As stated at the outset of this section (see p. 18), the influence of Hough, Lewis, and Niebuhr upon Michalson is immediately apparent. Yale's historian of Christian thought, Robert Calhoun, was also extremely influential.

> Calhoun brought him into contact with the whole sweep of the history of Christian doctrine and of western philosophy. Furthermore, Calhoun inspired him to attempt the art of lecturing without notes. On the occasion of Calhoun's retirement from Yale in 1965, Michalson expressed his appreciation to his revered teacher in these poignant words:
>
>> When I first heard you lecture, I told myself I would not be satisfied until I could teach like that. Twenty-four years have elapsed and I am still unsatisfied. However, I am not distraught, because I take pleasure in simply having known one such teacher.[59]

Though Calhoun shaped Michalson's thought less tangibly than Hough, Lewis, or Niebuhr, his influence should not be minimized. Calhoun taught Michalson to value the history of Christian doctrine in general, and broadened his knowledge of "Catholic orthodoxy" in particular.[60] The evangelical Methodism that nurtured Michalson has always tended to ignore the history of doctrine from the death of the last apostle to the Wesleyan revival,

---

[58] Ivey, "The Concept of the Holy Spirit," p. 75.

[59] Godsey, "The Legacy of Carl Michalson," pp. 78-79.

[60] See Hans Frie, "In Memory of Robert L. Calhoun," *Reflection* 82,1 (November, 1984):8-9, for an overview of Calhoun's thought and an indication of his importance to his students.

save for some reference to the Protestant Reformation. By introducing Michalson to this neglected segment of Christian history, Calhoun helped him appreciate the place of tradition, alongside scripture, experience and reason, in his Wesleyan heritage. Michalson's considerable teaching ability, which some consider his greatest gift,[61] was also inspired by and derived from Robert L. Calhoun. And Calhoun, with Niebuhr and Julian Hart, sat on Michalson's doctoral committee.

B. Systematic Principle: Michalson's Nature/History Distinction and its Importance to his Understanding of Responsibility in the World

Like his teacher, H. Richard Niebuhr, Carl Michalson's first theological concern was with theological prolegomena, i.e., theological method.[62] Michalson's theological method, which was quite dependent upon Niebuhr, contains a systematic principle that gives coherence to his thought and provides a framework for his understanding of responsibility in the world. This theological method is set forth succinctly in The Hinge of History, and dealt with again in The Rationality of Faith, and Worldly Theology. (Because these books represent a progression in Michalson's theological method, they will be dealt with sequentially.)

---

[61] See Robert T. Osborn, "Carl Michalson as Teacher," The Drew Gateway XXXVI, 3 (Spring-Summer, 1966):101-108.

[62] See Michalson, Hinge of History, p. 9. See also John Godsey, "The Maturity of Faith in Carl Michalson's Theology," The Drew Gateway 49,3 (Spring, 1979):1-9.

In *The Hinge of History*, Carl Michalson seeks to employ historical method and the category of history as a means for doing theology. Not philosophy, and not the natural sciences, but "historical method [is the] instrument of theological understanding."[63] Michalson calls his theology one of correlation (in so doing he admits to being open to the Barthian criticism) and thus makes history "the foundation for the relation between divine and human concerns."[64]

After describing four kinds of history, *The Hinge of History* is divided into two parts. In part I, Michalson speaks of "existential history as the exposition of meaninglessness in world history" and then in part II "develops eschatological history as the appearance of ultimate meaning through Biblical history."[65]

Attempting to set forth the historical structure of the divine-human encounter with which Christianity is concerned, Michalson states: "The first element in the spectrum is world history,"[66] that which happens and then is past. World history (history here being "an occurrence" and "a way of grasping that occurrence")[67] is both an object to be known, and also knowledge of the object. As such, it is both "outer" and "inner", i.e., it

---

[63] Carl Michalson, *The Hinge of History*, p. 8.
[64] Ibid., p. 9.
[65] Ibid., p. 10.
[66] Ibid., p. 24.
[67] Ibid. See p. 26.

is both <u>Historie</u> (this to the spectator), and <u>Geschichte</u> (this to the participant).

To say that history (as object and as knowledge of the object) is both outer event and inner event, is an important statement, for Michalson here alters the Cartesian subject/object split. Though he would discard outer history <u>as meaningful</u>,[68] he will not give up objectivity.

> History as inner event is to be distinguished from both subjectivism and objectivism in history. It is not an event created by a subject, a knower. Nor is it an event defined by an object without reference to a subject. The former would be too inventive to correspond to the realities of history. The latter would be too detached to admit of history as knowledge. History refers to events in which subject and object exist in a mode of togetherness.[69]

In other words: in history, "meaning <u>for me</u>" is denoted. World history is the (outer) fact to be appropriated and also the (inner) act of appropriation. But,

> The properly historical event is neither the [inner] subject nor the [outer] object, but the point at which subject and object come together "intentionally." The locus of history is where the purpose of the object coincides with the consciousness of the subject. That mode of togetherness is what is meant by historical "understanding," "meaning," "interpretation."[70]

Michalson, using Collingwood and Bultmann to good advantage, thus defines the historical <u>event</u> as central and sees both inner and outer aspects of history as crucial to the historical truth of that event. <u>The emphasis though is on inner history, i.e. con-</u>

---

[68]Ibid. See p. 33.

[69]Ibid. p. 27.

[70]Ibid., pp. 27-28.

temporary appropriation as primary and meaning-laden, with outer history's importance diminished.[71]

Michalson further characterizes history by distinguishing it from nature.

> Nature by definition is the world in so far as it is silent about the meaning of man. History is the world in so far as the question about the possibility of a meaningful life is opened up. . . .
> Nature does not mean simply the birds and the bees. It refers rather to anything that does not involve one's life in the question of meaning.[72]

Having distinguished history from nature, Michalson returns to the prior distinction between inner and outer history, and, as has been anticipated above, restates the dichotomy in even more radical terms.

> Inner history simply brackets out the question of the empirical, outer-historical existence of christological and ecclesiological realities. The question of outer history is not yet a properly historical question. It is a nature question. Inner history asks the question of meaning.[73]

Whereas inner history asks the question of meaning, outer history fails at precisely this point, asking simply of an event's facticity--i.e. the nature question--and thus missing entirely the question of meaning.

Michalson's embracing inner history as his theological starting point does not mean a total disregard for outer history. That would be subjectivism, rather than subjectivity, and "too

---

[71] Ibid. Again, see p. 33. Also see references to the reality of the resurrection, pp. 192-198.

[72] Ibid., pp. 31-32.

[73] Ibid., p. 33.

inventive to correspond to the realities of history."[74] Rather, Michalson seeks the meaning of the historical event which is found in the togetherness of subject and object. Simply asking what has happened in history truncates history by disregarding the subject's participation in and the eventfulness of history for mere facticity. Thus, Michalson is far more concerned with and concentrates his efforts on inner history, the realm of meaningfulness. Admittedly, this diminishes the importance of history's facticity, but it does not negate history's facticity, which remains a necessary background.

It is now clear that, for Michalson, the underlying, all-pervading questions of meaning are crucial, and the answers to these questions are the linchpins which hold our lives together and give them coherence. These (inner history) questions of meaning, and their answers, take precedence over the more mundane (outer history) cause-effect relationships with which we are wont to become satisfied. Michalson demonstrates their significance and insignificance respectively.

With (outer) world history as a necessary but distant background, Michalson's theological starting point is (inner) world-become-existential history. For Michalson, to be human is to be involved in a quest for meaning, and existential history is the realm where the quest initially takes place.

---

[74]Ibid., p. 27.

> Existential history is the dimension of history in which the cracks in the arch of world history are felt as some lack of completeness in one's own life, in one's own capacity to negotiate life with meaning. . . .One may be seeing world history as a road segmented here and there by washouts or as a vessel riddled in its hull by holes. World history becomes existential history the moment one sees oneself as already embarked upon that broken course, already afloat upon that ship.[75]

Existential history is thus paratactic--deficient in connectives. Existential history is an awareness of those gaps (the cracks) in world history which leaves one with a sense of incompleteness.

For Michalson, however, to be properly aware of (inner) history as the realm of meaning and to articulate (existential) history's questions is <u>still insufficient</u>. One must <u>appropriate</u> the eschatological in biblical history.

> <u>Biblical history</u> supplies what existential history finds lacking in world history. Biblical history is the witness to the occurrence of events in history which have the capacity to fill the paratactic gaps, to supply the revelation without which our life is all in pieces, all coherence gone. These are what might be called "the paradigmatic events." (Eric Voegelin). . .They are the events which more than any others provide the very form of our existence.[76]

Reinforcing the fact that inner history is the realm of meaning, Michalson goes on to state that:

> Biblical history. . .does not refer to events in general, but to special events. . . .They are unique in supplying the hinges between events which would otherwise leave our lives in paratactic incompleteness. . . .
> . . .Biblical events are trustworthy not because they are factual, but because these are the events in which God makes accessible to us a justifiable life. . . .
> . . .The historicity of the Christian revelation may be asserted within the categories of world history, but to do so is an act of bad faith which undervalues the truth of the

---

[75] Ibid., p. 35.

[76] Ibid., p. 39.

event which says Christ is the hinge of history, the paradigmatic event which supplies the very form of the Christian man's existence."[77]

With the appearance of Christ, "which supersedes all previous events and teleologically suspends all previous acts of obedience by an imperious claim to be the sole authentic form of existence,"[78] Michalson states that

> The Christian revelation is a "cosmic event," the event in which our whole existence finds its full summation. . . .It happens in the world to end the world in its old form. It gives all history its end, its meaning. The new creation into which the Christian is ushered by this event is an historical reality, but it is history lived eschatologically.[79]

In Christ, biblical history is superceded by eschatological history and thus loses its status. "Biblical history has lost its substantial significance as saving history now that God is present in Christ as the hinge of history."[80]

Michalson's argument (i.e. his theological method and systematic principle), as presented in The Hinge of History, can be summarized as follows: Given inner (world) history as the realm of meaning, and asking (existential) history's questions, God in Christ has become accessible to us, in (biblical) history. As such, he provides answers to the questions of (existential) history which can then be (eschatologically) appropriated.

---

[77] Ibid., pp. 41-42.

[78] Ibid., p. 45.

[79] Ibid., p. 46.

[80] Ibid., p. 47.

47

In his 1961 Richard Lectures at the University of Virginia, published under the title The Rationality of Faith, Michalson reviews his attempt at a prologomena to theology. Like The Hinge of History, The Rationality of Faith is aimed at clarifying a fitting theological method based on Michalson's distinguishing between nature and history. In The Rationality of Faith, Michalson

> seeks to develop and illustrate a "historical" understanding of the logic of faith. Arguing that "rationality is a contextual concept" and that "there is more than one logic," Michalson attempts to show that the perennial problem of faith and reason can be satisfactorily solved only when one sharply distinguishes between the "logic of nature" and the "logic of history." Given this distinction, any supposed conflict of faith with reason can be relativized as really a conflict with the reason appropriate to nature; and faith's own logic or rationale can be explicated as a "historical rationality."[81]

Michalson, then, reiterates, with DesCartes, Kant and Buber (among others), the fact that there are two dimensions to, or structures of, reality, which are apprehended in two different ways. (For Michalson, "it can still be said. . .that the 'conceptual distinction between objective and subjective reality is one of the greatest achievements of our western civilization.'"[82]) For Michalson, meaning is located in the two dimension's relationship (i.e. in subjectivity), and he points to the I-Thou

---

[81] Schubert M. Ogden, review of The Rationality of Faith by Carl Michalson. Perkins School of Theology Review XVII, 2,3 (Winter-Spring, 1964):45.

[82] Michalson, Rationality of Faith, p. 39.

relationship as genuine. With Buber he would say: "Life does not exist in virtue to activities. . .which [only] have something for their object."[83] That is, life does not exist in the realm of the *It*, but in the realm of the *Thou*. Again, with Buber Michalson would say: "when *Thou* is spoken, the speaker has no-thing-- he has indeed nothing. . .the speaker takes his stand in relation."[84]

Michalson's emphasis on history (i.e. the realm of the I-Thou relationship) rather than nature (the realm of the I-It relationship) does not preclude an interplay between the subjective and objective. In fact, Michalson's concept of subjectivity holds that the contrary is true!

> Historical language as interpretation rejects the gap between the subject and the object in order to relate them. Yet it does so without ever relinquishing either its fidelity to the object or its creative subjective responsibility to negate the object. The dialectical relation between subject and object in history is not an ordinary subject-object relation such as occurs in the monologue with nature. It is genuine dialogue, constituted by the fact that history is a record of a personal sort. The distinctive thing about history is neither loyalty to objective facts nor expression of subjective imagination but response to the subjectivity in the objects, which is their social, human character.[85]

Thus nature for Michalson is seen from within the context of history--re-related to from the (truly) historical perspective. The epitome of this rationality of faith is seen in Michalson's

---

[83]Martin Buber, *I and Thou*. (New York: Charles Scribner's Sons, 1963), p. 4.

[84]Ibid., p. 4.

[85]Michalson, *Rationality of Faith*, pp. 96-97.

use of the concept "speech-event," from the theologies of Fuchs and Ebeling.

> . . .Speech is not an object one analyzes but an event through which one understands. The theological significance of this formulation of "speech-event" is indeed far-reaching. Jesus can be said to be a "speech-event" who identifies himself with his words. The word of God is not a language in detachment from God but the very coming of God himself.[86]

In line with this understanding, encounter controls occurrence, and event makes up the total experience. In *The Rationality of Faith* Michalson attempted to clarify his theological method as set forth in his earlier work, *The Hinge of History*.

In *Worldly Theology*, Carl Michalson brings together strands of theologizing from the past fifty years to put forth a theological position rooted in "history," and culminating in a Christian "maturity." Here Michalson's theological method begins to express itself in constructive theology.

Again, Michalson's understanding of the faith as historical is an understanding opposed to seeing the faith as nature. In this understanding history is not knowable reality. That is nature. Rather, history is the meaning granted when the knower interacts with knowable reality to form an event. An historical event, encompassing both the subjective and the objective, yields

---

[86] Ibid., p. 91. See Chapter II C2 (p. 96ff) for a more complete delineation of the concept "speech-event." See also Michalson's footnote 22 in *The Rationality of Faith*, pp. 51-55 and footnote 34, p. 91 for additional references to "speech-event" and its companion concept the "new quest of the historical Jesus."

its meaning not through the objective, not through nature, but through existential appropriation--the subjective. Therefore Michalson rejects Heinrich Ott's penchant for theologizing about the reality behind faith. For Michalson "faith is eschatological and not ontological."[87] Faith's task is not the examination of events in order to establish a being to relate to in faith--the ontological task, nature's concern. Rather, faith seeks to find the meaning that is implicit in the historical event and to existentially appropriate the same. In being about the task of faith, Michalson employs existential philosophy, linguistic analysis, apologetics,[88] Bultmann's demythologizing, and Kierkegaard's subjectivity--faith's helpmates all.

What Michalson claims to be doing is to unite what James D. Smart has elsewhere called "the divided mind of modern theology."[89] Standing on what he conceives as a Barth/Bultmann axis, Michalson wishes to hold together in dialectical tension the subjective and objective aspects of the Christian faith. Standing between a revelational positivism on the one hand, and the faith's being reduced to anthropology on the other, Michalson seeks to have the faith address the modern world. To be sure, Michalson's "Barth/Bultmann axis" is weighted on the subjective pole, but, at the same time, he would criticize Fritz Buri for

---

[87]Michalson, Worldly Theology, p. 105.

[88]See footnote 5, p. ii above.

[89]See James D. Smart, The Divided Mind of Modern Theology (Philadelphia: Westminster Press, 1967).

negating the objective pole.[90] For Michalson, *something* happened, in Christ, that even today engenders a meaningful faith. The theologians's task is to encounter and proclaim the meaningfulness that results from the Christ *event*.

Given this theological method, Michalson's theology emphasizes responsibility for the world. Responsibility for the world results from the faith's granting us a new relationship to the world. The consequence of faith's meaningfulness

> . . .is a new accentuation of temporal existence, the creation of a new kind of world. The object of a Christian's love is not now God but the world. . . .The implication of faith is not preoccupation with the absolute but, in faithful relationship to the absolute, preoccupation with the relativities of the world. Kierkegaard has shown us how, through subjectivity, not simply to find ourselves, but how thereby to let God exist, and, as a consequence of that, to receive back the world we otherwise evaporate by our direct gaze upon it.[91]

In short, the faith relationship (i.e. meaningfulness) allows for our living (meaningfully) in the world. This is done by accepting our responsibility for the world. The result of a Christian's faith is a reorientation toward the world where one, anticipating a Wesleyan holiness, acts responsibly, maturely, in the world. Linking Bonhoeffer's "man come of age" to Wesley's concept of perfection, Michalson seems to be saying this: In Christ Jesus humanity is granted meaningfulness and the possibility not only of realizing but of inculcating the same. God has, in Christ, sown the seed and we have responsibility for tending

---

[90] See Michalson, *Worldly Theology*, p. 39.

[91] Ibid., pp. 125-126.

its growth. Christ is the final revelation. "The eschaton is an historical reality."[92]

Michalson's constructive theology, like his theological method, has the advantage of recognizing twentieth-century secularity, while clinging to biblical and Christian tradition. Firmly rooted in the dialectical relationship of reason and faith, his theology expresses itself in a dialectical eschatology which Michalson describes as follows: "In Christ God delivers up his rule to men, but he continues to reign."[93] This is to say that mature persons assume responsibility for the world under the continued grace of God. Michalson's theology as history thus culminates in historical responsibility, by a mature humanity in continued relationship to God.

---

[92]Ibid., p. 215.

[93]Ibid., p. 215.

CHAPTER TWO

Responsibility in the Thought of Carl Michalson

A. The Prominence of Responsibility in Michalson's Thought

1. Responsibility Defined

Responsibility for Michalson means primarily response to God.

> Man is a being created with the responsibility for reflecting the reality of God as in a mirror. . . .[This] means that man's life takes on a posture defined by the open acknowledgement that there is a God, and a demeanor consistent with the knowledge of who God is. The Christian man's responsibility is not to become like God. . .The Christian man holds his life in relation to God in such a way that others are influenced to see what he sees and to posture their lives in the same direction. "To be like God" is not man's responsibility; it is his sin. By that temptation the serpent originally sets man against his creator. (Gen. 3:5) To be responsible to God is man's task, and that task defines his very being as man.
>
> . . .God has made man a being who is responsible for reflecting His reality.[1]

Responsibility for Carl Michalson is also in relation to the world. Michalson calls on humanity to be responsible in and for the world. In short, Michalson's theology allows humanity to be ethically responsible. Freed from legalism, by and for God, humanity related to God can accept the world and move decisively into the future. Continually being related to God, humanity is called to assume ethical responsibilty for the world.

For Michalson, a Christian's life is illuminated by God in a way that alters not only who a person is, but what a person is as well. And responsible to God, for the world is "what the Chris-

---

[1] Michalson, Faith for Personal Crises, p. 8.

tian person is." For Michalson, responsibility is the Christian's task, a task performed in relation to God, and a task performed in relation to the world. Wrought by faith, responsibility is the Christian's task.

2. **Responsibility as an Abiding Concern and the Key to Michalson's Ethics**

The prominence of the concept of responsibility in Michalson's writings is indicative of its importance to him, and its legitimacy as a research tool for Michalson studies. It may be fairly argued that responsibility is a leading theme in the overall theology of Michalson. Certainly, Michalson's concept of responsibility was developed as his work progressed, and yet, responsibility was a continuous concern as well.

Michalson's M.A. thesis at Drew was entitled "Responsibility in Plato's Republic and the Synoptic Gospels." His Ph.D. dissertation at Yale (on Karl Heim and the problem of revelation and reason) contains references to and an appreciation for the practical in Heim's apologetic. While at Yale, Michalson also seems to have benefited from H. Richard Niebuhr's treatment of responsibility, though Niebuhr's work was unpublished at that time.[2] In Faith for Personal Crises, Michalson says responsibility is "that task which defines man's very being as man,"[3] and seeks to

---

[2] See H. Richard Niebuhr, The Responsible Self, (New York: Harper & Row, 1963).

[3] Michalson, Faith for Personal Crises, p. 8.

enable humanity to be responsible in crucial situations. In The Hinge of History, Michalson states the importance of the nature/ history distinction for the church and asks "what the church's responsibility is."[4] The Rationality of Faith concludes with a chapter entitled "Faith as Historical Maturity" (comprising almost one-third of the book). Here responsibility means maturity in the world, with reference to Gogarten and Bonhoeffer. Worldly Theology brings to fruition Michalson's concern for responsibility. Here Michalson speaks directly to the place of ethics and relates himself to Wesley. Finally, Michalson's posthumously published sermons on prayer reflect his concern for responsibility. Here Michalson understands prayer as the means whereby mature humanity, having assumed responsibility for the world, remains in relationship to the God who "continues to reign."

Responsibility was an abiding and central concern for Michalson. As the concept developed, its importance to his theology and its implications for ethics become increasingly apparent, until finally, and as will be seen, Michalson defined the Christian in terms of responsibility to God and for the world. Michalson's concept of responsibility then, is crucial to his theology and the key to his ethics.

---

[4]Michalson, Hinge of History, p. 244.

3. **Michalson's Concept of Ethics and its Relationship to Responsibility**

The term "ethics" should also be explained. Concerning the possibility of existential ethics, Michalson writes:

> In fulfilling this ethical program existentialists are. . .acosmic. . . .The world of the cosmologist is an out-there world into which a man is invited to fit as a coin fits in a box. Existentialists, however, believe the world is not something one is _in_. Worlds are modes of being-in. There is the world of politics, of sports, of religion, of art. There is no "world" of ethics because ethics is the study of modes of being-in which result in revealing the possibilities for the worlds one creates through his modes of being-in.
>
> The model from art comes the closest to exemplifying how an existential ethic works. The artist does not record a world that exists. He creates, through his aesthetic behavior, the possibility for a world one may not previously have known. . .The Acropolis mobilized the earth, sea, and sky of Periclean Athens into a significant human world. . . Ethics, like art, nihilates [sic!] the world as cosmos (earth, sea, and sky) in order to create the world as a mode of being-in (the Acropolis). Now it can be seen why it is a mistake to call existentialism an individualism, implying that is has no social ethic. The primary term for existentialist ethics is neither "individual" nor "social" but "world," a reality in which the distinction between individual and social disappears, for "world" embraces _all_ modes of being-in.[5]

In calling the Christian to responsibility for the world, Michalson calls the Christian precisely to the task of ethics, the task of "revealing the possibilities for the worlds one creates through his modes of being-in," the task of "creating the world as a mode of being in." Responsibility, then, may be seen as an entirely suitable tool for determining, treating, and evaluating Carl Michalson's ethics.

---

[5]Michalson, _Worldly Theology_, p. 33.

In the process of developing Michalson's ethics of responsibility, a variety of critical questions must be raised, some of which have already been indicated. What does Michalson mean by responsibility? How is responsibility related to ethics? Is responsibility for the world an adequate ethical formulation, or does it, as John Godsey has suggested,[6] remain too cerebral? Is existentialism an adequate conceptual framework for ethics, or, as Godsey implies, is it too individualistic and subjective for social and ethical thought? Does Michalson's ethics integral to theology really denote adequate attention to ethics?

Additional questions will be raised with regard to Michalson's relevance for recent Christian ethics. How does Michalson's seeking to maintain a "Word of God theology" as the basis for human responsibility square with those who emphasize context as so important (liberation theology)? Can Michalson's themes of secularization and worldliness be viable in climates of religious conservatism and fundamentalism (evangelical perfectionism)? How is Michalson's understanding of ethics related to the ethics of those who place such strong emphasis on the character and virtue of the ethical actor (Gustafson and Hauerwas)?

Finally, I will want to come to some conclusions about Michalson's theology and ethics. To what extent was he an existentialist and dependent upon Kierkegaard and Bultmann, or was he

---

[6]Godsey, "The Maturity of Faith," p. 7

post-Bultmannian? How Wesleyan was he? These and other critical questions will be asked as the study proceeds and develops.

B. Responsibility in the Context of Michalson's Historical and Theological Development[7]

The fact that responsibility was an important concept for Carl Michalson has been indicated. Responsibility for the world, as defined above, was an abiding concern for Michalson and central to his ethics. Now an attempt will be made to understand the origins and development of the concept of responsibility, the soteriological context of responsibility and, finally, the ethical implications of responsibility in Michalson's thought.

1. Methodist Piety

All who deal with Michalson biographically point to the lasting influences of Methodist pietism on him and his theology.[8] It is also generally held that Christian responsibility was a

---

[7] In order to more clearly delineate Michalson's historical and theological development, I have adopted, with slight modification, Olin Ivey's procedure of conceptualizing Michalson's theology as a series of "stages along life's way." (Ivey explains and defends this procedure in his dissertation, "The Concept of the Holy Spirit," p. 7ff.) As used here, these "stages" represent periods of growth and influence each of which produced a part of his thought's eventual shape. Michalson's final formulations had aspects of each of these themes and postures in it. They should therefore not be viewed as absolutely sequential or exclusive.

[8] See Godsey, "The Maturity of Faith," pp. 1-9. See also Ivey, "The Concept of the Holy Spirit," pp. 12-20; Maddox, "Carl Michalson: Author, Teacher, Churchman," pp. 30-32; Gordon Michalson, Introduction to Hermeneutics and the Worldliness of Faith, pp. ix-xiii; Pennington, "Carl Michalson as Churchman," pp. 109-113; Runyon, "Carl Michalson as a Wesleyan Theologian," pp. 1-13.

significant part of that pietism, though Michalson students disagree in their evaluation of this pietism's ultimate ethical import.[9] John Godsey, who sees Michalson's theology as ultimately lacking social and political significance, writes that:

> Carl Michalson's theology is a sophisticated elaboration of an evangelical piety typical of much of American Methodist thought, and certainly not foreign to what he experienced in his Minnesota homeland. By evangelical piety I mean a Christianity which emphasizes the converting power of the preaching of the gospel and a personal response which is experientially and morally meaningful. This type of Christianity is characterized by an urgent sense of mission, but the focus tends to be on the individual rather than society, on inner rather than outward events. It is a Methodism that was more affected by revivalism than by the social gospel movement, so that its social outreach was more philanthropic than political.[10]

Godsey goes on to point to futuristic theology as that which gives attention to the social and ethical implications of theology. In so doing, he contrasts Michalson's (hermeneutic) theology with futuristic theology -- a contrast which he sees as "stark, but not absolute."[11]

Theodore Runyon (who sees Michalson as a Wesleyan in closer proximity to current Latin American theologians) writes in response to Godsey. Runyon too points to the fact that Michalson's holiness heritage lacked social and political concern. But unlike Godsey, Runyon sees Michalson reacting against these tendencies.

___

[9] See especially Godsey, "The Maturity of Faith," and Runyon, "Carl Michalson as a Wesleyan Theologian."

[10] Godsey, "The Maturity of Faith," pp. 1-2.

[11] Ibid., p. 7.

> We can be sure that the standard holiness vocabulary of "religious experience," "sanctification," and "Christian perfection" was familiar terminology in the world young Carl Michalson inhabited. I have not found in Michalson's writings any direct and explicit discussion of his holiness heritage, but I suspect that some of his later preoccupations cannot be understood apart from his reactions against it as well as his appreciation of it. . . .his sensitivity to the issues of the relationship of law to faith and the resistance against coercion in faith can be traced back to questions of authenticity which he must have raised as a youth exposed to the high-pressure methods of revivals and the nagging demands of perfectionism.[12]

Runyon, then, sees Michalson's pietistic background as "positive and healthy. . .and [representing] a conscious effort to counterbalance the compulsion to deprecate the human which characterized so much of nineteenth-century holiness theology and preaching."[13] In short, Runyon sees Michalson's upbringing as Wesleyan in the best sense of the word--it was pietistic, but affirmed the self and the world, and thus could find expression in responsibility for the world. Runyon, while recognizing Michalson's pietistic heritage, wishes to maximize his ethical importance.

Both Godsey and Runyon agree that Michalson grew up in a pietistic Methodist atmosphere, and that this had a lasting effect. They disagree on Michalson's appropriation of Methodist piety and his ultimate ethical importance. To be sure, Godsey sees in Michalson's later theology,

> a vision of worldly faith more akin to Gogarten's theology of secularization [where] the intention of God's act in Jesus Christ is to turn the world over to humankind and to

---

[12]Runyon, "Carl Michalson as a Wesleyan Theologian," p. 2.

[13]Ibid.

have them assume responsibility for it as mature sons and daughters.[14]

In that Michalson's earlier existential approach gave way to his vision of worldly faith, Godsey's conviction is that

> he would have had to give much more attention to the social and ethical implications of his theology if that theology were to be truly "worldly." But whether he could do this without changing some of his presuppositions is a serious question.[15]

Godsey is also convinced that Michalson's "talk of 'world,' like Gogarten's, seems too cerebral."[16]

Runyon too thinks Michalson's late essays, especially the one entitled "The Hermeneutics of Holiness in Wesley"[17] represent a shift in his theological enterprise. But for Runyon this shift is toward a heightened social and political concern, totally commensurate with Michalson's Wesleyan heritage. Writes Runyon, "[Michalson's later writings] indicate that he is seeking in a positive way to put together the two realms, nature and history, which previously were kept so antiseptically distinct from each other."[18]

---

[14]Godsey, "The Maturity of Faith," pp. 6-7.

[15]Ibid. p. 7.

[16]Ibid.

[17]This is the title Michalson gave this article when it appeared in the Robert Calhoun Festschrift, The Heritage of Christian Thought, edited by Robert E. Cushman and Egil Grislis (New York: Harper & Row, 1965), p. 243ff. It was printed in Worldly Theology, under the title "Holiness and the Maturity of Faith--John Wesley's Theology," pp. 127-158.

[18]Runyon, "Carl Michalson as a Wesleyan Theologian," p. 9.

In support of this thesis, Runyon juxtaposes Lutheran justification against Wesleyan sanctification, and sees Michalson's later essays in the Wesleyan context.

> The concrete structures of love operative in the world, which Wesley sees as the fruits of sanctification and the telos toward which faith and the whole process of Christian perfection move, provide the later Michalson with the materials for his distinctively Wesleyan interpretation of a contemporary Christian faith that goes beyond the limitations of Reformation and neo-Reformation approaches. Pre-understanding, as he now interprets it, is no longer exclusively determined by existential questions of personal thirst but by world-historical questions of human responsibility.[19]

Michalson's later essays then, take seriously the fact that forgiven humanity must live in the world--and his later theology allows for precisely that, as Runyon points out:

> "Wherever holiness and not forgiveness has been the distinctive mark of faith," says Michalson, forgiveness is seen as only the first step along a way that leads to the fruits of the Spirit. These fruits are "fully historical realities," he claims, "which are lived out in men. Among them are love, joy, peace, patience, kindness, goodness, faithfulness, gentleness, and self-control. These are the attributes of a life of freedom, a life of responsibility," made available to us through the proclamation of the true son and steward, Jesus of Nazareth. "Life in Christ realized in these eschatological attributes is the maturity of history." This is why Michalson can claim that "holiness secularizes the world."[20]

The issues Godsey and Runyon raise are tremendously significant for this study. Godsey sees Michalson's theology as "a sophisticated elaboration of an evangelical piety.[21] As such, it

---

[19] Ibid., p. 11.

[20] Ibid., pp. 10-11.

[21] Godsey, "The Maturity of Faith," p. 1.

is bound to a "personal piety" heritage and existential presuppositions which preclude any real social and ethical concern. Runyon, on the other hand, views Michalson's theology more positively, in terms of social and ethical importance. He sees Michalson's heritage as a social pietism that "bears surprising resemblance to. . .Latin American liberation theology."[22] The question raised is this: Coming as it does, from a pietistic background, and maintained with existential presuppositions, to what extent is Michalson's theology socially and ethically significant?

Godsey seems to assume that because Michalson's approach was pietistic, existential, and subjective, it was individualistic and lacking in social significance. This is not true. For Michalson the subjectivity of Kierkegaard demands responsibility for the world.

> In the inwardness of subjectivity one's passion for the infinite is gratified by the God-relation. What is the consequence of this for Kierkegaard?. . .Oddly, the consequence for Kierkegaard is the opposite of monasticism. It is a new accentuation of temporal existence, the creation of a new kind of world. The object of a Christian's love is not now God but the world. . . .The implication of faith is not preoccupation with the absolute but, in faithful relationship to the absolute, preoccupation with the relativities of the world. . . .The religious individual does better to visit the local park than to enter a cloister, because "it is the humblest expression of his God-relationship to admit his humanity, and because it is human to enjoy oneself.". . .That is why it can be said of the Christian that "he belongs entirely to the world." His faith has translated him out of the world of unreality, of abstraction, of objectivity and ideality, which is not a world one lives, into the real world where one can grasp existence as a

---

[22]Runyon, "Carl Michalson as a Wesleyan Theologian," p. 11.

whole. "By faith I make renunciation of nothing, on the contrary, by faith I acquire everything."[23]

It is in harmony with his pietistic heritage and on the basis of his existentialism and subjectivity that Michalson builds his ethic. For Michalson,

> Kierkegaard has shown us how, through subjectivity, not simply to find ourselves, but how thereby to let God exist, and, as a consequence of that, to receive back the world we otherwise evaporate by our direct gaze upon it.[24]

Michalson's pietism does not necessarily lack social and ethical significance. In fact the contrary is true.

For Michalson, individual piety <u>must be</u> reflected in the world. Kierkegaardian presuppositions thus provide the framework for, and in fact necessitate his thinking about, responsibility and ethics. Michalson's move to a worldly theology was not only in keeping with his existentialism, with its focus in individuality and subjectivity, but in fact was necessitated by it. Thus pietism, channeled through existentialism, does not preclude ethics. As was true of Wesley's faith, the (pietistic, existential, subjective) faith that Michalson sought to understand, live and communicate was a faith that necessitated responsibility for the world.

Runyon's point is well taken. "There is no reason to consign [Michalson] to [personal] pietism and existentialism [narrowly defined]" and thereby determine that he has "little to

---

[23] Michalson, <u>Worldly Theology</u>, pp. 125-126.

[24] Ibid., p. 126.

contribute to current theological debate."[25] Based on an existentialist foundation, Michalson's theology is an attempt to make the Christian faith socially relevant. As such it has definite ethical implications. And this is especially true in the later essays. But Runyon goes too far when he judges Michalson's later essays as representing a *basic* shift in Michalson's theological enterprise,"[26] in light of which "the natural world, as well as the world of meaning becomes the object of salvation."[27]

For Michalson, humanity--standing betwixt and between history and nature--is the object of salvation! One's historical faith allows for a *re-relating* to the world--i.e. one's historical faith allows for our living *in* the world but not *of* it, for our gaining the world while *not* losing our souls! Participating in eschatological existence, through (historical) faith in Christ, allows not for the salvation of the (natural) world, but for humanity to live meaningfully as saved people in the world-- as we must! In this way, we live between the times.[28]

Michalson states this clearly in his posthumous *Worldly Theology*:

> To say it as Gogarten does, the Creator has given us the world as the locus of our responsibility to him. But we

---

[25] Runyon, "Carl Michalson as a Wesleyan Theologian," p. 12.

[26] Ibid. See p. 9.

[27] Ibid.

[28] See Carl Michalson, "Is American Theology Coming of Age?" *Drew Gateway* XXXVI, 3 (Spring-Summer, 1966):65-75. This article was included in *Worldly Theology*, pp. 13-25. See also Ivey, "The Concept of the Holy Spirit," pp. 214-217.

have worshipped the creature rather than the Creator, perverting our responsibility _for_ the world into responsibility _to_ the world. The effect of the advent of Jesus is to restore to us the proper relationship by reintroducing obedience to God as the new possibility for life in the world. In the new age, we must be in the world while not of it. We must live in the world "as if not" in the world. We must buy the things of the world "as if not" possessing them and have our wives "as if not" having them.[29]

Both Godsey and Runyon see Michalson's later writings as more attentive to responsibility for and maturity in the world. Godsey, however, doubts that Michalson's theology could speak to these concerns due to inadequate presuppositions, while Runyon ses Michalson's concern for responsibility in the world evolving into a concern for the natural world per se. A middle course seems the more plausible one. It is possible to identify, in Michalson, a consistent but developing ethic of responsibility from his Minnesota Methodism to Worldly Theology. In this regard, Michalson saw the Christian faith as (necessarily) responsible for the world precisely because of his presupposing faith's subjectivity. But his seeing the Christian as responsible for and mature in the world was an understanding that stopped short of making the natural world the object of salvation.

2. Neo-Orthodox Expressions

Michalson's studying with Edwin Lewis, at Drew, marks his introduction to Neo-Orthodox thought and its influence on him.

---

[29]Michalson, Worldly Theology, p. 171.

Michalson came to Drew in 1936. Following the publication of A Christian Manifesto in 1934, Lewis' thought reflected more and more the dialectical or Neo-Orthodox theology of the Continent,[30] particularly as expressed by Emil Brunner. These influences were not lost on Michalson. The evangelicalism he brought to Drew from John Fletcher College was tempered and deepened--girded up by philosophy and literature, and given a sound theological basis.

Along with Michalson's deepened evangelicalism, Lewis also conveyed to him an emphasis on ethics and the demands of Christian living. Writes Godsey,

> Under the stimulus of Lewis, who taught a course on Platonism, Michalson wrote an M.A. thesis on "Human Responsibility in the Republic of Plato and in the Synoptic Gospels." The influence of Emil Brunner, three of whose books are listed in the bibliography, is unmistakable on Michalson. At one point in his Conclusion he approvingly quotes this statement from Brunner's Man in Revolt: "The Christian doctrine of man is simply a doctrine of responsibility."[31]

---

[30] "The [Neo-Orthodox] movement is usually regarded as having begun in 1918 with the publication of Karl Barth's commentary on St. Paul's Epistle to the Romans. . . .Its theme was "God is God," which Barth thought meant three things: (1) that there is an infinite qualitative difference between God and man; (2) that sin is the attempt to obscure this difference, whether by religious experience, mysticism, or moral idealism; (3) that the realization that there is this gap and that it can only be bridged by God and not by man is itself saving faith. Each of these three theses constituted a full-scale assault on. . . the prevailing [Liberal] tendency to interpret Christianity as the highest product of Western culture. (Van A. Harvey, A Handbook of Theological Terms [New York: Macmillan Company, 1964], p. 163.)

[31] Godsey, "The Maturity of Faith," p. 2. Godsey goes on to say, "Of course, the cutting edge of evangelical pietism has always been moral living. The question is only how that morality is understood and practiced." (p.2) Godsey thus preserves his ambivalence toward Michalson's ethics, stated above (pp. 58-59,

The 1940 M. A. thesis was Michalson's major statement on responsibililty during his Neo-Orthodox period, and clearly reflects Edwin Lewis' concerns and influence. Here, Michalson's aim is to "hint at certain critical distinctions which are implicit in the Republic of Plato and in the Synoptic Gospels with respect to human responsibility."[32] The thesis is organized around what Michalson considers to be

> the central considerations in the problem of responsibility . . . .freedom of choice [and] the reality to which freedom of choice is answerable. Obviously, only where there is moral freedom is there moral responsbility. And, the nature of the reality to which the one choosing is obligated greatly determines the nature of the choice itself and hence the nature of responsiblity.[33]

In chapters one and two, Michalson "attempts to see man in the particular societal relations provided in the Republic and in the Gospels of Jesus,"[34] and to determine the freedom of choice afforded in each. He examines the ___ of the Republic and ___ of the Synoptic Gospels to this end, concluding that "The truth about human responsibility is more apparent in the idea of the ___ than in the ___."[35] For Michalson,

> The whole strategy of the Republic is that the entire citizenry will be subjected to whatever is discovered by the knowing groups to be the summum bonom for society. . . . How

62-64).

[32]Ibid.

[33]Ibid.

[34]Ibid.

[35]Ibid., p. 23.

precarious this superimposition of the ideal upon society would be to the responsibility of the individual becomes cumulatively apparent.[36]

According to Michalson,

> Jesus looks at his kingdom not from the standpoint of a glorious superstructure to be imposed on humanity but from the standpoint of the man who must enter it. He has an obligation to meet, preparation to undergo, before he may enter. Berdyaev places great stress upon this fact of man's creative activity and responsibility in entering the kingdom. The Gospel "elevates" man, for "seeking for the kingdom is the core of Christianity." He says very plainly what marks the difference between the Republic and the kingdom from the standpoint of human responsibiity. "At the time of ancient civilization, in Greece and Rome, men were entirely dependent upon the State, the city: religion was a State religion, and possessed no inner spiritual freedom."[37]

Chapter three "pursues and analysis of the idea of the Good, the ultimate object of man's choice"[38] and is largely descriptive.

> . . .the telos for humanity in the Republic is the Idea of the Good, a rationalistic abstraction of what ought to be. The telos for humanity in the Synoptics is the Person of God, the living reality of what ought to be, supremely attested to and revealed by Jesus.[39]

Given these ideas of the Good, Michalson again sees the Gospel as encouraging and providing impetus to human responsibility.

> God's Fatherhood not only to Jesus but to all men was the chief contribution Jesus made to thought about God. By that designation he placed men under the condition of a filial relation to one another and a relation of sonship to God, provisionally.

---

[36]Ibid., p. 8.

[37]Ibid., pp. 28-29.

[38]Ibid., pp. ii-iii.

[39]Ibid., p. 45.

. . .the ethical implications for human life in his vivid experience of the Fatherly God was that God is a person, and the good that he is may be sought by persons.[40]

In chapter four Michalson "unfolds the implications for responsibility inherent in the relative Platonic and Christian concepts of the "Good."[41] This chapter is basically a comparison of the concept of   in the Republic with the concept of   in the gospels.

> The conclusive aspect of the whole discussion of the   is the one fact that it is "an upward movement of the soul," exclusively one-directional. . . .That means, finally, as it was discovered to be true in the Republic, that the grounds for knowledge of the end of life, the idea of the good, the ens realissimum, is no more than the labor of man's striving. . . .
> To what extent, then, can a society of men who are not disciplined philosophers ever come into the direct sense of responsibility to the good? The "bourgeoise," as Berdyaev calls the masses, cannot be responsible because the contemplation necessary to seeing "the Good" is unkown to them.[42]

A   , on the other hand, encourages response and responsibility.

> The Good which the Gospels of Jesus would have to be known is a living reality of what ought to be, and the condition of its being known partakes of the nature of a personalism which ultimates in a two-directional process of divine revelation and human acceptation. Irrespective of contingencies that appear in phenomenal affairs, God makes himself known under the condition of   and man responds in faith. It is the Christian faith that all men everywhere will be confronted with the moment of free choice by which they may determine their course of life.[43]

---

[40]Ibid., pp. 41, 42.

[41]Ibid., p. iii.

[42]Ibid., pp. 55-56.

[43]Ibid., p. 64. In line with his understanding the faith as "a two directional process" where God makes himself known. . .and man responds in faith," Michalson quotes Brunner regarding responsibility: "Responsibility. . .is not first of all a task but

Michalson concludes his thesis by dealing "briefly with the nature of the individual as observed apart from his societal relations, as well as the provisions in the respective documents for the final judgment on one who has or has not accepted his responsibility."[44] It is in his conclusion that he makes use of the Brunner quote cited by Godsey: "The Christian doctrine of man is simply a doctrine of responsibility."[45] Of Plato's Republic, Michalson remarks that "critical thought may never cease to reveal the respects in which the humanism which has no theistic reference will be betrayed by its own weaknesses, however unwittingly."[46]

Utilizing Brunner as opposed to Barth (whom Michalson identifies with Plato's "fallacy of the one directional"[47] which precludes responsibility) Michalson's M. A. thesis demonstrates a serious concern for ethics that goes beyond "pietistic lip service." It is without question an example of pietism and meaning-

---

a gift; it is not first of all a demand but life; not law but grace." (p. 59) Thus Michalson has inextricably bound reponsibility to the gospel and vice versa. From henceforth, this conclusion is inescapable to him and forces him to theologically account for human responsibility.

[44]Ibid., p. iii.

[45]Ibid., p. 71.

[46]Ibid., pp. 75-76.

[47]Ibid., See pp. 59-60 esp. For Michalson, Barth's refusal to acknowledge the role of general revelation as a point of contact (Anknupfungspunkt) between God and humanity in the salvation process, is fallacious. Michalson, with Brunner, understands the salvation process as two directional pointing to the importance of human acceptance and responsibility for its completion.

ful ethics going hand in hand, and clearly represents Michalson's beginning to set forth an understanding of ethics based on and bound to subjectivity.

The implications of Michalson's having written so conclusively on human responsibility and the Christian faith in his M.A. thesis are enormous. Not only does his thesis indicate that responsibility is an important concept for the Christian faith, it concludes that the Christian faith is <u>by nature</u> responsible. The concept of responsibility is woven into the fabric of Christianity in such a way that it cannot be removed lest the faith unravel. The Christian faith cannot but be responsible. From henceforth this conclusion proved inescapable for Michalson and forced him to theologically account for human responsibility. But more than forcing him to simply account for responsibility, his conclusions here regarding the necessary and natural relationship between responsibility and faith led him, finally, to understand the faith in terms of responsiblity for the world.

In Carl Michalson's life and work, there is a continuing and constant concern for the problem of faith and works. However, the porblem of faith and works (i.e. responsibility) was not Michalson's <u>only</u> concern. As his doctoral dissertation shows, he demonstrated a concurrent concern for problems relating to theological method. Yet even when occupied with the question of theological method, as in his doctoral dissertation and later in <u>The Hinge of History</u> and <u>The Rationality of Faith</u>, Michalson's abiding concern for responsibility is demonstrated.

Michalson's doctoral dissertation, "The Problem of Revelation and Reason in the Theology of Karl Heim" is a study of Heim's theological method. Michalson presents Heim as one who seeks to hold revelation and reason together in a dialectical relationship, similar to that which Karl Barth attacks as Emil Brunner's negative point of contact between human reason and God's revelation.

> According to Brunner's former explanation, man's aptitude for the revelation of God consists only in the fact that in the rational existence of man there is a diacritical point where this existence can become discontinuous, where it can issue in a 'negative point,' where its most essential truth, its 'fundamental condition', i.e. despair, can come to light, where this despair can be theoretically described as true and felt to be so by the conscience, and where the knowledge of God, which is bound up with it from the start, can 'become uncertain'.[48]

Indeed, Michalson makes precisely this point when he says,

> The point of contact [heretofore discussed as allowing for the continuity of revelation and reason] is [in Heim] completely negative as well as unsalutary, but it is nonetheless a point of contact and a basis of appeal for the Christian Gospel.[49]

Heim uses the negative "point of contact" apologetically, in what Michalson calls a "radical questioning of the rational criticism."[50]

> By unsparing, aggressive rational criticism, the apologist takes the battle to the grounds of the foe. By a "process of fundamental questioning" rational criticism pursues

---

[48] Karl Barth, "No!" in *Natural Theology* (London: The Centenary Press, 1946) p. 80.

[49] Carl Michalson, "The Problem of Revelation and Reason in the Theology of Karl Heim." (Ph.D. dissertation, Yale University, 1945) p. 77.

[50] Ibid., p.68.

> the antagonist from his own premises to their ultimate conclusions. In this fashion, secularism, as an instance, when allowed to proceed to its own conclusion, breaks. Rationalism is overcome by rationalism. Knowledge meets knowledge.
> . . .
> Heim regards this as the "maieutic" method of Socrates--intellectual midwifery which clears away all inadequate knowledge as a basis for the reception of adequate knowledge, not-knowing as a basis for knowing.[51]

In other words, competing (rational) pursuits of ultimate meaning are pushed to their limits. (The pursuit of ultimate meaning Heim sees as a universal quest in which all disciplines are finally engaged.) When at these limits (the limits of rationalism, really), and thus thoroughly negated, one stands on the threshold of the solution.

> An emptiness is induced by radical criticism and the faith-witness offers the fact of God's solution. The solution comes not as proof or as postulate, but as pure factuality.[52]

In standing before God's solution, which, for Heim, is Christ, one is confronted with a choice: to choose God or to reject God by building another rational pursuit.

Heim has thus sought to hold revelation and reason in tension, in a polar relationship. On the one hand, one cannot, by rational means, arrive at revelation. This quest is finally negated and despair is its result. On the other hand, Heim sees this negation of reason as a real point of contact with revelation, for precisely at this point of emptiness, space is made for

---

[51] Ibid., pp. 66-67. Michalson later uses the term "maieutic" to descirbe his own theology in Faith for Personal Crises.

[52] Ibid. p. 68.

revelation. Put another way, it is only by death that one is resurrected!

Michalson is critical of Heim's dialectic, summarizing his criticism as follows:

> When [Heim] speaks of the relation of continuity between revelation and reason, he presupposes a pre-established harmony between human aspirations and divine gifts. For this conviction I believe he is dependent upon the prior actuality of the divine gift, the revelation. When he speaks of the relation of discontinuity, either he presupposes that there is nothing salutary in the human spirit, and for this presupposition I believe that either he is dependent upon the datum of revelation as given in the reformation belief in justification by faith alone, or, he contradicts his conclusions about the incapacity of the reason in his own dependence upon the operation and achievement of the reason.[53]

To say that Michalson is critical of Heim's dialectic is not to say that he is unsympathetic to it, however. Michalson's thesis ends with a recitation of three positive factors in Heim's thought, that amounts to an affirmation of Heim's theological method and agenda.

> (1.) Heim deals in epistemological categories that validate theoretically the possibility of the real knowledge of God. While he has made that knowledge of God unilateral, in the sense that it can be given only by God, at least it must be conceded that he finds it possible to affirm the reality of God, even though on the basis of revelation, and that this conviction is a controlling principle throughout his thought.

> (2.) Second, Heim has contributed to the understanding of the nature of religious truth. . . .The truth of the ultimate to which the life of man capitulates, is in a completely different dimension from general truth. That is, revealed truth is not a species of the genus, truth. It is a genus by itself.

---

[53] Ibid., p. 310.

> (3.) Third, Heim has insisted that the practical motive is inseparable from the theoretical, that the intellectual life ought not leap over high moral seriousness. . . .
> . . .In the nature of personal existence defined as existence in decision, every moment demands that a man live in the light of his chosen ultimate.[54]

In summary, Michalson affirms Heim's contention that revelation and reason are related, he affirms Heim's understanding of the nature of religious truth, and, as well, he affirms Heim's contention that religious truth, because it is related to reason, is inseparable from responsibility for the world.

In the dissertation on Heim, Michalson, again reflecting Brunner, is concerned with the necessity of bringing the world into relation with the gospel and vice versa. To be sure, human responsibility is mentioned only in passing in Michalson's doctoral dissertation. But the fact that responsibility is mentioned at all, in a document such as this, points to its importance on Michalson's theological agenda. This reference, in and of itself, does not constitute a viable ethic, but, together with the M.A. thesis, it demonstrates a genuine concern for human responsibility, from the beginning of his scholarly career. References to responsibility in Michalson's theses constitute the beginning of a patterned concern that finally finds expression in Worldly Theology and worldly responsibility.

3. Existential Expressions

---

[54]Ibid., pp. 312-313.

The second general period of Michalson's theological career covered the span of years 1953 to 1960.[55] This period saw Michalson engaged in several significant projects. The Hinge of History, published in 1959, was developed over the seven years prior, according to Michalson's preface.[56] Faith for Personal Crises published in 1958, was a concurrent work, five of the chapters comprising the 1957 Willson Lectures at Southwestern University, Georgetown, Texas. While these two books represent Michalson's major efforts during his existential period, he also edited two books (Christianity and the Existentialists, in 1956 and The Witness of Soren Kierkegaard, in 1960) and wrote numerous other pieces.[57]

In this period of his life, Michalson sought to understand the Christian faith from the standpoint of history through existential interpretation. In line with this understanding, Michalson's first book concerning theology as history (The Hinge of History) was a prolegomena to theology that set forth "a method of thinking about the Christian faith."[58] He subtitled The Hinge of History "An Existential Approach to the Christian Faith."

---

[55]See Ivey, "The Concept of the Holy Spirit," p. 8.

[56]Michalson, Hinge of History, p. 10.

[57]See Wynne's bibliography in The Implications of Carl Michalson's Theological Method, Appendix, part A, p. 329ff.

[58]Michalson, Hinge of History, p. 9.

As stated above, in <u>The Hinge of History</u> Carl Michalson seeks to employ historical method and the category of history as a means for doing theology. Not philosophy, not the natural sciences, and not emotion, but "historical method [is the] instrument of theological understanding." Michalson calls his theology one of <u>correlation</u> and thus makes history "the foundation for the relation between divine and human concerns."[59]

Through the use of history, Michalson seeks to avoid the Cartesian dichotomy of subject and object and tries to "drive a wedge" between the theological/philosophical choices of <u>fideism</u> and rationalism. Finally this is the existentialist approach. Though Michalson (in accordance with his introductory chapter in <u>Christianity and the Existentialists</u>[60] and his disclaimers in <u>The Hinge of History</u>[61]) would perhaps feel more comfortable terming his approach existential/eschatological, the point of departure for his theology is existentialism. In keeping with the tenets of his existential approach, Michalson asks of the meaning of events, rather than inquiring of their facticity. In historical terms, his concern is with <u>Geschichte</u> rather than with <u>Historie</u>, as the instrument of theological understanding.

Having set forth his understanding of theology as history (see above, Chapter I, p. 40ff. for a more thorough analysis),

---

[59]Ibid.

[60]Carl Michalson, <u>Christianity and the Existentialists</u> (New York: Charles Scribner's Sons, 1956), p. 19ff.

[61]Michalson, <u>Hinge of History</u>, p. 51ff. See also p. 117ff.

Michalson ends The Hinge of History with a chapter entitled "The Creativity of Preaching" and a "Conclusion" entitled "The Mission of the Church." Given the nature of faith, preaching is necessary for faith to come to expression and is the only appropriate means for faith to be expressed.

> The ability of contemporary man to enter into that history is in a large sense dependent upon the historiographical finesse with which one reiterates the event. . . . Preaching is historiography in an evangelical form, testifying to the good news of the eschatological event in such a way as to give rise to the eschatological history. To say it with utter simplicity, the preaching of the gospel is the telling of a story of God's turning to man in Jesus of Nazareth. In a single report it tells us to whom we really belong and saves us from being lost. Preaching is the witness to the gospel. By that witness the paratactic gaps which existential history exposes in world history are filled with the presence of God.[62]

The cruciality of preaching, for Michalson, cannot be overemphasized. Not only is preaching the reiteration of the Christ event, but, given the nature of faith as history, preaching is alone appropriate to the communication of the gospel. Michalson quotes Paul and Luther in this regard.

> It was the Apostle Paul who laid down this formula. "How are they to believe in him of whom they have never heard?... So faith comes from what is heard, and what is heard comes by the preaching of Christ." (Rom. 10:14 and 17) Or, as Luther says it in his commentary on this passage, "Faith is an acoustical affair."[63]

---

[62] Ibid., p. 213.

[63] Ibid., p. 217. Michalson's emphasis on preaching as alone appropriate to the communication of the gospel should not be interpreted as a denial of the other means of grace, i.e. other outward ordinances whereby the faith is conveyed. By defining preaching as "any act of communication in which the intention is present to bear witness to the meaning of the Christ event for our ongoing lives" (Hinge of History, p. 214), Michalson accounts for other means of grace. Preaching, for him, is a broad rubric,

Quite simply, Michalson is saying that because the faith is history and not nature, it's truth must be heard rather than seen. The Christian faith, by definition, cannot be conclusively, objectively demonstrated. If so, it would not be faith. Rather, faith comes from hearing, i.e. the hearing of preaching. Says Michalson in this regard:

> My friends, the Christian message is a proclamation that strikes the ear of the world with the force of a hint! Some get it. Some do not. And, to those who do, it is the power of God unto salvation.[64]

Given the fact that preaching is necessary for the faith's coming to expression, and alone appropriate to communication of the gospel, it stands to reason that Christian responsibility involves preaching first and foremost.

> A Christian is one who acknowledges that God has turned to man in Jesus and who takes upon himself the responsibility of turning to the world with that report. Hence, to be a Christian is to be involved in the responsibility of the communication of the gospel.[65]

In The Hinge of History, responsibility is, unmistakably, an integral part of Michalson's theologizing. Because the cruc-

---

that includes enacting the story in the sacraments, as well as reciting the story from the pulpit. (See Hinge of History, p. 237) By thus establishing the sacraments and additional ordinances in relation to and in the context of preaching, Michalson supports his point that given the nature of faith, it must be heard (Paul), and that faith is an "acoustical affair" (Luther), while not denying other means of grace.

[64]Michalson, "Faith Must be Risked" in The Witness of Radical Faith, p. 94. See also "'Mere Words' and the Event of Faith," p. 75ff.

[65]Michalson, Hinge of History, p. 214.

iality of preaching is undeniable, and preaching is identified with responsibility, responsibility holds a lofty place in Michalson's theological schema. According to Michalson, since the Christian cannot but preach, the Christian cannot but be responsible.

Faith for Personal Crises demonstrates again the importance Michalson placed on responsibility as he worked out his "Existential Approach to the Christian Faith" that was The Hinge of History. Written concurrently with The Hinge of History, Faith for Personal Crises represents a practical theology--a "faith stance" set forth in terms of Christian responsibility--that complements and "concretizes" Michalson's existential theological method.

Faith for Personal Crises relates the Christian faith to the crucial situations of "the man in the street"--i.e. to anxiety, guilt, doubt, vocation, marriage, suffering and death. These crises are seen as "inescapable. . .requiring decisiveness," situations "in which it is being determined whether one will live or die," and such situations always carry with them the "dimension of ultimate significance."[66]

Three personality types (rebellious, recessive, and resigned), understood in relation to "the more general anxiety producing situations of life (the cosmic, social, and ontic),"[67] are

---

[66]Michalson, Faith for Personal Crises, pp. 3, 5, 6.

[67]Ibid., See pp. 24-25.

examined in relation to the seven particular crises. The Christian faith then is brought to bear on these issues.

Michalson sees the Christian faith as pertinent to people confronting life's crucial situations because it "unifies one's life interiorly."[68] Says Michalson,

> Our very life can be lived under the knowledge that every major threat to our being, to our abundant life, is overcome in God. . . .Revelation, reconciliation, and Resurrection are the three R's of the Christian faith."[69]

Our burden of guilt can be born "because man is not meant to bear it himself."[70] Christ bears the burden for us.

The aim of <u>Faith for Personal Crises</u>, then, is "to pattern the mind with the resources in the Christian faith for meeting personal crises."[71] In so doing, Michalson seeks to convey the Christian faith's answers to the two questions which "interpenetrate in every crucial situation."

> As I have said, in every crucial situation a judgment, a decision is required. But in the New Testament, the judgment referred to is never simply the judgment man must make. It is always the judgment God has made. . . .No crucial situation is adequately lived through, therefore, which does not take into consideration the dimension of the God-relation. "What does God intend?" "What, therefore, must I do?" These two questions interpenetrate in every crucial situation.[72]

---

[68]Ibid., p. 19.

[69]Ibid., p. 36.

[70]Ibid., p. 51.

[71]Ibid., p. 12.

[72]Ibid., pp. 6-7.

Michalson thus seeks to allow for humanity's reflecting the image of God, which is to say he seeks to allow for humanity's being responsible in the world.

> Man is a being created with the resonsibility for reflecting the reality of God as in a mirror. . . . [This] means that man's life takes on a posture defined by the open acknowledgment that there is a God, and a demeanor consistent with the knowledge of who God is. The Christian man's resonsibility is not to become like God. . . .The Christian man holds his life in relation to God in such a way that others are influenced to see what he sees and to posture their lives in the same direction. "To be <u>like</u> God" is not man's responsibiity; it is his sin. . .To be <u>responsible</u> to God is man's task, and that task defines his very being as a man.
> . . .God has made man a being who is responsible for reflecting his reality.[73]

Michalson's <u>Faith for Personal Crises</u> is an attempt to communicate the gospel's message to people in special need, i.e. to people confronting life's personal crises. By so doing, he hopes to enable humanity to transcend oft-times debilitating personality types and be responsible in the world (even in the face of the crisis of death).

During this second general period of his theological life, Michalson sought to interpret the Christian faith, as history, from an existentialist posture. Responsibility was featured prominantly in this endeavor. At the same time, and in line with his existential approach, Michalson developed a practical theology that had Christian responsibility at its center. Thus, for Michalson, faith is history, existentially interpreted, and faith is responsible.

---

[73]Ibid., p. 8.

4. Phenomenological and Hermeneutical Expressions

In many ways The Rationality of Faith, written in 1963, and marking the start of Michalson's third theological stage, is a recasting of The Hinge of History. At the same time, there are important additions. Phenomenology and hermeneutics play a significant role in The Rationality of Faith and it contains Michalson's first extended discussion of "Faith as Historical Maturity." In this text, Michalson pays increased attention to the phenomenology of Merleau-Ponty (and others), aligns himself with the New Hermeneutic of Fuchs and Ebeling, and, especially important to this study, exhibits the influence of Friedrich Gogarten.

Michalson's relationship to Gogarten is widely recognized. Ivey says that Gogarten "was as influential on Michalson as any other person."[74] Theodore Runyon, writing about Gogarten in A Handbook of Christian Theologians, calls Michalson Gogarten's "foremost American admirer" and says that "The Rationality of Faith, a programatic study of faith's relationship to history, has given most explicit expression to Gogarten's concerns."[75]

The relationship of Michalson to Gogarten is especially crucial to this study, because Michalson's understanding of faith as historical maturity and his understanding of responsiblity for

---

[74]Ivey, "The Concept of the Holy Spirit," p. 10.

[75]Theodore Runyon, "Friedrich Gogarten," in A Handbook of Christian Theologians, ed. Martin Marty and Dean Peerman (Nashville: Abingdon, 1965), pp. 443-444.

the world can be traced directly to Gogarten. In short, when Michalson (who had recently translated Gogarten's The Reality of Faith) makes reference, in The Rationality of Faith, to historical maturity and responsibility for the world, he is referring to Gogarten.[76] Michalson's ethics bear a striking resemblance to, and are in some measure dependent on Gogarten's. Thus, to fully understand Michalson's references to historical maturity and responsiblity in The Rationality of Faith, and to understand Michalson's ethics, it is necessary to deal with Gogarten.

Gogarten believes that faith is history, and that history "designates. . .the process of interaction in which being and meaning are created ever anew."[77]

> The reality of history is neither the reality of ideas in the mind of the interpreter, who by virtue of these ideas makes the facts fit together in a meaningful pattern (sub-

---

[76] See Michalson, The Rationality of Faith, p. 131ff. See also Worldly Theology, p. 179ff; and Runyon, "Carl Michalson as a Wesleyan Theologian," p. 10. Though Michalson's ethics are clearly traceable to Gogarten, as Michalson himself admits, Runyon's point regarding the difference between Gogarten and Michalson is well taken, and will make itself felt. Unlike Gogarten, "Michalson's basis for rethinking the relationship of humanity to the world is not Luther's two realms but Wesley's doctrine of sanctification." (Runyon, "Carl Michalson as a Wesleyan Theologian, p. 10) This fact, though largely academic, points again to the importance of ethics for Michalson's theology. In precisely the same way he was committed to responsibility, Michalson was inherently committed to maturity in the world, and as a Wesleyan could integrally relate maturity in the world to his theology.

[77] Runyon, "Friedrich Gogarten," p. 430. My account of Gogarten's theology is heavily dependent on Runyon's Gogarten article, due to Michalson's endorsing its occurrence. (See footnote, The Rationality of Faith, p. 132.) Though Runyon's article may not be the best way to treat Gogarten in and of himself, it is without question an excellent means of linking Gogarten and Michalson, as it was written with precisely that link in mind. (Again see Runyon, "Friedrich Gogarten," pp. 443-444.)

jectivism and idealism), nor the reality of the "facts" in themselves in their detached isolated state (objectivism and positivism). The truth cannot be known by coming down on one side or the other of a fence between subject and object -- or better, in the case of God and man, between Subject and subject. Reality is an event which happens in the "between," in history.[78]

For Gogarten, "man is understood as receiving his being from the God whose creative Word calls man not just into existence but into an existence-in-responsibility."[79]

In his book Political Ethics, Gogarten examines the implications of humanity's being called into responsibility by an historical faith.

> . . .the problem of relativity as it concerns Christian faith is solved not by escaping from history into a realm of absolute ideals and universals but by living in history the responsible life of faith. . . .
> . . .From Gogarten's standpoint, . . .historical contingency--while undermining an absolutist ethic--is not inimical to ethics as such. Indeed, the fact that history is composed of contingent relationships is what makes it unavoidably ethical. One has his being in creative encounter--being is always being-from-the-other--and his continuing existence in being-with-another. These are not secondary modes of existence preceded by a primary mode of being-in-and-for-oneself; rather, individuality is secondary and the interpersonal is primary.
> Accordingly, ethical decisions and actions are the result not of adhering to abstract, nonhistorical standards of what one does or does not do, but of responding to each situation out of the being which one is in the relation to God and neighbor. The Christian life is a life of openness and obedience. The two go together. . . .In ethics as elsewhere, therefore, the problem of relativity is overcome not by substituting nonhistorical absolutes for the relativities of history but by facing each situation as a call to responsible action in history out of the being one has in faith.[80]

---

[78]Runyon, "Friedrich Gogarten," pp. 430-431.

[79]Ibid., p. 434.

[80]Ibid., pp. 431-432.

Gogarten, then, sees the Christian faith as an historical phenomenon wherein God calls humanity to be responsible in the world. And, for Gogarten, a contextual ethics results from this necessary relationship between faith and responsibility for the world.

Following World War II, Gogarten's interest in history was directed less toward the problem of historical relativism and more toward what he considered the major problem confronting the modern age: the relation of Christian faith to secularism.

> While the popular attitude toward secularism regards it as the archenemy of the faith, Gogarten asks whether a certain kind of secularization is not implicit in the Christian gospel itself. For example, the secular view sees the world as depopulated of those spirits once thought to have the world's well-being under their control. The task of maintaining the order of the world passes out of the hands of the demons, angels, "principalities and powers" and into the hands of man, who takes over the responsibility of ordering and caring for the world in accordance with his own needs and desires. Such a secularization is, . . .by no means foreign to the Christian faith. . .[81]

In fact, the contrary is true, for the Christian faith calls humanity precisely to this responsibility--the responsibility of sonship.

> A son is distinguished from a child in that, whereas the child is completely dependent upon the parent for his continued existence, the son--who has come of age and received an inheritance which is his to manage--has the ability to stand on his own, to be independent, no longer bound to the father by the necessities of his physical survival. The inheritance bestowed upon man is the world; he is given dominion over it and charged with the responsibility to "till it and keep it." His position with regard to the world thus frees him for a mature and noncompulsive relationship with the Father, while his filial relation to the

---

[81]Ibid., pp. 433-434.

Father frees him for a mature and noncompulsive attitude toward the world.[82]

The problem with secularism, according to Gogarten, is not that it lacks religion, but its tendency to give to the world the honor due to God alone and thereby "enter into a compulsive relation to the world." Humanity then becomes enslaved by a world that holds sway and is, in effect, a religious object.

> Christian faith proposes to keep the world truly secular and thus safeguard man's freedom toward the world through a certain kind of existence, existence as a mature and responsible son under the Creator-Father.[83]

With Gogarten as his point of departure, Michalson in *The Rationality of Faith* does indeed "give explicit expression to Gogarten's concerns," especially his concern regarding the secular person's assuming responsibiity for the world. In the first two chapters of the book Michalson discusses, literally the rationality of an historical faith. Larry Shiner summarizes his position:

> From the phenomenologists Michalson learned to distinguish nature and history. . .as two modes of man's being-in-the-world. . . .
> What [he] was driving at can perhaps be illustrated by the story of the three baseball umpires. One, an incipient empiricist, asserted, "I calls 'em as I sees 'em!" The second revealed his deep metaphysical passion when he indignantly objected, "I calls 'em as they *are*!" Both turned to the third, each hoping for an endorsement of his own position, only to experience a phenomenological shock to their natural standpoints: "They ain't nothin' until I calls 'em!" To the rationalist and empiricist alike this sounds like a crude subjectivism, but, as Michalson was constantly pointing out, such an objection fails to perceive the wide gulf separating subjectivism and subjectivity. . . .Subjec-

---

[82] Ibid., p. 434.

[83] Ibid., p. 436.

tivity. . ."includes the self in what it grasps." Subjectivity is not a matter of letting one's personal preferences intrude on his research (that would be subjectivism), but of approaching problems which involve the meaning of being human with the human passion to understand.[84]

Having phenomenologically reiterated that "the faith is historical" and having discussed the logic peculiar to an historical faith, Michalson concludes his book with a chapter entitled "Faith as Historical Maturity."

One who obeys the implications in Christ's obedience will anchor himself firmly in history, that is, assume the responsibility for shaping a world. In Jesus of Nazareth such responsibility is revealed to be the meaning of history. One can now judge history from an end that is present. . . . The purposes of God are now explicit. . . .God through the faithful ministry of Jesus of Nazareth has turned the world over to men. As the Apostle Paul told the Galatians, "You are no longer a slave but a son, and if a son then an heir" (Galatians 4:7). In this event the intention of creation is radically fulfilled: henceforth man is to subdue the earth. . . .To be a "child of God" is. . .the possibility in history which Jesus' announcement of the end of history commences. To be "a child of God" is to be set within an historical framework in which one begins to assume his responsibility for a world which God has turned over to him.[85]

Michalson's point is that humanity comes of age when it accepts responsibility in and for the world, and that responsibility in and for the world is eschatological. "Jesus of Nazareth is the open door by which the whole of history may live a history of wholeness."[86]

In short, a Christian is one who knows the fruits of the spirit. These fruits are structures of existence, not intellecutal data. They are fully historical realities which

---

[84]Larry Shiner, "Carl Michalson's Contribution to Theology," Religion in Life XXXVI, No. 2 (Spring, 1967):86.

[85]Michalson, Rationality of Faith, pp. 131-132.

[86]Ibid., pp. 134-135.

are lived out in men. Among them are love, joy, peace, patience, kindness, goodness, faithfulness, gentleness, and self-control. These are the attributes of a life of freedom, a life of responsibility prepared for in God's final word to history in Jesus of Nazareth. They are the eschatological attributes.[87]

Worldly Theology, a posthumous volume edited by John Godsey, follows closely the line of thought established in The Rationality of Faith. In many ways, it summarizes Michalson's theological career. In Worldly Theology, Michalson examines fifty years of theology in retrospect, and then offers a truly worldly theology for the future.

Regarding responsibility for the world, Michalson reiterates what was said in The Rationality of Faith.

> The contemporary theologian must influential in my delineation of this of worldly faith has been Friedrich Gogarten. While details in my presentation vary from him, the main lines are instructed by his view. Let me summarize it as it is stated in his recent volume, The Reality of Faith.
> What is the nature of the reality in which Christians participate when they have faith? How does this reality differ from the reality of the world in general, or from sheer human invention? Gogarten's answer is that the Christian faith involves a relation to the man Jesus Christ, who experiences the nothingness of the world. Acting in complete obedience toward God, Christ takes the nothingness of the world upon himself and thus introduces into history a new kind of reality, the reality of freedom from bondage to the world. The freedom from the world and for God is the reality of faith.[88]

John Wesley's emphasis on holiness also informs Worldly Theology. Michalson identifies Wesleyan holiness with maturity in the world, and the world's coming of age (from Bonhoeffer),

---

[87]Ibid., p. 139

[88]Michalson, Worldly Theology, p. 179.

and in terms of his historical and theological growth, uses Wesley to develop a "hermeneutics of holiness."

Michalson's hermeneutics of holiness is "a method of interpretation which relates to the Biblical text in such a way that the text interprets the reader effecting a significant change in his situation."[89] Utilizing the hermeneutics of holiness, Michalson concludes that "when the Bible is allowed to express its intention, the result for the world is transforming. The world is brought to maturity."[90] Michalson sets forth his hermeneutics of holiness by building upon the distinctive Wesleyan themes of holiness and perfection. According to Michalson, holiness augments the hermeneutical circle, holiness is a type of demythologizing, and holiness secularizes the world.

The hermeneutical circle, according to Michalson, is the relationship between man's preunderstanding (Vorverstandnis) and God's word.

> The relation between man's pre-understanding and God's word is a circle because the circuit of understanding is never complete where either functions in independence of the other.[91]

In the hermeneutical circle, humanity is addressed by God's word. Holiness augments humanity's being addressed by God, because it adds a new dimension to the circular strategy of hermeneutics. In short, Wesley's concept of holiness provides for a "newer and

---

[89] Ibid., p. 151.

[90] Ibid.

[91] Ibid., p. 144.

higher stage of the Christian life," and the hermeneutical circle then becomes "a spiralling transcendence."[92]

Michalson's hermeneutics of holiness is first "the exercise of interpreting human existence in the light of a text," but it also provides "a critical procedure for evaluating a text." If holiness is the text's fundamental concern (and Michalson says it is), then the text can judge itself in light of its adherance to this basic concern. Michalson, seeing himself in the tradition of Wesley, can thus reinterpret "passages which are, on the surface, deficient in scriptural holiness."[93]

Finally, holiness secularizes the world. Holiness liberates the Christian from the world in such a way that responsibility for the world can be assumed. The world is no longer of ultimate concern and in danger of becoming an idol. Rather, holiness frees the believer from the world so that the believer can assume dominion over it, live in it with the perspective of grace, and thus be responsible for it. Again, Michalson relates his task to Wesley's:

> The question being raised here is the same question Wesley himself once raised: "Would not one who was. . .sanctified be incapable of worldly business?" The answer Wesley gave: "He would be far more capable of it than ever, as going through all without distraction." Question: "Would he be capable of marriage?" Answer: "Why should he not?"
> Which is to say, the problem is the same, and so is the solution: when you buy, you will hold what you possess as if not possessing, when you marry, as if not married. Christian worldliness removes the distraction of idolatry and thus liberates a man to assume responsibility for the

---

[92] Ibid., p. 147.

[93] Ibid., pp. 148, 149.

world. Without that liberation, one could turn the world into an idol to which he felt responsible, thus losing his capacity to be responsible for it.[94]

What Michalson has done with his hermeneutics of holiness is to systematize his concern for responsibility. Given the logic of his hermeneutics, Christianity points finally to responsibility for the world. According to Michalson, responsibility for the world, having been born of scriptural holiness is the warp and woof of Christianity.

> Holiness, without disparaging the world, is committed to orienting the world to God in order not to turn the world into the very idol, exclusive devotion to which obstructs the sense of responsibility for it.[95]

C. Responsibility in a Soteriological Context

It has been shown that responsibility was an abiding concern for Carl Michalson. As a student at Drew with Edwin Lewis, at Yale with H. Richard Niebuhr, and throughout his career as a teacher, lecturer, and published theologian, Michalson sought to bring the faith to fruition in responsibility. His Wesleyan heritage demanded it, Lewis and Niebuhr encouraged it, and his later theologizing out of Gogarten and Wesley sought to understand, how the Christian, having been freed *from* the world by Christ, can assume responsibility *for* the world. Stanley Hopper, in his Memorial Service meditation, captured the essence of Michalson's thought when he said, "Theology becomes parable and

---

[94]Ibid., p. 155.

[95]Ibid., p. 157.

preaching. . . .We are now responsible, and mankind (in God's eyes) is now mature."[96]

An awareness of Michalson's continued concern for responsibility points to its importance in his theologizing. But to fully appreciate and understand the importance of responsibility in Michalson's thought, the concept must be seen in a soteriological context. Responsibility was an integral part of Michalson's theology. His understanding of the Christian faith was such that human response to God's call and responsibility in Christ were crucial to the expression of faith.

In Chapter I (p.40ff.) and again in Chapter II (p.58ff.) I have attempted to show that Michalson saw the faith's occurrence within history alone. Ivey summarizes this aspect of Michalson's thought as follows:

> Revelation happens within history and history alone. Faith, which is the ongoing interrelationship with revelation, is to be explained in historically conceived constructs. . . .To be Christian is to stand squarely, completely, and openly within history. History does not refer to past events but is that reality which addresses itself to the question of meaning for the human being. Both natural and supernatural categories are considered foreign to the rationality of the Christian faith. Natural categories, as Michalson defines them, are silent about the meaning of personhood. Supernatural and metaphysical categories divert one's attention away from the reality within which life occurs. To state what it means to be a Christian--what it means to be truly human--in any terms other than historical is to betray the very reality of the Christian faith.[97]

---

[96]Stanley Hopper, "Memorial Meditation," Given at Madison Methodist Church, Nov. 11, 1965. <u>Drew Gateway</u> XXXVI, 3 (Spring-Summer, 1966):114-121. Also on cassette tape in Drew University library.

[97]Ivey, Introduction to <u>Witness of Radical Faith</u>, p. 11.

Since Christian faith occurs within history alone, Michalson sought to discover and explicate the rationality of the Christian faith, the peculiar way one knows as a Christian. According to the dustcover of The Rationality of Faith:

> Michalson argues that faith and reason do not conflict, but that historical reason and scientific reason are fundamentally different. . . .By keeping [Christianity in the realm of historical reason], the theologian avoids any conflict with scientific reason.[98]

1. Existential Nothingness

Michalson understood the Christian faith (within history alone and with a rationality all its own) as first and foremost an illumination of human existence. Faith, elucidates what it means to be truly human, grants self understanding and personhood, and in so doing illuminates human existence. As Ivey puts it:

> When Michalson made the claim that history was the locus of operation for the Christian, he was faced with the depravity and utter shipwreck of so much of human occurrence. . . .As a theologian, he sought. . .the best way to structure the search that ought to characterize such human void. Existentialism provided the means for him to do this. Existentialism as a _way_ of life is the experience of the quest for meaning. Existentialism as a _view_ of life is the philosophical attempt to uncover meaning in the midst of the meaninglessness of life and to give philosophical structure to that.[99]

Michalson, himself says

> There are cracks in the orderliness of being through which man sees the possibility of powerfully unpredictable impul-

---

[98]Michalson, The Rationality of Faith, dust jacket.

[99]Ivey, Introduction to Witness of Radical Faith, p. 11.

ses toward himself. Their presence evokes in him unquenchable heroic instincts to leap against his fate.[100]
Existentialism (as a way of life) is the inevitable awareness that these cracks exist. Existentialism (as a view of life) is the unsuccessful search for meaning in the cracked orderliness of a flawed world. The Christian faith is that leap against fate that fills the void of meaninglessness with meaning, and gives our lives purpose and hope.

2. Christian Encounter and Meaningfulness

a. Christology, Soteriology and Eschatology

The meaningfulness provided by an historical faith comes in Jesus of Nazareth. In Jesus the quest for meaning is fulfilled. By his obedience to God's love, Jesus calls human existence into question and challenges humanity to itself become obedient and responsible. Jesus offers humanity the opportunity to live a new and meaningful life received from and with reference to God. Humanity need no longer be dependent on the world for life's meaning. Rather, meaning is found in Jesus who frees people _from_ the world in order for them to be responsible _for_ it.[101]

As can be seen from his describing the importance of Jesus, Michalson's Christology emphasizes not the person of Christ, but the work of Christ. This is intentional, for in theology as

---

[100]Michalson, The Hinge of History, p. 69.

[101]See Michalson, Worldly Theology, pp. 159-163. See also Ivey, Introduction to Witness of Radical Faith, p. 13.

history the accent falls not on Christology, but on soteriology, which is eschatological. That is, the importance of Christ resides primarily in his functioning or "working" to unite humanity to God eschatologically.

According to Michalson, "To behold Jesus is to understand oneself as a man in the presence of God. To discern him is to discern God. To hear him is to hear God. He and the father are one. . . ." God is thus uniquely present in Jesus, who "had the authority to speak and act for God"[102] and who called humanity, on behalf of God, to responsibility. The point of juncture between humanity and God is Jesus of Nazareth in whom God is calling the world into eschatological existence, and who allows humanity to understand itself as responsible for the world as an inheritance.

Having defined history as both past facticity and interpretation of past facticity, Michalson was confronted with the difficulty of conceptualizing that historical encounter where subject and object meet, when subject and object are really Subject and subject--i.e. God in Jesus and humanity. Not only is the past facticity of Jesus lying behind the texts impossible to lay hold of; but when the claim is made that Jesus is the Christ, history is in double jeopardy. In the face of this "history

---

[102]Michalson, Worldly Theology, p. 164. This material (Chapter nine, section two of Worldly Theology) was originally published as "Jesus Christ as Word Became Flesh," The Christian Century (May 3, 1961):552-553. See also Godsey, "The Legacy of Michalson," p. 83ff. See also Runyon, "Michalson as a Radical Theologian," p. 94.

problem," Michalson utilizes the "new quest of the historical Jesus," where Jesus (the point of juncture between humanity and God is referred to as "speech-event or "word-event." By so doing, he seeks to re-relate his theologizing to (outer) world history and reclaim its facticity.

b. The New Quest and Word Event

Precisely at the point where (inner) eschatological history seems to have lost its objective point of reference, Michalson seeks to re-establish its past facticity. "The concern with existential and eschatological dimensions of history is not meant to be a denial of world history and Biblical history."[103] Though "world history is not concerned with the final (eschatos) meaning of events"[104] (When it is so concerned it becomes existential history.), and though Biblical history is superseded and reduced by our finding meaning in Christ as the (inner) eschatological event, Michalson's historical faith nonetheless seeks to maintain contact with both (outer) world history and Biblical history--and necessarily so!

Michalson maintains contact with world and Biblical history (and thus keeps his understanding of faith truly historical) by reference to the historical Jesus as discussed by the "new quest of the historical Jesus." According to Michalson, one cannot

---

[103] Michalson, The Hinge of History, p. 180.
[104] Ibid.

"experience the 'sheer happened-ness' of faith without a prior knowledge of some historical facts."[105] And for him, the two concepts are related on the basis of the "new quest of the historical Jesus" which, with its references to Jesus as word-event, performs a mediating function between (outer) world history and Biblical history on the one hand, and (inner) existential history and eschatological history on the other.

Michalson recognized the post-Bultmannians as responsible for and definitive of the "new quest:"

> . . .the pupils of Bultmann. . .do not search for the world-historical Jesus behind the confessional and sermonic form in which the testimony to his existence appears in the New Testament. They search for Jesus _within_ that form. This is fully consistent with any historian's method who finds the data of diaries and letters more primary and illuminating historically than accounts by journalists and court clerks. Nor do they search for some object in the past which is undeniably there as any other world historical object. They simply let the data be, as sensitive historians would, and in the process Jesus emerges as the Christ, the source of meaningful existence, the eschatological event.[106]

---

[105]Ibid., p. 182.

[106]Michalson, _Hinge of History_, p. 181.

Gerhard Ebeling was especially important to Michalson[107] and serves here to detail the "new quest."[108]

Ebeling, and others involved in the "new quest," utilize Bultmann's historical-critical method, but recognize the insufficiency of a strictly existential interpretation and understanding as its result. There is, in fact, no significant difference in Ebeling's and Bultmann's use of the method; Ebeling's complaint is not that it is erroneous, but that it is insufficient. For example, in answering the question, "What did Jesus in fact say?" (What are the authentic logia?"), Ebeling and Bultmann are essentially identical. The difference appears in what is done with the logia after they have been determined or authenticated. Ebeling would agree with Bultmann that you cannot get behind the kerygma in order to find historical facts as proof, but he goes on to say that Jesus is more than mere facts.

---

[107]See Michalson, Rationality of Faith, footnote 22, pp. 51-56. Here Michalson refers to his adaptation of Ebeling's "new quest" formulation and comments at length on the "new quest." See also Rationality of Faith, p. 91ff; and Gordon Michalson, preface to Witness of Radical Faith who quotes Ebeling as having recognized Carl as "my beachhead in America." (p.5) The closeness of Michalson to Ebeling is also seen in Ebeling's having written for the Michalson Festschrift Hermeneutics and the Worldliness of Faith. (Ebeling, "Against the Confusion in Today's Christianity," Drew Gateway 45:1,2,3 (1974-1975):pp. 203-229.

[108]For a comprehensive treatment of the "new quest of the historical Jesus," see Gerhard Ebeling, "The Quest of the Historical Jesus," Word and Faith (Philadelphia: Fortress Press, 1963), p. 290ff. See also James M. Robinson, A New Quest of the Historical Jesus (London: SCM Press, 1959; reprint ed., 1971); James M. Robinson and John B. Cobb, ed. New Frontiers in Theology, Vol II: The New Hermeneutic, (New York: Harper & Row, 1964), esp. article by Ernst Fuchs, "The New Testament and the Hermeneutical Problem, pp. 111ff.

For Ebeling to have to do with Jesus means to have to do with nothing but the Word. The task of bringing to expression what came to expression in Jesus is a hermeneutic task which concludes in the word-event. It is the word-event, and its coming to expression which enables historians and theologians to come together without destroying the purity of historical method or the basis of theological assertions.

> When. . .theology approaches history in a proper way, i.e. with the question what it was that came to expression, and when it understands this coming to expression as something that happens in the word-event, then it is pursuing the hermeneutic task in a way that begins to bridge the modern gulf between the historical and the dogmatic.[109]

The attempt to get behind the kerygma is not an attempt to get to objective facts but to get to that which has come to expression in the kerygma.

> If we carry out our attempts to get behind the primitive Christian kerygma in a proper manner, then we shall not be looking for facts which confirm the Word, but we shall be looking beyond a word which needs interpretation for the word-event which is presupposed within it.[110]

The question of the historical Jesus should not seek to get <u>behind</u> the Word of proclamation, but to penetrate further into the Word, in order to truly hear the challenge and understand the kerygma as the <u>Word of God</u>. Jesus thus <u>appears</u> in the confessional and sermonic form of the New Testament and <u>emerges</u> as the Christ.

---

[109]Ebeling, "The Quest of the Historical Jesus," <u>Word and Faith</u>, p. 295.

[110]Ebeling, <u>Theology and Proclamation</u> (Philadelphia: Fortress Press, 1961), p. 46.

In the "new quest for the historical Jesus," Ebeling posits the word-event as the "object" of the faith, and as a source of common ground for the historian as historian and the theologian as historian. Word-event is the mediator between history as history and theology as history. Behind this, of course, is the Heideggerian metaphorical attribution of "life" to language. The assumption that "language speaks," is an assumption of a potentiality in language to "happen" as word-event. Thus to come into language is, literally (really, truly) to come to expression.

The self-hood of Jesus and his identity as Christ <u>are available</u> to us through his word and message, because language (as his language) causes the word-event (then) to re-occur (now). The word-event contains the self-hood of Jesus and his identity as Christ, and makes Jesus Christ "real" for us. Thus, word-event is a common ground that both the historian as historian and theologian as historian can affirm.

The "new quest of the historical Jesus" was "tailor-made" for Michalson's theology as history.[111] Its use of word-event,[112] to characterize the encounter of God in Christ with humanity, meets Michalson's definition of history as past facticity <u>and</u> interpretation of that facticity. And it allows for the meeting of subject and "object" (which is really the meeting

---

[111] See especially Michalson, <u>Rationality of Faith</u>, p. 91ff and <u>Worldly Theology</u>, p. 165ff. for Michalson's adaptation of Ebeling's (and Fuchs') formulations.

[112] See ibid. Michalson calls the word-event "speech-event."

of Subject and subject) which an <u>historical</u> faith demands.[113] It is thus in the context of the "new quest of the historical Jesus" that Michalson states that God is present and encounters humanity in the obedience (i.e. work) of Jesus Christ. This encounter is an historical one, because as word-event, it is an encounter which <u>literally</u> contains the selfhood of the historical Jesus and his identity as the Christ. By this encounter people understand themselves as sons and daughters of God, called to responsibility for the world. The significance of the word-event is not that God be known to humanity as father, but that human beings understand themselves as heirs, responsible for the world as an inheritance.

3. Holiness and Maturity

For Michalson, the drama of salvation concludes with "Holiness and the Maturity of Faith" i.e. responsibility for the world. In discussing "Holiness and the Maturity of Faith" in <u>Worldly Theology</u>, Michalson treats approvingly several major themes in Wesley's thought: faith works in love; the Gospel reappropriates the law; and perfection as a process, rather than an end.

---

[113]Because of the word-event's ability to <u>historically</u> bridge the gap between God and humanity, it has tremendous implications for Christian theology. Its significance for eschatology has been touched on here (see above, pp. 96-97; see also <u>Rationality of Faith</u>, p. 135ff). Michalson also speaks of the impact of a consistently historical faith on the doctrine of the Holy Spirit (see <u>Rationality of Faith</u>, pp. 51-56, footnote #22; see also <u>Rationality of Faith</u>, p. 150ff).

Says Michalson:

> Life under grace, in holiness, was not a condition of conformity where one was successfully fulfilling moral principles. Life under grace was a life in love where the most benevolent simplicity was introduced into all one's affairs. Holiness, therefore, in Wesley's doctrine of Christian perfection, is a life of truth where truth is understood to be beauty and not ideas. It is a life of energy where energy is the expression of beauty, a beauty which is neither innate (Descartes) nor derived from experience (Locke), but which more closely resembles what "belongs to the substance of the spirit" (Shaftesbury). It is, in short, a life of simplicity, characterized as "faith, humility, willingness to be taught, and freedom from all evil reasonings."[114]

Michalson thus concludes his discussion of "Holiness and the Maturity of Faith" with reference to a hermeneutics of holiness which emerges from Wesley's emphasis on holiness, referred to above (See p.91ff).

Finally Michalson characterizes holiness and the maturity of faith as freedom. "When persons choose Jesus of Nazareth as the beginning of their history, they undergo an ascent from the old age to the new. This transition is experienced as freedom."[115] This freedom, according to Michalson, is freedom from the world, freedom from the law, freedom from sin and freedom from death. It is in this regard that Michalson summarizes Friedrich Gogarten:

> The contemporary theologian most influential in my delineation of this view of worldly faith has been Friedrich Gogarten. While details in my presentation vary from him, the main lines are instructed by his view. Let me summarize it as it is stated in his recent volume, The Reality of Faith.

---

[114] Michalson, Worldly Theology, p. 140.

[115] Ibid., p. 168.

What is the nature of the reality in which Christians participate when they have faith? How does this reality differ from the reality of the world in general, or from sheer human invention? Gogarten's answer is that the Christian faith involves a relation to the man Jesus Christ, who experiences the nothingness of the world. Acting in complete obedience toward God, Christ takes the nothingness of the world upon himself and thus introduces into history a new kind of reality, the reality of freedom from bondage to the world. The freedom *from* the world and *for* God is the reality of faith.[116]

D. Ethical Implications of Responsibility in Michalson's Thought

1. The Necessity of Christian Responsibility

I have sought to demonstrate that Michalson's theology (especially when seen soteriologically) depicts the Christian faith as inextricably bound to human responsibility. Systematically, responsibility is a necessary consequence of an historical faith. Responsibility necessarily follows that encounter between Subject and subject that defines historical faith. Michalson seems to have adopted this understanding from Kierkegaard,[117] but it is also found in Gogarten. An historical faith that is grounded in responsibility avoids the problems of relativity and subjectivity.

> [The Christian's faith translates] him out of the world of unreality, of abstraction, of objectivity and ideality, which is not a world one lives, into the real world where one can grasp existence as a whole. "By faith I make renun-

---

[116] Ibid., p. 179.

[117] See Soren Kierkegaard, *Fear and Trembling* and *The Sickness Unto Death*, trans. Walter Lowrie (Princeton: Princeton University Press, 1941). See also *The Journals of Kierkegaard*, ed. Alexander Dru (New York: Harper & Row, 1959).

ciation of nothing, on the contrary, by faith I acquire everything."[118]

What has been said of Gogarten can be said of Michalson.

> . . .the problem of relativity as it concerns Christian faith is solved not by escaping from history into a realm of absolute ideals and universals but by living in history the <u>responsible</u> life of faith.
>
> Likewise, faith. . .cannot be labeled "subjective," for faith is not a subject's affirmation of an object but rather its being confronted by the Word from beyond itself and incorporated into a relationship--into a new history--fundamentally conditioned by the history of Jesus Christ (as that history has just been described). Faith therefore transcends subjectivism by virtue of the fact that it is a historical mode of being, a being-from-the-other and with-the-other. Apart from this "other" and the historical interaction there is no genuine faith.[119]

Michalson also views faith as responsible <u>by nature</u>. In his M.A. thesis, Michalson utilizes Emil Brunner to show that Christianity by its very nature begets responsibility. In his later writings (specifically <u>The Rationality of Faith</u> and <u>Worldly Theology</u>) Michalson, utilizing Gogarten, points to Paul's concept of Sonship (Gal. 4) as paradigmatic and sees Sonship as necessarily begetting responsibility. "In this event [of sonship] the intention of creation is radically fulfilled: henceforth, man is to subdue the earth."[120] Michalson, on numerous occasions and in a variety of ways, sought to identify the Christian faith with human responsibility. I will now seek to explore the ethical implications of this responsibility born of faith.

---

[118]Michalson, <u>Worldly Theology</u>, p. 126.

[119]Runyon, "Friedrich Gogarten," pp. 431, 442.

[120]Michalson, <u>Rationality of Faith</u>, p. 131.

2. **Christian Responsibility in Terms of Ethics: Responsibility Transcends Ethics**

On first glance, Michalson's concept of responsibility does not seem very promising in its implications for Christian ethics. Michalson's understanding of responsiblity is defined and set forth in The Hinge of History, and is, by his own admission, ambiguous.[121] In The Rationality of Faith, Michalson says emphatically that Christianity's being responsible for the world is not a code of conduct and that maturity in the world transcends morality.[122] And in Worldy Theology, where Michalson shifts his focus toward the world, there is a decided ambivalence toward the ethical consequences of his concept of responsibility.[123]

Throughout his writings then, Michalson is reluctant to think of responsibility in terms of morality and/or codes of conduct. These imply standards other than Christ as authoritative for Christian life. And for Michalson, Christ abrogates all other authority. Responsibility cannot be understood as moral responsibility or responsibility in line with a code of conduct. Rather, responsibility is historical responsibility in line with historical faith and the Christ of history whose word of grace transcends and makes mute all others. Responsibility for the

---

[121] See The Hinge of History, p. 241ff.

[122] Michalson, The Rationality of Faith, p. 138.

[123] See Worldly Theology, esp. p. 140. See also p. 168ff.

world is in reality, response-ability--wrought by Christ and lived in Christ alone.[124]

3. **Ethics in Terms of Christian Responsibility:**
   The Possibility of a Christian Ethic

Does Michalson's ambivalence toward the ethical implications of "responsibility for the world", mean that he is not concerned about ethics? No not at all. Rather, Michalson sees the Christian's responsibility for the world as transcending the ethical much like Kierkegaard saw the Religious Stage as transcending the Ethical Stage.[125] This approach is known as "transvaluation".[126] Far from disregarding ethics, Michalson calls for usual notions of morality to be transcended and advocates a heightened sense of the ethical--a distinctly _Christian_ ethics, if you will. Michalson's concept of responsibility for the world then, is far from being ethically irrelevant. In fact, and as will be seen in Chapter III, quite the opposite is true. For Michalson, Christian responsibility for the world is ethical, in a higher sense of the word.

_____

[124]The sense in which Michalson uses the word responsibility is primarily response to God or responsiveness -- quite literally response-ability, or the ability to respond to God. Thus responsibility is first retrospective; it looks (back) to God as its source. At the same time, and as will be seen, responsibility is prospective; it looks (forward) to the world as its outlet. This is in keeping with my initial definition of responsibility as _to_ God and _for_ the world (pp.53-54).

[125]See Kierkegaard, Fear and Trembling.

[126]Edward L. Long, A Survey of Christian Ethics, (New York: Oxford University Press, 1967), pp. 33-34.

Michalson's concept of responsibility, representing a distinctly Christian ethic that transvaluates the ethical situation, is also contextual. "Value is determined by the persons or beings for whom something is good; it is not a rigid category of right."[127] Again, what Runyon has written of Gogarten in this regard, is also true of Michalson:

> . . .ethical decisions and actions are the results not of adhering to abstract, nonhistorical standards of what one does nor does not do, but of responding to each situation out of the being which one is in the relation to God and neighbor. The Christian life is a life of openness and obedience. . .whose action is a creative response to what he hears. In ethics as elsewhere, therefore, the problem of relativity is overcome not by substituting nonhistorical absolutes for the relativities of history but by facing each situation as a call to responsible action in history out of the being one has in faith.[128]

For Michalson, responsibility for the world is necessary to, and integrated with the Christian faith. Humanity, called by God's grace in Jesus Christ, responds to God's call by being responsible in the world, (i.e. by "faith's working" in love) and by seeking to attain holiness. Responsibility is preaching; it is prophetic and redemptive; it is freedom from the world and for God. As such, responsibility is humanity's receiving the world

---

[127] Ibid. p. 34. Ellis B. Johnson writes that Michalson articulated a contextual ethical stance as early as 1947. "In a book review in that year he questions C. S. Lewis' call for men to obey absolute values." (Johnson, "Carl Michalson's Concept of History as a Theological Method," p. 224). See also Carl Michalson, review of The Abolition of Man, by C. S. Lewis. Drew Gateway XIX, 1 (Autumn, 1947):13.

[128] Runyon, "Friedrich Gogarten," pp. 431-432.

(with all its ambiguity) back from God so that "henceforth man [can] subdue the earth."

Michalson's understanding of responsibility in and for the world has definite ethical implications--in fact, responsibility, for Michalson, supersedes, or transvaluates ethics as to become (contextual) <u>Christian</u> ethics in its own right. In the next chapter I will further examine Michalson's ethics of responsibility and evaluate it.

CHAPTER THREE

Ethics in Carl Michalson: Theory, Substance and Application

A. The Ethics of Responsibility: Theory and Substance

For Carl Michalson, responsibility for the world is the <u>necessary</u> conclusion to the Christian faith's drama of salvation. And responsibility for the world, as proposed by Michalson, has definite ethical implications. In fact, responsibility for the world transvalues ethics and itself becomes contextual Christian ethics. This chapter will further define and clarify Michalson's ethics of responsibility by examining his ethics in theory and substance and by examining the application of his ethics of responsibility. Finally, this chapter will evaluate Michalson's Christian ethics of responsibility.

<u>Theoretically</u>, Michalson writes about existential ethics and ethics integral to theology. <u>Substantively</u>, he sees preaching as the means whereby the Christian meets the world and, thus, the basis of a contextual ethics that, ultimately, is expressed as historical maturity (sanctification). In line with this he also speaks of ethics in terms of social responsibility, justice and power, human rights, economics, politics, war and peace, and world community. These ethical formulations are then <u>applied</u> to the specific problems of racism and alcohol.

1. *Theory*

a. The Ethics of Responsibility as Existential Ethics

Michalson makes very few theoretical references to ethics. In an article for the <u>Dictionary of Christian Ethics,</u> which was later incorporated into <u>Worldly Theology</u>, he puts forth a sympathetic understanding of existential ethics. In <u>Rationality of Faith</u> he refers to ethics as being integral to theology.[1]

---

[1] In addition to these citations, there are several folders in Drew's "Michalson Collection" pertaining to ethics. The first two such folders, numbered 43 and 67, are entitled, "Christian Ethics" and "Moral". These are related to a two semester course Michalson taught from 1943 until 1951 entitled "The Doctrines of Sin and Salvation." The course description for this course was as follows:
> First semester: After a brief review of the biblical teaching and of the doctrinal development, the course will center on various modern interpretations with a view to understanding the moral, social, psychological and religious meanings of the doctrine.
> Second semester: A critical evaluation of historical and contemporary viewpoints on the place of Christ in human salvation. (Drew University Catalogue, 1943-44)

The folders in question contain Michalson's lecture notes on the moral meaning of the doctrine of sin. He treats the subject historically, and deals with the positions of Kant, Schleiermacher, Ritschl, and Tennant, among others, in seeking to set forth the moral meaning of the doctrine.

The third folder in the Michalson Collection that pertains to ethics is number 248, and contains collected book reports on ethics texts that were apparently written for H. Richard Niebuhr while Michalson was at Yale. Niebuhr's comment regarding these reports is instructive. "These are exhaustive summaries of the works in question and indicate your careful study. Since you have added little in the way of evaluation or criticisms, I need make no comment. HRN."

In both of these instances, the Michalson student is acquainted with Michalson's background in the field of ethics, but aside from this, the material is not especially useful.

When Michalson does speak theoretically of ethics, he reiterates what has been said regarding responsibility for the world, and thus, confirms the fact that responsibility for the world is a transvaluated and contextual ethical construct. In the article entitled "Existentialist Ethics", Michalson favorably compares Christian and existentialist ethical thought, claiming that "Even the alleged acosmism, individualism and atheism of Existentialism have meanings which are closer to the Christian position than the casual observer generally concedes."[2]

The first point Michalson makes regarding existentialist ethics has to do with its opposition to legalism.

> Living by laws, . . .is regarded by existentialists as 'bad faith'. . .A legalistic ethic abridges freedom by taking decisions out of the hands of responsible selves. Soren Kierkegaard's treatise, Fear and Trembling, anticipated this view. Abraham was a knight of faith because he remained open to God's word. His willingness to murder his son out of obedience to God is higher than ethics because it does not force the future to conform to revelations of God given for the past.
> In contemporary Existentialism what Kierkegaard called 'the teleological suspension of the ethical' is itself ethics. Openness to the future has primacy over conformity to the past.

For Michalson "Christian ethics has accomplished the same movement away from legalism." Michalson sees this movement rooted in Paul's "reducing of the whole law to the one word 'love'" and related to such contemporary formulations as Ramsey's "ethic with-

---

[2]Carl Michalson, "Existentialist Ethics," in The Dictionary of Christian Ethics, ed. John Mcquarrie (Philadelphia: Westminster, 1967), p. 124.

out laws" and H. Richard Niebuhr's "responsivity", among others.[3]

Existentialist ethics is also acosmic, says Michalson.

> Existentialists. . . believe the world is not something one is *in*. Worlds are modes of **being-in**. There is the world of politics, of sports, of religion, of art. There is no 'world' of ethics because ethics is the study of modes of being-in which results in revealing the possibilities for the worlds one creates through his modes of being-in.
> The model from art comes the closest to exemplifying how an existential ethic works. The artist does not record a world that exists. He creates, through his aesthetic behaviour, the possibility for a world one may not previously have known. . . .Ethics, like art, nihilates the world as cosmos (earth, sea and sky) in order to create the world as a mode of being-in.

According to Michalson, this acosmism points to the fallaciousness of saying that existentialism is an individualism without a social ethic. "The primary term for existentialist ethics is neither 'individual' nor 'social' but 'world', a reality in which the distinction between individual and social disappears, for 'world' embraces all modes of being-in."[4]

Finally, Michalson says that existentialist ethics are atheistic. But atheism does not mean "that men have killed God." Rather,

> it means that men have used a static concept of God in order to endorse effete causes whose prolongation is murderous to men. . . .Kierkegaard was a theist for the very same reason that existentialists today are atheists. . . .Because if there is a God, nothing else can be absolutized. All one's relations will be relative. Old worlds, like Isaac, must be allowed to die in order for new worlds to be born. In this case relativism does not mean the absence of stan-

---

[3] Ibid. See also Michalson, "Christian Faith and Existential Freedom," *Religion in Life*, XXI, 4 (Autumn, 1952), p. 524.

[4] Ibid., p. 124.

dards, but the freedom, that is, the responsibility for creating in one's time the relevant mode of being-in.[5]

What Michalson says about existentialist ethics is almost identical to what has been said about responsibility for the world. Responsibility for the world is in contrast to legalism, and is a free response to grace. Responsibility for the world, as the warp and woof of an historical faith, is precisely the existentialist's acosmism--i.e. opposed to the world of the cosmologist. . ."an out there world into which a man is invited to fit as a coin fits in a box."[6] Finally, Michalson's theism is predicated on the same assumption as existentialism's "benign" atheism. And like existentialism's atheism, Michalson's theism relativizes ethics. Michalson says, "If there is a God, nothing else can be absolutized". Thus, responsibility for the world is a relative relationship established by the freedom that Christ grants us from the world when he relates us to the absolute God. This freedom from the world allows us to assume responsibility for the world and "subjugate it."

b. The Ethics of Responsibility Integral to Theology

The Rationality of Faith reference to ethics points, first to the importance of ethics for Michalson.

> In contemporary hermeneutics, understanding and exegegis are merged. One does not first understand, then explain. The understanding must be self-explaining. Thereafter, what becomes of the responsibility for applying what is under-

---

[5] Ibid., pp. 124-125.

[6] Ibid., p. 124.

stood? If historical understanding is an act of decisiveness, meaning ought not be looked upon as an intellectual preface to action. Meaning is itself a kind of action; meaning is realized in action. Theologians endorse this method of interpretation when they refuse to separate theology and ethics: faith _is_ what a man does that is meaningful. . . .Faith is _not_ what a man does _with_ the claims of the gospel. Faith is the act of being claimed by the gospel in such a way as to have one's life illuminated. In matters of faith, one does not understand, then decide. Nor does one decide, then understand. Understanding is itself decision and decision is itself the form of understanding.[7]

For Michalson to say that being faithful is being ethical, and vice versa, is to say again that being faithful is being responsible, and vice versa. Ethics, for Michalson, is woven into the fabric of the faith so as to be imperative. Ethics is crucial to the Christian's being Christian and, in fact, is the faith's coming to expression.[8]

By refusing to separate theology and ethics, Michalson has indicated the importance of ethics. He has also reiterated his understanding that faith transvaluates ethics. That faith is action means further that action is faith--i.e. that all meaningful action is informed by and necessarily reflects the faith understanding concurrent with it. Just as faith necessarily

---

[7]Michalson, The Rationality of Faith, p. 80. All through his writings, Michalson maintains that ethics grows out of theology, and if theology is done correctly, ethics will naturally follow. See also Carl Michalson, Review of Foundations for Reconstruction, by D. Elton Trueblood, The Drew Gateway, XVIII, 4 (Summer, 1947):71.

[8]The fact that Michalson understands responsibility as "imperative" to Christian faithfulness should be understood in the context of his Wesleyanism. This, in no way, shape, or form implies a "works righteousness" inflection in Michalson's theology.

acts, ethical action is necessarily faithful. And because action is faithful--because action is informed by and reflects the faith--it can be said (again) that faith transvaluates action.

Michalson's references to ethics per se reiterate what was said in chapter two. Because his understanding of ethics so closely parallels his understanding of responsibility for the world, it can be stated conclusively that Michalson's concept of responsibility is an ethical construct. For Michalson, ethics is responsibility and vice versa. Therefore his is an ethics of responsibility. In his speaking of ethics per se, Michalson's presupposition is clearly subjective (i.e. historical) faith, which he defends as altogether appropriate. His ethics of responsibility is an ethics of grace that is opposed to legalism; it is acosmic; and it is relativized by the absoluteness of God, therefore contextual. When Michalson says, "The teleological suspension of the ethical is itself ethics", he says again that the Christian faith transvaluates ethics. Michalson's "ethics integral to faith" reference points again to the importance of ethics/responsibility and restates his understanding of faith's informing (transvaluating) ethics.

2. Substance

It has been determined that, for Michalson, responsibility is a necessary part of the Christian faith, theologically and soteriologically. And responsibility has implications for Christian ethics. In fact, Michalson understands responsibility as a transvaluation of ethical concerns that expresses itself as a contextual Christian ethic.

Michalson's writings on ethics per se, by reiterating what was said about responsibility and effectively identifying ethics with responsibility, allow for the recognition of responsibility as an ethical construct. Having established the fact that responsibility is an ethical construct, I will examine Michalson's ethics of responsibility substantively, examine Michalson's ethics of responsibility as applied, and evaluate his Christian ethics of responsibility.[9]

The Hinge of History, and an antecedent article, 'What Doth the Lord Require Of Us?"[10] contains the first substantive reference to responsibility. In The Hinge of History, Michalson understands preaching as the sine qua non of historical (or Christian)[11] responsibility.

---

[9] The delineation of theory and substance on the one hand and application on the other is roughly the same as that of formulation and implementation, utilized by Edward LeRoy Long, Jr. in A Survey of Christian Ethics. I have further delineated Dr. Long's categories, to more clearly characterize Michalson's ethic, and because Michalson's presentation of the material seems to demand it. In Chapter Four (p. 145ff.), when Dr. Long's categories are used to evaluate Michalson's ethics, references from my schema will be placed appropriately.

[10] The article "What Doth the Lord Require of Us?" appeared in The International Review of Missions XLV, No. 178 in April, 1956 (pp. 145-154), and forms the basis for chapter ten in The Hinge of History.

[11] In accordance with the discussion above, regarding responsibility's transcending morality, and, according to Michalson, forming the basis of a distinctly Christian ethic (see pp. 107-110), Michalson distinguishes between moral responsibility and historical (or Christian) responsibility in The Hinge of History.

A Christian is one who acknowledges that God has turned to man in Jesus and who takes upon himself the responsibility of turning to the world with that report. Hence, to be a Christian is to be involved in the responsibility of the communication of the gospel.[12]

Because Michalson understands preaching as the church's primary task, it stands to reason that "The Mission of the Church" centers on preaching.

. . .the Christian witness creates history. But it does so not without constituting a meaningful and responsible community. It becomes the mission of this community to bring God's end, which is Christ, to all peoples in such a way as to constitute their beginning.[13]

Since Michalson understands preaching as the faith's coming to expression, as the faith's being lived, and as the faith's beginning to actually assume its responsibility, preaching is uniquely capable of characterizing Christian responsibility *toward* God and *for* the world. (Indeed, in Michalson's sermons the faith does become remarkably alive.[14]) Therefore, it is in preaching--where the responsible Christian actually, contextually, meets the world--that Christian ethics begins. For Michalson, preaching, by virtue of its actually giving life to faith, is the point of departure for his *Christian* ethics of responsibility, that is integral to theology.

For Michalson, preaching creates and is at the center of the church's mission, and according to Michalson, "we blunder if we

---

[12]Michalson, The Hinge of History, p. 214.

[13]Ibid., p. 239.

[14]See Michalson, The Witness of Radical Faith in its entirety.

underestimate the breadth of relevance for our world in this simple charge."[15] In concluding The Hinge of History, Michalson characterizes and defines preaching's relevance for the world and in so doing speaks substantively of responsibility and Christian ethics.

> There are a proliferation of mandates to the church, both negative and positive, in the confession of Christ's Lordship.
> Negatively, it means that as a church we must refuse to allow ourselves to be drawn so deeply into the discussions of the time that we lose the very perspective which redeems time, the perspective of the fulness of time. We must refuse to become the mouthpiece or the ideological champion of any social, political, or economic party, program, or interest. . . .
> Positively, the Lordship of Christ means that we must be genuinely prophetic and genuinely redemptive in today's life.[16]

Even as Michalson recognizes the cruciality of preaching, he also recognizes that:

> In the effort to fulfill that commission under present day conditions, however, [the church] is running against a containing wall of ambiguity. . . .
> One ambiguity is that the church must get very near to the hostile forces of the world in order to be heard by them, yet when it gets too close, it hazards kidnap and silencing. Being "an acoustical affair," however, faith must have a voice.
> Another ambiguity is that the church must speak freely, yet it must also accept support from sources alien to its mission. . . .
> Still another ambiguity is that wherever the church carries the word, it creates history, but not without re-creating community, and the re-creation of community is a revolutionary threat to all existing communities. . . .
> To cite one more ambiguity, the political enforcement of religious pluralism in many quarters of the world is requir-

---

[15]Michalson, The Hinge of History, p. 244.

[16]Ibid., p. 244.

ing of the Christian movement a curtailment of its propagandistic and proselytizing techniques.[17]

Michalson's attempt to deal with these ambiguities is, itself, somewhat ambiguous. He calls on the church and its preaching to be prophetic and redemptive, participating in the world's miseries.

> By prophetic I mean we must insist that a maximum of justice be achieved within the concrete conditions of this present time. . . .
> By our redemptive role I mean that we must proclaim the reality of God's mercy to a world from which mercy is always a waning reality. . . .We must participate, through the universal body of Christ, in the miseries of humanity everywhere in the world. . . .The church is fulfilling its redemptive mission in the world when the body as a whole becomes patterned after God's own self-emptying in Christ.[18]

At the same time, he calls for patience and waiting.

> We must provide an atmosphere of calm and sensitivity in which clear vision and resolute will may be achieved. Above all we must not succumb to the temptation of impatience, losing faith in the very forces that constitute what meaning now supports our life. . . .Patience is a situation in which man is doing nothing, nothing is being done. There are times when simply to wait is to give God time to do something.

Finally, Michalson urges "prayer and fasting, and. . .the steady witness of the believing community."[19]

In *The Hinge of History* and its antecedent article, Michalson states unequivocally that historical responsibility, is expressed through preaching. And preaching, for Michalson, is of tremendous consequence for the world because it is prophetic and

---

[17]Ibid., pp. 241-242.

[18]Ibid., pp. 244-245.

[19]Ibid., pp. 245-246.

redemptive. In characterizing the prophetic and redemptive nature of preaching though, Michalson is cautious. He sees preaching and responsibility as fraught with ambiguity; he is tentative in his calls for prophetism and redemption; and he encourages patience and waiting.

Michalson is cautious at this point for several reasons. His contextualism and aversion to legalism dictate an ethic that accounts for and has a healthy regard for the ambiguity of the world. As will be seen in substantive texts that follow, and in his applied ethics, Michalson clearly states that Christian ethics is not legalistic. Rather, the gospel's word of love and reconciliation addresses a given situation in such a way that it transcends and transvaluates the law. This is the very essence of responsibility.

Michalson's understanding of the nature of ethics thus dictates a certain degree of caution. But something more is at work here too. In The Hinge of History and its antecedent article, Michalson goes beyond a healthy respect for the ambiguity of ethical action, calling for the patience to do nothing and emphasizing prayer and fasting to the exclusion of "human manipulation of the mystery in history."[20] This is a far cry from maturity in the world, where the world has been turned over to humanity.

---

[20]Ibid., p. 246.

Michalson's caution here is to avoid any semblance of works righteousness. This reflects his theological emphases at the time and impending theological development. At this point, Michalson's Wesleyanism, with its emphasis on sanctification, lies dormant. As Runyon has correctly pointed out and as this segment of The Hinge of History verifies:

> Up to [the early 1960's] he had espoused a relatively straightforward Bultmannian position, which asserts that the New Testament's eschatological language is understandable only if it is translated into the language of existential encounter. . . .
> However, when we arrive at his late essays. . . .The focus has shifted from the more formal existentialist category, "human meaning as such," to the implicitly more normative "holiness history,". . . .It is no longer the individual and his or her felt needs that are the object of salvation for Michalson, but. . .the individual's participation in the redemptive processes of God depends upon his or her new orientation toward the world." . . .
> This leads to a second way to describe the same change in Michalson's theology, namely, by tracing the shift in the meaning of eschatology. Whereas previously the definition was more formal--eschatology referred to a personal crisis of meaning in which one's taken-for-granted existence is suspended in the face of new possibilities--now it is more concretely teleological.[21]

In The Hinge of History (written between the years 1952 and 1959) Michalson has not yet consummated the marriage of meaningfulness and responsibility in the world. His preoccupation with

---

[21] Runyon, "Carl Michalson as a Wesleyan Theologian," p. 8. Again, though in basic agreement with Runyon, I think he pushes Michalson's "theological shift" a bit too far. I see Michalson as shifting his focus from "human meaning as such," to human existence in the world, rather than to the world itself. This distinction allows for responsibility in the world without allowing the world to dominate human existence, and is in keeping with Michalson's concern that the world not become a religious object. It is also in keeping with his understanding the faith as transvaluating ideas of morality and government. See again, Worldly Theology, p. 171.

ambiguity, his ambivalence regarding prophetism and redemption, and his encouraging prayer, fasting and the steady witness of the believing community indicate, as Runyon says, a relationship of humanity to the world based more on Luther's two realms than on Wesley's doctrine of sanctification, where simul justus et peccator "preempts the Christian telos of the Kingdom of God as the decisive hermeneutic."[22] Here Michalson sees clearly the need for Christian responsibility, but Christian responsibility is not yet identified with maturity and holiness wherein eschatological fulfillment is a reality. At this point Michalson speaks of the possibility that eschatological history brings,[23] but has not yet identified that new life with God's handing over the world to humanity. Here faithfulness is Michalson's goal rather than eschatological fulfillment. Thus he aligns himself here with the reformers, rather than with Wesley, and is more concerned with justification than with sanctification.

Michalson's emphasis on justification rather than sanctification during the years prior to The Rationality of Faith is not to be confused with antinomianism or quietism however. (Neither is Luther's, for that matter). As early as 1955, in his social ethics particularly, one encounters themes that are later integral to his understanding of eschatological fulfillment as maturity in the world. In a series of articles entitled "New Tes-

---

[22]Runyon, "Michalson as a Wesleyan Theologian," p. 10.

[23]Michalson, Hinge of History, p. 143ff.

tament Teaching for Modern Living", published as the October, November, December, 1955 issue of Christian Action, which represents his clearest and most concise statement on ethics, Michalson defines and details responsibility and ethics.

Writing against the imitation of Christ as an adequate ethical precept, he says two things are wrong with this quietistic tactic.

> . . .to follow Jesus in the New Testament sense simply does not mean imitation. It means discipleship: accepting Jesus Christ as Lord, as a sign of the coming rule of God on earth, being obedient to his law of life, and revering him as the Righteous One who himself fulfills the law. . . .
> The other thing that is wrong with the interpretation of "following Jesus" as "imitation" is that it tends to pull out the rug of social relevance from under the Christian cause. . .One must realize that the problems of Jesus' time could not have been at all points like the problems of our time, so that to imitate him would make us peculiar in our day in an ineffective way.
> . . .Therefore, I say, if you were simply to follow the example of Jesus in the world today you would render the Christian cause socially inept.[24]

Michalson goes on to speak to the issues of social responsibility, justice and power, human rights, economics, politics, war and peace, and world community. In so doing, he sets forth his Christian ethic of responsibility.

Recognizing the complexity of applying God's command to "love your neighbor" at the social level, Michalson subscribes

---

[24]Carl Michalson, "New Testament Teaching for Modern Living," Christian Action 10,4 (Oct. Nov. Dec., 1955):24-25. See also Carl Michalson, review of Man Against Mass Society, by Gabriel Marcell, in Religion and Life, XXII, No. 4 (Autumn, 1953): 629; and Johnson, "Carl Michalson's Concept of History as a Theological Method," p. 429ff. for additional references to Michalson's concern for social ethics.

to the (Reinhold) Niebuhrian compromise.

> Neighbor love at the social level will take the form of the highest legislative equivalent of love. We will not call this love, but rather "justice." However, we will not forget that there is the _intention_ and quality of Christian love in social justice.[25]

For Michalson there are only two alternatives to this position, and neither is satisfactory. There is monastic withdrawal and there is martyrdom, but "The effectiveness of either is limited to exceptions."[26]

Michalson goes on to characterize the meaning and relevance of justice and power. The Christian person is called by God to spread the good news of God's mercy and righteousness. In assuming this responsibility at the social level, he will find it necessary to use economic and political techniques (the mechanisms of justice). Given the sinful nature of the world and its people, Michalson says these mechanisms serve more to restrain than to reconcile and are efforts to create a social situation "where there will be a maximum of equality of opportunity." He recognizes the inevitability of a clash between existing social orders and the ideals of justice and equality and thus endorses _limited_ "rebellion against the social structure, revolt against the prevailing definition of rights, an overthrow of the existing balance of power."[27]

---

[25]Michalson, "New Testament Teaching," p. 26.

[26]Ibid.

[27]Ibid., p. 29.

Power, like money and authority, is morally neutral, but it is not morally innocent, says Michalson. "Power is a constant temptation to evil. Power inspires pride and pride inspires the will to power and the inordinate use of power, which is itself injustice." Given the dangers of power, Michalson says that "any human use of power--even when in the interests of what is believed to be justice--must come under the judgment implicit in the sinfulness of man and in the sole goodness of God."[28]

Michalson begins his discussion of human rights by stressing the importance of other-worldliness in the Christian's life and the consequence of other-worldliness for worldly living.

> To live with one's mind on things above the earth is to live in the earth with a new nature, a new kind of integrity, that is, a new perspective for all one's relations to others in the world.
> Quite clearly, the other-worldliness in the Christian's life does not translate him out of the world. It does not make him less responsible to the world, but more.
> The Christian's vision is bifocal. He is to keep one eye on "the Kingdom which is not of this world," and he is to keep the other eye on life in this world. From one eye he gets his orders. With the other eye he develops the strategy along the lines of which the orders will be carried out.[29]

The perspective communicated by other-worldliness for worldly living is one that recognizes that God is the Creator of humanity. Michalson then asks:

> What is the implication in the New Testament message for such earthly concerns as civil liberties, for the protection of the rights in a situation where all men are known to be creatures of one God. . .?

---

[28]Ibid., p. 30.

[29]Ibid., p. 31.

> . . . .The Christian will preach the truth that God is Creator, hence man as creature is responsible to God. . . . This strategy will be the only thing that will at last provide the wholesome conditions, the conditions of integrity on the basis of which the rights of others are recognized.
>
> The Christian will also, however, judge with severity the unjust condition of unequal rights that is perpetuated within the very household of faith, the church. . . .
>
> And when he has done these. . .things, there will be left to him one major. . .responsibility. The Christian will use all available earthly agencies, in an expression of neighborly love, to see to it that all. . .are allowed to live by their rights as creatures of God, whether they seem to desire it or not.[30]

Freedom, says Michalson is both spiritual and physical, and the truth that is "not of this world" guarantees freedom in both its aspects.

In his discussion of economics, Michalson examines Christendom's understandings of wealth from New Testament times to date. Today, he says, the church must confront the fact that

> Wealth. . .has become not simply a diversion from spiritual interests but a source of power over the lives of men. . . .
>
> The story of the last two or three decades has been the story of the increased sense of the injustice of unequal wealth and the struggle of society to overcome the smart of that injustice.

Communism and democracy are portrayed as competing solutions to this struggle with Michalson concluding that "it seems both reasonable and essentially Christian that, on the basis of the democratic process, economic inequalities will not be allowed to become so great that human rights will be jeopardized.[31]

---

[30]Ibid., p. 33.

[31]Ibid., pp. 36, 37.

Michalson's discussion of politics focuses on the role of the state as a political entity, and to what extent the state can be expected to further God's rule and the quality of life that love and justice demand.

> The state is, as Reinhold Niebuhr has said, a "dyke against chaos" in the sinful world. "All of us," according to Emil Brunner, "even Christians, need the state as a protection against our own unrighteousness." The state maintains a minimal kind of justice. It does so not because it is kind or because it loves justice. . . .It does so simply to stem the chaos which would otherwise result in a world where God's rule is continually challenged by rebellious humanity.[32]

To those who understand American democracy as the Christian form of government, Michalson again quotes Brunner:

> "The Christian state never has existed and never will." The point [Brunner] makes is that "Christian" is applicable only where the law of love is in force. . . .it is not possible to say "Christian state," where justice is the goal, and a justice with no necessary relation to the sources of Christian inspiration.[33]

Michalson admits that some political systems are more congenial to the faith than others. He finds this congeniality in democracy's willingness to hear words of judgment and its ability to judge itself through its system of checks and balances.

Speaking about war and peace, Michalson writes,

> Here is the real nub of the war and peace issue. If one strikes you on the cheek, you can afford to turn the other cheek, within the requirements of obedience to God. But when one strikes your neighbor on the cheek, what shall you do? Do you hear, under God, the command, "Do not resist one who is evil"? Or is not your action toward the evil one dictated rather by the command, "Love your neighbor"?

---

[32] Ibid., p. 39.

[33] Ibid., pp. 40-41.

In dealing with this dilemma, Michalson reminds his readers that a) justice is the Christian's goal at the societal level and b) that the state has been vested as the "agent of justice". The state's responsibility then is to define and decide what constitutes the "better" and "more just" response. Having implied that war can be the "more just" response, Michalson then deals with the concept of "just war," and concludes that

> States will not deal with the question of war and peace at the level of moralizing in the abstract about the right or wrong of war. They will ask in the context of practical conditions existing at any given time, "Under these circumstances, is war justified?'
> The issue of war and peace must, therefore, be dealt with at two levels: one, how to prevent war from breaking out; the other, how to decide who is the thief and who is the molested merchant in case war should break out.[34]

Michalson concludes "New Testament Teaching for Modern Living" with a brief discussion about world community.

> Christians can and ought to bring [their] ultimate perspectives to bear upon the events of life today. The message about God's kingdom is not an invitation to sloth, a kind of patient waiting for God to clean up the whole mess of human history. The message about God's kingdom is a call to discipleship in the situation in which we find ourselves.
> . . .This game of the political balance of power which could destroy the world, could at the same time infuse the world with the widest and highest access of economic and political justice that it has ever known.[35]

Michalson also spoke substantively about ethics in a sermon/lecture entitled "Faith Must be Expressed in Works of

---

[34]Ibid., pp. 43, 44, 45.

[35]Ibid., pp. 47-48.

Love."[36] This piece is an attempt to define Christian love and thus to characterize the Christian ethic. In this regard, his subheadings are "Christian Love is not Legalistic," "Christian Love is not Humanitarianism," "Christian Love is not Based on Feeling" and "Love in Social Relations." Parts of this sermon--especially the section entitled "Love in Social Relations"--are excerpted from the booklet "New Testament Teaching for Modern

---

[36]This lecture/sermon has been transcribed from recording tapes and is included in the book The Witness of Radical Faith. It also exists in manuscript form as "How to Love Your Neighbor," having been delivered at Penn State University, April 28, 1963. The tapes were recorded at the United Congregational Church, Seattle, Washington (1964) and a meeting of the New England Student Christian Movement (June, 1965). See Wynne, The Implications of Carl Michalson's Theological Method, Appendix, Part A, pp. 329ff.

Drew University's Michalson Collection possesses numerous tapes of Michalson's speaking engagements. The tapes contain several versions of oft delivered speeches, with only slight variations distinguishing them. Also, multiple copies of the exact same lecture/sermon exist. This occurred due to Drew's appeal for Michalsonia through The Drew Gateway, which resulted in alumni and friends sending duplicated recordings and/or different recordings of the same lecture. Finally, Michalson students using the materials have rerecorded and duplicated items already in the collection.

As can be seen, Drew University's Michalson tape collection resulted from diverse contributions occurring over the course of several years. Therefore, while it is possible to know Michalson's lecture topics and specific times and places for a given lectureship (Again, see Wynne, Appendix, Part A, pp. 329ff), it is sometimes difficult, if not impossible, to coordinate a specific taped speech with a given lectureship.

In cases where manuscripts and transcripts exist in addition to or instead of tape recordings, some provide bibliographical information, others do not. When variant material from Drew's Michalson tape collection (as well as the Michalson Collection at large) is used in this study, I have attempted to document items as completely as possible and have included this information in footnotes.

Living." However, there is additional material here that needs to be presented.

In "Faith Must be Expressed in Works of Love," Michalson contrasts Christian love with legalism, humanitarianism, and pietism, saying that each of these alternatives endorses irresponsibility because each limits love. "Once we have kept [a] limited set of laws, we have no further responsibility." Humanitarianism is based on "one's love-worthiness," and if the neighbor ceases to be worthy, we stop loving him. Pietism limits love by basing it on "feelings of affection." In contrast to these, Christian love is "an ethic of responsibility to which there is no terminus."[37] Love is a free response to God's grace that is done not out of compulsion, or worthiness, or feelings of affection.

> . . .a Christian is one who has been mobilized by God's love toward us, and by our love toward him. Loving him, we will do anything he says. That is the love basis of the Christian faith. He has commanded us: "Thou shalt love thy neighbor." We will do it, if only for the reason that the one we love has commanded it.[38]

Having characterized love of neighbor, Michalson then speaks of love in the neighborhood, i.e. of love at the social level. In so doing he reiterates what was said before: at the social level, justice is "the highest possible equivalent of

---

[37] Michalson, Witness of Radical Faith, p. 99.

[38] Ibid., p. 97.

spontaneous love." He then argues for legislation as the "way to get justice in society in a democracy."[39]

Michalson argues again against monasticism and martydom as ineffective, and, finally, speaks of love in the face of agression:

> We must identify the aggressor and throw all our power against him, not to annihilate him but to annihilate his injustice, to neutralize those forces of aggressive injustice while still loving the aggressor.

In advocating the neutralization of agressive forces Michalson speaks against pacifism (and in so doing restates his contextualism). "Pacifism as an ethical principle is made up in advance of a given situation and that is always dangerous. We must make up our ethical principles in relation to real life situations."[40]

The substance of Michalson's ethics of responsibility is set forth in *The Hinge of History*, "New Testament Teaching for Modern Living" and the sermon "Faith Must be Expressed in Works of Love." In these writings Michalson advocates a contextual ethic that centers on works of love offered as free response to God's grace. At the social level, justice represents "the highest possible equivalent of spontaneous love" and is the Christian's goal. (Reinhold Niebuhr, Emil Brunner, etc.) Power, judiciously employed, is directed toward the establishment of justice in the

---

[39]Ibid., p. 106.

[40]Ibid., p. 107. See also Michalson, *Hinge of History*, p. 240ff, esp. pp. 244-245.

fields of human rights, economics, politics, and war and peace (among others). In this regard, the state, with its "minimal kind of justice" is required by the Christian to "hold its power under the criticism of enlightened standards of justice."[41] While he rejects the notion of a Christian state, Michalson advocates Christianity's impacting the state with world community as its aim. Because of Christ's injunction to "love your enemies, "Christians keep the hope of world community alive among the nations.

Michalson understands the Christian's attempt to establish justice as complemented and enhanced by the virtues of democracy and involvement in the legislative process. However, he does not rule out resistance to and even rebellion against the existing balance of power as an "alternative to the Christian endorsement of injustice."[42] Related to this is his tacit acceptance of the concept of a just war.

Throughout, Michalson's Christian ethics of responsibility is tempered by a watchfulness and concern that God be present in all ethical action. This concern was stated forthrightly in The Hinge of History, and in the fact that his ethics is derived,

---

[41] Michalson, "New Testament Teaching," p. 40.

[42] Ibid., p. 27.

literally, from New Testament teaching for modern living. Serious Bible study stands behind every ethical injunction.[43]

As Michalson reappropriated Wesley's Hermeneutic of Holiness, responsibility and ethics became increasingly important to his theological enterprise, which culminated in his understanding maturity in the world as eschatological fulfillment, wherein responsibility represents the denoument of faith. These understandings are set forth in an article entitled "How Our Lives Carry Christ's Resurrection: Atonement, Redemption and Ethics", which became the substance of chapter nine in *Worldly Theology*.

In *Worldly Theology* (and also in *The Rationality of Faith*), Michalson's ethics are integrated with Wesleyan theology, where "the Christian telos of the kingdom of God [becomes] the decisive hermeneutic."[44] Here the basis for and context of humanity's relationship to the world becomes Wesley's doctrine of sanctification and its attendant holiness preunderstanding; and responsibility for the world is seen as maturity in the world and eschatological fulfillment. Does this theological development, which places increased importance on responsibility and ethics, change Michalson's concept of responsibility for the world or alter the

---

[43] It is clear from the structure of his articles on "New Testament Teaching for Modern Living" that serious Bible study lies behind Michalson's ethical injunctions. Each section begins with scriptural texts, which are examined historically and critically, before being applied to modern living.

[44] Runyon, "Michalson as a Wesleyan Theologian," p. 10.

content of his ethic?

Runyon sees this theological development as making the natural world, as well as the world of meaning, the object of salvation. My reservations in this regard have already been stated.[45] Runyon also implies a shift from the first to the third use of the law: "I think these changes represent something more basic in Michalson's theological enterprise than simply a shift from the first to the third use of the law."[46]

I find very little evidence of Michalson's having adopted a third use of the law when he adopted Wesley's hermeneutic of holiness. Granted, a third use of the law would be in keeping with Wesley's theology. But Michalson's adopting a third use of the law (wherein the law is reappropriated and utilized under the aegis of grace) would have significantly altered his contextual ethic. Comparison of his 1960's sermon "Faith Must be Expressed in Works of Love" with the earlier "New Testament Teaching for Modern Living," and careful study of his entire ethical corpus, indicate that this is simply not the case. Legalism in all forms

---

[45] See especially pp. 10ff, 64-66, 123 (footnote 21) above.

[46] Runyon, "Michalson as a Wesleyan Theologian," p. 9. (For the uninitiated, the reformers, especially Calvin, set forth the following three uses of the law: The spiritual use of the law is to convince humanity of its sinfulness, so that despairing of their ability, persons cling to the mercy of God in Christ. The civil use of the law is its ability to specify what society needs for peace and order. The third use of the law is its positive function as a guide to the Christian life, wherein it is reappropriated under the aegis of grace.)

is decried.[47] Therefore, while his developing theology gave increased importance to responsibility and ethics, Michalson did not adopt a third use of the law and change the character of responsibility and ethics. Substantively, Michalson's ethics of responsibility was consistent, although his Wesleyanism, by establishing its context, increased its importance dramatically.

Given the increased importance of ethics in Michalson's theological schema, and his relating salvation so closely to responsibility in the world, it is tempting to view him, with Runyon, as having shifted his focus to the salvation of the world, with the world's being the only relevant soteriological concern. At this point, more so than earlier, this might seem to be indicated. Again, however, this is simply not the case, as is evidenced by an examination of Michalson's last writing, on prayer.

In the Fall Semester of 1961, Michalson introduced a course entitled "Theology of Prayer". In 1964 he wrote a sermon series of six sermons for First Methodist Church in Plainfield, N. J. The topic, of his own choosing, was prayer.[48] These sermons are of considerable interest to this study, for in them prayer is understood as a paradigm for the structure of human existence,

---

[47]See "Faith Must be Expressed in Works of Love," in Witness of Radical Faith, p. 107. See also "New Testament Teachings," pp. 26ff, 30ff, and 38ff.

[48]Edward J. Wynne, Jr., Introduction to Prayer for Today's People by Carl Michalson, p. xiv.

wherein meditation and ethics, withdrawal and engagement meet. In short, Michalson considers prayer as "the Christian's mode of being in the world."[49] In prayer, the Christian receives (from God) the duty that is directed toward neigbbor.

> The content of prayer is that God gives us the world as our responsibility. In his <u>presence</u>, God turns the world over to man. . . .God's answer to our prayers has been given before we have sought him. The Christian is not like the pagan who cries to his god and his god does not answer. . . . The Christian is one who prays to a living God who has already answered our prayers in giving us the world as our responsibility. . . .
> If prayer is definable as the act in which God turns the world over to us as our responsibility, then the really querelous question about prayer is not, does God answer prayer, but do you? God has moved; the next move is yours.[50]

I see in Michalson's understanding of prayer and prayer's implications for ethics, further evidence of his reluctance to allow humanity's responsibility for the world to degenerate into responsibility <u>to</u> the world. His delineation of prayer provides a structure for his understanding of humanity's being responsible for the world while God still reigns and thus precludes humanity's immersing itself totally in the world. The Christian's perspective on the world is maintained by prayer. Therefore, while living in the world is of utmost necessity, Michalson avoids the world's dictating its own soteriology. Responsibility

---

[49]See pp. 53-65 of <u>Prayer for Today's People</u>, entitled "A Theology of Prayer," for a summary of Michalson's understanding prayer as paradigmatic for Christian existence and transcending the dualism of meditation and ethics.

[50]Ibid., pp. 42-43.

for the world _in the sight of God_ is the substance of Michalson's Christian ethic of responsibility.

It is clear that Christian ethics was a continuous and crucial concern for Michalson, from early in his life up to the time of his death. Whether or not this concern would have manifested itself in a work devoted to ethics is something no one knows. It can be surmised that, given the centrality of ethics to Michalson's theological schema, ethics would have had to play a significant role in the constructive theologizing that he was beginning at the time of his death. As it is, Michalson's ethics is a patchwork of sorts, gleaned from various and sundry references in his biography, his articles and books, and his sermons and lectures. Nonetheless, it represents a substantial contribution to the field. Based on the subjectivity of Kierkegaard, Michalson's ethic combined Wesley's doctrine of holiness with Gogarten's (and Bonhoeffer's) world-come-of-age, in such a way that the Christian faith not only remains valid in the face of mounting skepticism, but also makes a significant difference in the world and its affairs.

B. Ethics of Responsibility: Application

Because Michalson's ethic was conceived as integral to his theology, and expressed primarily through his theologizing, rarely did he address and involve himself in actual, concrete ethical dilemmas. There are, however, at least two recorded instances of his applying his Christian ethics of responsibility.

1. <u>Racism</u>

In March, 1965, Bernhard Anderson, Howard Clark Kee and Carl Michalson represented the Drew Theological School faculty at a civil rights march in Montgomery, Alabama. Upon returning to Drew they addressed the Drew community in an attempt to "Focus on a Revolution."[51] Michalson's trip to Montgomery and his report of that experience offer a clear example of his ethics in action.

In his remarks, Michalson asks and then comments on three questions. These questions are: "Why did I go?", "Would I do it again?" and "What will we do on other occasions?". Michalson claims he went to Montgomery "not to integrate Alabama, but to demonstrate on behalf of the freedom to demonstrate." He says he went as a theologian, and because "the existence of God is at stake in what men do in history. One cannot do theology today without involving God in just such historic causes." His returning to Montgomery and going elsewhere to demonstrate are distinct possibilities, for, like pastoral calling, the civil rights issue "invites repeated acts of responsibility."[52]

---

[51]These dated addresses, collectively entitled "Focus on a Revolution," are on recording tape as part of the Michalson Collection at Drew University's Rose Memorial Library. A transcript of Michalson's report, taken from the tape, is included below as "Appendix A."

[52]Ibid., pp. 254-250.

Michalson recognizes a problem in one's <u>immersing</u> oneself in such causes, saying that one cannot be a theologian without involvement in such causes, but at the same time wondering if one can remain a theologian if only involved in such causes. Finally though, he likens the civil rights struggle to the first century's struggle against legalism, and thus sees it as "the one big opportunity for the expression of faith in our time."[53]

Having recognized the importance of civil rights issues, Michalson suggests that it be made a priority in Drew Theological School's curriculum and field work, and that the school participate in activities supporting the civil rights movement. By so doing he says, responsibility is fulfilled and God has a chance to be born again.

2. <u>Alcoholism</u>

In an article for <u>Concern</u> magazine entitled "The Maturity of Sonship" and published seven days after his death, Michalson discusses the Methodist Church and alcohol from a theological standpoint. Sonship, says Michalson, is the Christian's condition, and it is "a condition in which the son must be responsible for developing the details of his relation to the world." In line with his existence as mature son, the Christian knows what is expected of him, but he is not told what to do." Christian ethics then, represents the Christian's assuming responsibility

---

[53]Ibid., p. 255.

for the world with "the freedom to discern the form that the responsibility will take in any given situation."[54]

The tactics of Evangelical Christianity's legalism do not constitute a responsible approach to alcohol, according to Michalson. Scolding the practice of drinking, offering forgiveness for the sin of it, and promising divine power to overcome it, have no "intrinsic force." In fact, says Michalson, "To withhold the celebration of the world because of the evils to which human perversion can carry it [is] the heresy called Manichaeism." And "In walling in the world to protect its weak. . .the Christian may be. . .creating the conditions that nurture and perpetuate weakness."[55] When catering to weakness, maturity is prevented.

A responsible approach to alcohol, according to Michalson, will recognize the distinction between private taste and social justice. It will recognize, as well, the problems associated with bondage to drinking and allergy to alcohol.

> The fault of irresponsibility in driving is not in the drinking, but in the driving when drinking. The fault in habitual drinking. . .is not in the drinking, but in the painful sense of meaninglessness in one's life for which drink becomes the anesthesia.[56]

While respecting "private tastes" and the responsible exercise thereof, the church's push for social justice will not allow private tastes to jeopardize the public good. Nor will the

---

[54]Carl Michalson, "The Maturity of Sonship," *Concern* VII, 20 (Nov. 15, 1965):10.

[55]Ibid., pp. 10-11.

[56]Ibid., p. 11.

church condone self defeating and self punitive habits. It will utilize civil law and medicine to fight these respective battles. "A Christian. . .should be able to distinguish the public and private dimensions of his responsibility." Likewise, a Christian should be able to distinguish responsible use of alcohol from bondage to drinking. "In sum, he ought so to act that others may be allowed to be responsible while himself remaining responsible."[57]

When Michalson addresses the issues of civil rights and alcohol, he speaks as a theologian for whom involvement in the world is a necessity. The fact that Michalson speaks as a theologian and the fact that faith impelling action is his primary concern, is clearly stated in both articles. The one real sin, he says, is "default in responsibility to God, forfeiture of Sonship, . . .failure to love."[58] At the same time he recognizes the danger a theologian faces "if all he does is get involved in such causes."[59] Thus responsibility for the world with perspective from outside the world is again advocated.[60]

---

[57]Ibid., p. 14.

[58]Ibid., p. 10.

[59]Appendix A: Transcript of Michalson's report, "Focus on a Revolution," p. 255.

[60]Michalson's thoughts regarding the necessity of a Christian's having perspective from outside the world in order to function *for* the world are set forth in "New Testament Teaching for Modern Living:"
". . .the advantage a Christian has in taking his orders from a point outside the world is that he can know something

Michalson's contextualism and opposition to legalism are also evident in these instances of applied ethics. Racism in Montgomery demanded a rebellion against the law, in which he was willing to participate. His call to distingtuish between private taste and public good, and between private taste and bondage to drinking in "The Maturity of Sonship," also indicates a contextual approach to ethics.

In addition to reflecting Michalson's ethical theory, these articles also reflect the substance of Michalson's ethics. Though the articles' brevity precludes a point by point comparison, it can be said that here, justice (as an expression of love) is a primary concern and power is judiciously employed. His statements on human rights and economics are commensurate with actions taken and advocated here, and legislation is a factor in the resolution of these problems, but not the only factor. Therefore, the law can be demonstrated against as well as advocated.

---

about the world that the world does not know about itself. Serving with the artillery on the front lines, he is so involved in battle, he cannot quite see where to aim apart from a perspective communicated to him from reconnaissance flights over enemy positions." ("New Testament Teaching," p. 31.)

CHAPTER FOUR

Ethics in Carl Michalson: Evaluation

Michalson's Christian ethics of responsibility clearly represents a significant and actively expressed theological concern. Questions have been raised about its adequacy however. In order to speak to these criticisms and further delineate Michalson's ethical thought, I will now seek to evaluate his ethics in terms of its character and adequacy. The character of Michalson's ethic will be stated with regard to its formulation, implementation, and appropriate sub-categories.[1] The adequacy of his ethic will be stated with regard to his theoretical and substantive formulations, and his implementation of them.

A. Character of Michalson's Ethic

1. Formulation of Ethical Norm

In formulating his ethics, Michalson clearly subscribes to the relational motif.

> In relational ethics the direction of action is shaped by the sense of excitement or gratitude which arises from a live, dynamic, and compelling encounter with the source of moral guidance. When a leader or a group proves attractive and exciting or when an event induces a profound sense of indebtedness or appeal, men are frequently given new motives for their actions and new insights concerning the scope of their obligations. . . .

___

[1] These categories and subcategories are from Edward L. Long's *A Survey of Christian Ethics*. As Dr. Long's typology is a recognized standard in the field of Christian ethics, I feel my use of his terminology will serve to clarify Michalson's ethics in relation to the ethics of others, and provide a common denominator for stating his possible contribution to more recent Christian ethics.

> . . .There is a real sense in which ethics in the relational motif ceases to be ethics in the normal sense of the word. Instead of setting forth a norm to which men must aspire, it understands an ethos in which they live. Ethics involves a style of life from which naturally flow certain responses appropriate to that style, rather than a process of analysis and prescription.[2]

It is not surprising that Michalson saw ethics in relational terms, since he studied with H. Richard Niebuhr, who "developed what may be the most reflective and theoretical conception"[3] of this motif. Michalson's relationalism is also a reflection of his being influenced by Kierkegaard's "teleological suspension of the ethical," a clearly relational concept. In Michalson this concept is expressed as transvaluation, referred to above.

Surprisingly, Wesley is less a factor in the formulation of Michalson's ethic than one might think. Insofar as Wesley's is a relational ethic that stresses grace as prompting an active faith, and since Wesley emphasizes the importance of response and responsibility, he stands behind Michalson's ethical theory. By informing Michalson's final conception of responsibility as holiness and maturity, Wesley also provides Michalson's ethics with a context. But Michalson, as discussed above, does not have the legalism of Wesley.[4]

---

[2]Long, Survey of Christian Ethics, pp. 117,119.

[3]Ibid., p. 118. See also H. Richard Niebuhr, The Responsible Self.

[4]See Long, Survey of Christian Ethics, p. 110 ff. Long classifies both Wesley and Kierkegaard as modified forms of prescription emphasizing "the imitation of Christ"; i.e. prescription informed by relation. Michalson's criticism of "the imitation of Christ" as a workable social ethic has been discussed above (pp. 125-126) and can be found in "New Testament

Michalson's relationalism is expressed in several ways. It expresses itself first as <u>response to the divine initiative</u>,[5] and in this regard reflects Nygren's influence.[6] The divine initiative lies of course in the Christ event, that for Michalson, makes possible an historical faith, of which response is a necessary part. Michalson then seeks guidance in determining what is appropriate to that response.

Ethical guidance, for Michalson, comes from God's command to "Love thy neighbor as thyself," <u>and</u> from the context of the ethical dilemma. Since Michalson reduces the law to the formulation "Love thy neighbor as thyself," his view of ethics is less prescriptive than, say Brunner's (or Barth's or Bonhoeffer's) ethics of obligation, where divine command "has the semblance of continuity and law," and where law has a "penultimate importance."[7] Michalson's formulation is more akin to Bultmann's concept of "radical obedience" as response to the dawning of the Kingdom of God, and eschatological deliverance in Christ.

Bultmann's argument stands behind Michalson's at this point, to the extent that they are almost identical. In Jesus Christ, the Kingdom of God has broken into human existence, and because

---

Teaching for Modern Living," pp. 23-26.

[5] See Long, <u>Survey of Christian Ethics</u>, p. 129ff.

[6] Ibid., p. 138ff. See also Michalson's M.A. thesis, "Human Responsibility in the Republic of Plato and in the Synoptic Gospels," Chapter 4, p. 49ff.

[7] Long, <u>Survey of Christian Ethics</u>, pp. 146-157.

of this development, humanity lives eschatologically, in radical obedience to God. Jesus has opened up to humanity the possibility of experiencing the Kingdom of God. This possibility completely alters human existence, and gives life an eschatological dimension before which all else pales. Thus radical obedience to God is thrust upon humanity as a crucial choice and becomes ultimately important, to the extent that radical obedience defines Christian life, ethically and otherwise.[8]

> The obedience of which Bultmann writes must be understood in relationship to the will of God. It is a response, in concrete and particular circumstances, to the divine word as made known to the man of faith in the situation or moment in which he finds himself. It involves the entire selfhood of the obedient man and cannot be the mere performance of predefined duty. While the obedient man may bring to his decision an awareness of standards from the past, these must be questioned as all else is questioned in the moment of decision.[9]

In line with the above, Michalson's responding to the Christ event in love is also guided by <u>context</u> ("the situation or moment in which he finds himself"[10]). His devaluation of law to the

---

[8] Rudolf Bultmann, <u>Jesus and the Word</u> 2nd ed. (New York: Charles Scribner's Sons, 1958), p. 35ff. See also Long, <u>Survey of Christian Ethics</u>, p. 155ff.

[9] Long, <u>Survey of Christian Ethics</u>, p. 156. See also Bultmann, <u>Jesus and the Word</u>, p. 155ff.

[10] Michalson's contextualism is stated in precisely these words (initially used by Long, above, to characterize Bultmann's ethic) when he discusses the necessity of the Christian's establishing world community.
"The message about God's kingdom is not an invitation to sloth, a kind of patient waiting for God to clean up the whole mess of human history. The message about God's kingdom is a call to discipleship in the situation in which we find ourselves." ("New Testament Teaching," p. 47.)

formula "Love thy neighbor" is directly related to his contextualism, where the situation dictates the content of love. Michalson is very clear in this regard, as is evidenced in his article, "The Maturity of Sonship," as well as in "New Testament Teaching for Modern Living" and the sermon "Faith Must be Expressed in Works of Love."[11]

2. <u>Implementation of Ethical Norm</u>

In implementing his ethics, Michalson is institutional and operational. He recognizes the necessity of the state as a "dyke against chaos" (Reinhold Niebuhr) and the necessity of economic and political techniques. At the same time he recognizes the role that power plays in the world, and that at times power is necessary to move institutions to change. These tendencies are seen clearly in his article "New Testament Teaching for Modern Living" and in his applied ethics as well. He is just as clearly leary of intentionalism, and in this regard openly criticizes monasticism, martyrdom and pacifism.[12]

Characterizing Michalson's ethics as predominately institutional or predominately operational is difficult. Michalson is cautious in sanctioning the use of power. His designation of power as "a constant temptation to evil," and his concerns for

---

[11]See Michalson, "Maturity of Sonship," p. 10; "New Testament Teaching," p. 26ff; "Faith Must Be Expressed in Works of Love," in <u>The Witness of Radical Faith</u>, p. 98ff.

[12]Michalson, "Faith Must be Expressed in Works of Love," pp. 106-107.

the legislative and democratic processes are institutional formulations. His affinities with Reinhold Niebuhr, on the other hand, indicate operationalism. His understanding of justice as the "highest legislative equivalent of love," is clearly Niebuhrian, and Michalson's quest for justice is set in Niebuhrian terms. In "New Testament Teaching for Modern Living," Michalson writes about "justice and power" as necessary to the assumption of social responsibility. The linking of these themes (again clearly Niebuhrian) points toward a recognition of political organizations as operations of power.

Michalson's view of the state is also operational (and Niebuhrian). He quotes Niebuhr in calling the state "a dyke against chaos," and sees it as only establishing "a minimal kind of justice." This understanding of the state implies the need to augment it, to impact it, and to direct it. Thus "emphasis is placed upon the power configurations of social and political maneuverings by which laws are enacted and decisions made,"[13] and operationalism is enacted. Finally, Michalson's seeking justice in the picket lines in Montgomery represents a clearly operational technique.

---

[13] Long, Survey of Christian Ethics, p. 216.

B. Adequacy of Michalson's Ethic

1. Adequacy of Formulation

a. Theoretical Adequacy. Michalson's ethic has been criticized on several counts, but perhaps the most significant criticism is that leveled by Godsey regarding the adequacy of its subjective base. This criticism (touched on in Chapter II, p.62ff) can be summarized as follows: Godsey charges that Michalson's theological presuppositions--subjectivity and individuality--are lacking in social, political and ethical significance.

Michalson, perhaps anticipating such a criticism, makes a case for the "worldliness" of subjectivity.

> In the inwardness of subjectivity one's passion for the infinite is gratified by the God-relation. What is the consequence of this. . .retreat from the world?. . . Oddly, the consequence. . .is the opposite of monasticism. It is a new accentuation of temporal existence, the creation of a new kind of world. The object of a Christian's love is not now God but the world. . . .The implication of faith is not preoccupation with the absolute but in faithful relationship to the absolute, preoccupation with the relativities of the world. . .[the Christian's faith translates] him out of the world of. . .abstraction, of objectivity, . . . which is not a world one lives, into the real world where one can grasp existence as a whole."[14]

In Michalson's rebuttal to Godsey's charges we see that his individuality (as is Kierkegaard's) is conceived in opposition to the <u>universal</u>, and not in opposition to the <u>social</u>. Subjectivity in this instance allows for and in fact generates ethical concern.

---

[14]Michalson, <u>Worldly Theology</u>, p. 125-126.

According to Michalson,

> To say that faith is a decision for subjectivity. . . .is to say that faith involves the question of reality-as-a-whole, that is, reality inclusive of the self. Faith is a totalizing act which includes the self in the whole of the reality embraced, standing over against the detotalizing act characteristic of the objective, cognitive process. . . .
> . . .Faith is not the grasping of objects but the appropriation of a reality inclusive of oneself.[15]

Christian faith, then, denies us objective certainty. And

> By refusing to allow our infinite passions to be satisfied in worldly [objective] processes, which always only approximate, the whole world of relativity is given a new character of finality.[16]

The world becomes critically important because it is precisely in the relativities of the world that subjective faith is born and fostered. The Christian (ethically and otherwise) cannot fall back on objective rules (ethical or otherwise) but must continually confront the world's dilemmas (ethical and otherwise) and hopefully, like Kierkegaard's knight of faith, rise above them.

Like Gogarten, who Godsey criticizes as "too cerebral," Michalson pointedly bases his ethics on the subjective (i.e. historical) faith relationship.

> . . .the problem of relativity as it concerns Christian faith is solved not by escaping from history into a realm of absolute ideals and universals, but by living in history the responsible life of faith. . . .
> . . .Historical contingency--while undermining an absolutist ethic--is not inimical to ethics as such.

---

[15]Ibid., p. 121.

[16]Ibid., p. 125.

Indeed, the fact that history is composed of contingent relationships is what makes it unavoidably ethical. One has his being in creative encounter. . .[17]

It is without doubt that Michalson's ethic, based on individuality and subjectivity represents a valid and even heroic position. His formulation of ethics in this regard puts ethics at the center of his theological enterprise, and in the tradition of Kierkegaard, challenges humanity to be faithful in ways that have stood the test of time. Given the fallacious alternatives of subjectiveness and universalism, Michalson's case for subjectivity and its consequences are continually timely and apropos. But are his ethics, so carefully crafted and formulated, adequately expressed?

Whether Michalson's understanding ethics as integral to theology gives adequate expression to ethical concerns and problems is difficult to ascertain. Michalson saw ethics as a natural and necessary outgrowth of the theological task, and claimed that if the theological task is properly done, the ethical task must follow. And in spite of the fact that his life and work ended prematurely, there is ample evidence that Michalson was seriously engaged in the integration of theology and ethics in precisely this way.

There are those, I am sure, who would disagree with Michalson's formulation because it seemingly reduces ethics

---

[17]Runyon, "Friedrich Gogarten," p. 431.

to an adjunct of theology. Michalson, I think would be the first to agree that theology and ethics, with their various subdisciplines, can legitimately be considered separate fields of study. To this end he identified himself as a theologian, rather than a theologian/ethicist and in this regard, ethical inquiry, for Michalson, was far from comprehensively considered, even though it was central to his theology. The actual expression of ethical concerns could not keep pace with the theological necessity of same.

On the other hand, Michalson's formulation of ethics-integral-to-theology states and treats something fundamental to the Christian faith, namely that faith must be expressed in works. Due to his early death and the nature of his task, Michalson could not get involved in Christian ethics to the extent that he was involved in Christian theology. But his formulation is a continual reminder that to the extent the Christian can, the Christian must express his or her faith in works.

The criticism that Michalson is not an ethicist and that his formulation does not do justice to ethics is, to an extent, justified. But this does not mean that Michalson's thought has no ethical significance or merit. For Michalson, responsibility is integral to Christian faith and crucial to faith's existence. By characterizing theology as necessarily ethical, Michalson accounted well for the necessity of so relating faith and works. Though ethics could not be treated as comprehensively by Michalson's conceiving it as integral to theology, there is, in fact, a sense in which his conception is the only legitimate one.

Michalson, in challenging the theologian to the necessary task of Christian ethics, and conversely challenging the Christian ethicist to the necessary task of theology, lifts up an ideal that cannot be disregarded. His expression of ethics as integral to theology is in keeping with something fundamental to the nature of faith. Ethics as integral to theology states quite simply that faith must be lived and expressed, that faith must be borne out in response. Thus Michalson's formulation, in spite of its inadequacies, is and must be, of genuine concern to all Christians.

b. Substantive Adequacy of Michalson's Formulation.

Having discussed the adequacy of Michalson's ethical formulations from a theoretical standpoint, questions regarding the substantive adequacy of Michalson's ethical formulations also need to be considered.

Since ethics is an outgrowth of theology, preaching is central to the substance of Michalson's ethics. But Michalson sees preaching as the faith's being lived and assuming its responsibility in addition to its bringing the faith to expression. To this end, he treats various and sundry ethical themes, among them social responsibility, justice and power, human rights, economics, politics, war and peace, and world community. This list, though far from comprehensive, points again to the fact that Michalson's ethic has a social dimension, as even his sharpest critics admit.[18]

Substantively, Michalson's Christian ethics of responsibility took its cue from scripture and sought to lift up relevant themes in a meaningful way. Reinhold Niebuhr's influence, though more important for the implementation of Michalson's ethics, begins to be felt at this point in much the same way that Kierkegaard, Gogarten, Bultmann, et al. influenced Michalson's ethical theory. Wesley's influence is here too--providing, finally, a context for Michalson's (substantive) ethics.

Michalson's ethic as substantively (and theoretically) formulated would meet with opposition from deliberationists and prescriptionists.[19] On the other hand, his relational approach is a bona fide ethical option and is recognized as such. As indicated above, it has its strengths as well as weaknesses, and can be positively recognized as contributing to the field of ethics. Michalson's ethic, I think, is especially noteworthy from a theoretical standpoint, and because of his adoption of Niebuhrian constructs and a Wesleyan context, is substantively

---

[18] Johnson, "Michalson's Concept of History," pp. 229-230.

[19] Michalson's contextualism, which is the most controversial aspect of his ethics, especially to prescriptionists, will be treated below. I have chosen to deal with Michalson's contextualism as an aspect of the implementation of his ethics, rather than as an aspect of the formulation of his ethics, because it is in the context of the implementation of ethics that his contextualism has been criticized.

adequate as well, especially when considered from a relational perspective.

2. Adequacy of Implementation

The sharpest criticism regarding the adequacy of Michalson's ethics comes from Ellis Blane Johnson, in his Boston University dissertation. Johnson, who relied primarily on the article "Maturity of Sonship" for his understanding of Michalson's ethics, raises several questions in regard to Michalson's applying his ethics to the problem of alcohol.

Johnson's first question is related to Michalson's assertion that alcohol can be "celebrated as a part of God's creation--that which God has made. . ."[20] Johnson claims that in taking this position, Michalson moves outside theology as history, and reverts to a "nature" concept of creation, as justification for an ethical decision.[21]

Michalson's understanding of the mature son's and daughter's responsible use of the world of nature, in no way denigrates his theology of history. There is no contradiction here. The person who is faithful lives in the world of nature as surely as in the world of faith, uses the world of nature and effects his/her dominion over it. In so doing, direction is taken from God in Jesus Christ as to the use of nature, and nature no longer

---

[20]Michalson, "The Maturity of Sonship," p. 11.

[21]Johnson, "Michalson's Concept of History," pp. 240-241.

dictates or holds sway, but nature can and must be utilized for life to occur and be lived.

The fact that the fruit of the vine is part of God's creation allows it to be used as nature can and must be used. The fact that the person using it is a person of faith prohibits its abuse--i.e. prohibits nature's gaining control and dominating historical existence.

Johnson's second criticism of Michalson is also related to his article on Methodism and Alcohol. Says Johnson:

> . . .when Michalson makes the crux of his treatment of ethics the question of choosing between matters of social concern and matters of private taste, it is reasonable to expect from him some guidelines for deciding into which category a particular issue falls. In asking for such, one can distinguish between guidelines and rules.[22]

Johnson's fourth criticism is related to his second (thus they are considered together), but is cast in a larger context.

> . . .Michalson's statement that the church can never tell people "what to do" appears to be an unwise one when the dimension of social action is given due consideration. This writer suggests that Michalson. . .could profit from a consideration of that which John C. Bennett and others call "middle axioms". . .[23]

Johnson's questions regarding the propriety of rules, are really questions regarding the propriety of contextualism--and Michalson is subject to the criticisms leveled at contextualists.[24] Michalson's response to these questions would be that to

---

[22]Ibid., p. 241.

[23]Ibid.

[24]See Harvey Cox, ed., The Situation Ethics Debate (Philadelphia: Westminster Press, 1968).

counsel legalism (even in a compromised form) endangers responsibility. He sees legalism as the promoting of irresponsibility by its encouraging only minimal compliance to minimal standards of justice. This response is typical of contextualism, when criticized by prescriptionists.

Going beyond the debate between contextualists and prescriptionists, it can be said that Michalson endorsed a very limited use of rules and law. Even though his understanding of responsibility in the world transcends the state, Michalson recognizes the state as a political reality with "minimal standards of justice." The state and its laws then, function as <u>a point of departure</u> for social justice. To be sure, civil disobedience is possible and may be required, in Michalson's schema, but primarily he uses power to influence, rather than destroy the state's authority, and then builds his ethics of responsibility on top of that. Also, to the extent that he builds his ethics of responsibility as a result of God's commands within a relational context, he utilizes laws and rules again. As recognized above, context, rather than command, is the more important factor in his relational ethic, but the element of divine command is present and is taken into account.

Finally (really thirdly), Johnson criticizes Michalson's "separation of issues into those things which have to do with faith and those which do not."[25] Michalson, in "The Maturity of

---

[25] Johnson, "Michalson's Concept of History," p. 241.

Sonship" states that

> [Faith does not] deplore enforcement of traffic regulations pertaining to drunken driving, or the regulation of liquor advertising for the honesty and deglamourizing of its claims. These are prudent ways of preventing men from exploiting and hurting each other in forms of social collision. But they classify more with civil law than with faith.[26]

Johnson sees this separation as endorsing

> a dangerous dichotomy between a "sacred" and a "secular" realm which would destroy the theological basis for social action, and thereby defeat the purposes of one who advocates a "worldly theology."[27]

In fact, quite the contrary is true.

Much like his understanding of the interplay between nature and faith in the life of a believer, Michalson also understands the relationship of civil law (the state) and faith. Persons of faith must live in the state and, insofar as is faithfully possible, comply to the state's minimal standards of justice. Because people of faith transcend these minimal standards, and at times rebel against them, does not dichotomize the sacred and secular--in fact the opposite is the case. It is precisely in transcending the state's minimal standards of justice that theology becomes worldly. In gaining and practicing perspective on the state, the church, as stated above, augments, impacts, and directs the state (while itself being impacted).

It seems clear that Michalson's Christian ethics of responsibility is applied in concert with its formulation. Again,

---

[26] Michalson, "The Maturity of Sonship," p. 11.

[27] Johnson, "Michalson's Concept of History," p. 241.

there are those who would disagree with Michalson--among them intentionalists, as well as strict institutionalists and strict operationalists. But, as was true of the formulation of his ethics, the way in which Michalson implements his ethics represents a legitimate and certifiable approach, with strengths as well as weaknesses. I have tried to lift up Michalson's strengths, while recognizing his ethic's weaknesses.

CHAPTER FIVE

Ethics in Carl Michalson: Summary
(A Michalsonian Model for Theological Ethics)

Carl Michalson's ethics of responsibility can make a significant contribution to the ethical reflection associated with liberation theology, evangelical perfectionism,[1] and the ethics of character and virtue. In this chapter, I will use Michalson's ethics, as set forth above, to construct a (Michalsonian) model of theological ethics, showing (a) Michalson's understanding of good and evil; (b) how he addressed both individual and systemic evil; and (c) how he actually promoted the good. In chapter six I will set forth an agenda of current ethical issues and concerns, and bring Michalson into dialogue with these more recent formulations in order to explore his relevance. Finally, in chapter seven, I will state his contribution to the field of theological ethics.

In chapter twelve of Worldly Theology, "Theology and the Worldliness of Faith--The Prospect for a Theology as History," Michalson states the task of systematic theology. He also establishes the basis and context for theological ethics conceived as Christian responsibility. "Theology and the Worldliness of

---

[1] Evangelical perfectionism describes the program of intentional Christian ethicists who "radically challenge the accommodation to principalities and powers that began when Constantine recognized the church and Augustine worked out the theory of the two cities." (Long, A Survey of Recent Christian Ethics, p. 82.

Faith--The Prospect for a Theology as History" thus provides the starting point for a Michalsonian model of theological ethics.

Michalson starts his article on the task of systematic theology by stating that "the reality of faith is historical."[2] After reiterating his understanding of theology as history, rather than nature, Michalson further states that "New Testament theo-logy is a doctrine of salvation. . .a doctrine of God-in-his-word, of God-for-us."[3] In short, there is, for Michalson, no sense in talking of God other than as God encounters us--in history.

Given this understanding, Michalson draws two methodological conclusions. Theology as history is "theology resolved to make no statements about reality which do not involve the question of the meaning of man's existence." Also, theology as history is "theology resolved to import no criteria into the interpretation of the Biblical faith which the Bible does not itself supply or confirm." From these resolutions, two consequences flow.

> One is that in theology as history there will be no norms and authorities. There will be only a frame of reference, that being the Bible and its hermeneutical aid, the history of its interpretation. . . .
> The second consequence for theology from its historical method will be that proof and explanation in theology must give way to clarification and illumination."[4]

---

[2]Michalson, Worldly Theology, p. 217.

[3]Ibid., pp. 218-219.

[4]Ibid., p. 219.

Michalson then asks, "Why is systematic theology warranted as an independent discipline in this definition of theology as history?[5]

For Michalson, the (historical) encounter of God with humanity is something that comes to us through a process. Its source is scripture. <u>Exegesis</u> of the scripture results in <u>dogma</u> (the church's official basis for self-understanding), which is expressed in <u>doctrine</u> (the faith actually confessed by the church), which encounters the world through <u>preaching</u>. Systematic theology clarifies the church's doctrine by forcing its continual encounter with dogma and scripture (through exegesis), so that it might result in preaching. In a word, systematic theology brings the encounter of God with humanity--i.e. it brings history--to the fore, by marshalling various fragmented theological functions to aid its final expression, preaching.[6]

For Michalson, the Christian faith, aided by systematic theology, is an historical encounter that is expressed in and through "the practice of preaching, broadly viewed."[7] This proclamation of the historical encounter between God and humanity is, for Michalson, the <u>sine qua non</u> of the Christian faith.

---

[5]Ibid., p. 220.

[6]Michalson's understanding of the process wherein God encounters humanity is found in <u>Worldly Theology</u>, p. 220ff. See especially, <u>Worldly Theology</u>, p. 223.

[7]Michalson, <u>Worldly Theology</u>, p. 223.

Preaching is the faith's coming to fruition and it's engagement with the world.

As the faith's coming to fruition and engaging with the world, preaching is also the motivation for and the enactment of responsible living and action in the world. Thus, preaching is also the *sine qua non* of Michalson's Christian ethic of responsibility,[8] where the world is confronted with a choice between the Good and (systemic) Evil. The model proposed below, is designed to clearly delineate how Michalson conceived of preaching as a basis for ethical concern in and by individuals and communities, i.e. as a basis for social justice, human rights, economics, politics, war and peace, and civil rights. In short, this model seeks to summarize how Michalson's theology is actually integrated with ethics in a way that allows it to "exist in the service of God. . .and express itself in the constitution of a meaningful world."[9]

A. Michalson's Understanding of Good and Evil: (The Object of Faith)

As explained above (Chapter I, page, 28ff), in the last stage of his theological career Edwin Lewis set forth a radical reinterpretation of the problem of evil. In response to the (Augustinian) tradition that regards evil as without status, and as the negation of being, which, because it comes from Pure

---

[8]See Chapter III, pp. 117ff., above.

[9]Michalson, *Worldly Theology*, p. 25.

Being, must be good, Lewis posits a metaphysical dualism. He argues that evil be recognized as having an irreducible ontological status alongside the divine.[10]

Though Carl Michalson benefited greatly from Lewis' tutelage, it is evident that, on this point, Michalson was an Augustinian. For Michalson, the Good that is God is experienced in the world as God's creation, the world as the object of God's love. Evil for Michalson, is the denial of God, expressed as the denial of the world as God's creation and an object of God's love. His (subjective) theology of secularization, from Gogarten,[11] is a testimony to this understanding.

Michalson's theology of secularity sought to demonstrate that turning to God is effected by turning to the world, and that in turning to God there is, necessarily, a turning to the world. The two are identical insofar as one cannot be done without the other. As stated above, (Chapter II, p. 105) from his Drew M.A. thesis onward, Michalson viewed the faith as necessarily responsible (or worldly) both systematically and by nature, utilizing Kierkegaard and Gogarten respectively.

Systematically, responsibility is a necessary consequence of an historical faith.

> [The Christian's faith translates] him out of the world of unreality, of abstraction, of objectivity and ideality,

---

[10] See Edwin Lewis, The Creator and the Adversary. (New York: Abingdon Press, 1948). See also Charles Hardwick, "Edwin Lewis: Introductory and critical Remarks," pp. 98-99 and Marvin Green, "Contemporary Theories of Evil," p. 323ff.

[11] See Chapter II, pp. 84-90, above.

which is not a world one lives, into the real world where one can grasp existence as a whole. "By faith I make renunciation of nothing, on the contrary, by faith I acquire everything."[12]

Michalson also views the faith as responsible by nature, pointing to Paul's concept of sonship as paradigmatic in this regard. "In this event [of sonship] the intention of creation is radically fulfilled: henceforth man is to subdue the earth."[13]

For Michalson then, the Good is what comes about when people live out the gospel. The Good is faith, hope and love abiding in the hearts and minds of people committed to Christ. <u>The Good is God's presence in the world by virtue of the church's preaching</u>.

Evil, for Michalson, is a denial of the Good that is God's presence in the world. It is expressed as the world in love with itself, as faithlessness, and as God's good world turned into an idol. Michalson cites Gogarten in precisely this regard.

> To say it as Gogarten does, the Creator has given us the world as the locus of our responsibility to him. But we have worshipped the creature rather than the Creator, perverting our responsibility *for* the world into responsibility *to* the world. The effect of the advent of Jesus is to restore to us the proper relationship by reintroducing obedience to God as the new possibility for life in the world. In the new age, we must be in the world while not of it. We must live in the world "as if not" in the world.[14]

---

[12]Michalson, <u>Worldly Theology</u>, p. 126.

[13]Michalson, <u>Rationality of Faith</u>, p. 131.

[14]Michalson, <u>Worldly Theology</u>, p. 171.

B. The Means for Bringing About the Good
and Combatting Evil:
(The Faith in Action Through Preaching)

The importance of preaching, for Michalson, cannot be overstated. In fact, preaching is the key to his whole theology. For Michalson, the nature of faith is such that it must be preached. Since faith is not objective, but subjective, it cannot be seen, but must be heard. As Michalson is so fond of saying, "Faith is an acoustical affair." In line with this, preaching is also central to his understanding of responsibility[15] and to his understanding of ethics: For Michalson, the Good occurs when the world is engaged by preaching.

These theological and ethical understandings are reflected, further, in Michalson's ecclesiology. The church, as a gathered community in the midst of the world, is energized and motivated by preaching, and thus engages the world. All else the church is and does is seen in light of its being the place where preaching engages the world.

Michalson envisioned the church, through its preaching, as creating a new climate in the world, where the Good could come to expression and where evil could be overcome. Thus preaching, as an expression of the Good, is the act of addressing individual and systemic evil. Preaching represents care overcoming self concern, it represents the abolition of idolatry and faithlessness, and the world's no longer loving itself and denying God's

---

[15] See p. 79ff., above

lordship. It is in and through preaching, rightly conceived (as history) and broadly conceived (as the church's engaging the world) that maturity is realized and people are freed for responsibility.

Preaching, for Michalson, is not an end in itself. Rather, it is the essence and epitome of responsibility.[16] It is the Christian faith's being engaged with the world, prophetically and redemptively.[17] It is the faith's liberating, engaging and motivating people for God and for the world. It brings about new self understanding and new relationships to others. It is an affirmation of the Good that seeks to address evil.

For Michalson, preaching is the sine qua non of responsibility, in that preaching effects the right way of being in the world.

> The responsibility for the world burdens man as a fate when man lacks the freedom for God from whence that responsibility originally arises. Modern man is right to feel responsible for the world. The preaching of the church makes it possible for man to remain free for that responsibility by receiving it from God.
>
> Preaching creates the very possibility of the transition from the old age to the new. In continuity with the living word of Jesus, it is a sign that we are now in the new age and that because of Jesus the situation in the world has radically changed.
>
> The preacher is the one who is vested with the responsibility of renewing [a] call. He is. . .not a reporter of past events but a herald who announces the intention of God in Christ in such a way as to precipitate the new age among us. Proclamation (kergyma) is not the message simply, nor even

---

[16]See Chapter III, p. 117ff. above.

[17]Ibid.

the act of preaching. Proclamation includes the call to life in the new age which comes as a claim upon the hearer.[18]

The sermon "Faith Must Be Expressed in Works of Love" is perhaps the key example of Michalson's preaching a faith that changes self understandings and, in turn has social relevance and begins to confront systemic evil. Here Michalson depicts the Christian as mobilized by God's love to "Love thy neighbor." (Sinfulness, on the other hand is a denial of God's love and direction, as exemplified by Luther's <u>cor incurratum in se</u> "the heart all curled up inside itself."[19] Michalson goes on to characterize love for neighbor as "an ethic of responsibility that has no terminus,"[20] and to speak of the importance of expressing love for neighbor at the social level, in terms of justice (which is "the highest possible equivalent of spontaneous love"[21]).

"Faith Must Be Expressed in Works of Love" thus clearly demonstrates the logic and necessity of Michalson's theological ethics. Preaching creates new self understandings, which necessarily affect our personal relations with others <u>and</u> our relations with the world at large. Preaching thus engages the world and the (Augustinian) evil that threatens it.

---

[18]Michalson, <u>Worldly Theology</u>, pp. 180-181.

[19]Michalson, "Faith Must be Expressed in Works of Love," in <u>Witness of Radical Faith</u>, p. 97.

[20]Ibid., p. 99.

[21]Ibid., p. 105.

Chapter nine of Worldly Theology, "Jesus of Nazareth and the Word of Faith," is another example of Michalson's perception that preaching engages the world with the gospel. Here, he speaks of faith as "the reality which has the task of liberating man from. . .bondage to the world."[22] And the propositions of preaching are seen to be "the occasions for. . .meaningful participation in [this] new age."[23]

Michalson's book Faith for Personal Crises is also a study of how preaching, broadly conceived, addresses the world. As discussed above (Chapter II, p. 81ff) Faith for Personal Crises sees to "pattern the mind with the resources of the Christian faith for meeting personal crises."[24] Michalson accomplishes this by bringing the God-relation to bear--i.e. by preaching the gospel--in the midst of these crises. Faith for Personal Crises is thus an attempt to communicate the gospel's message to people in special need, wherein Michalson hopes to enable humanity to transcend oft-times debilitating personality types and be responsible in the world--responsibility in the world being the task that defines a person's very being as a person.[25]

---

[22] Michalson, Worldly Theology, p. 180.

[23] Ibid., p. 182.

[24] Michalson, Faith for Personal Crises, p. 12.

[25] See Ibid., p. 8.

C. The Good that is Realized by Responsible Faith: (The Telos of Preaching)

Preaching, for Michalson, has as its end, being in the world in faith, hope and love--i.e. engagement with the world and maturity. This translates into individual action vis-a-vis particular others.[26] It also translates into social action wherein the church is motivated and energized for engagement with systemic evil.

1. The Definition of Engagement with the World

Admittedly, Michalson is not always clear and precise, as to the shape and definition of the action that is the telos of preaching. The fact that he was a charismatic and hermeneutical theologian-ethicist, with strong Neo-orthodox ties, meant that the bulk of his energies were given to theology as a prologomena to ethics. So the church's living out its responsibility and the world repentant under the freedom of the gospel are seen more as possibilities than realizations. As an avowed Methodist however, Michalson was confident that a changed self understanding meant a changed world understanding that addressed systemic evil. And in this respect, he made several significant forays into the realm of social action and ethics that were in conjunction with his week by week addressing of the powers from the pulpit. Together, these exercises in "preaching, broadly conceived" suggest and

---

[26]See Ibid.

begin to set forth a Michalsonian social ethics that is, in fact, relevant today.[27]

Several of the texts cited above indicate *how* preaching is engaged with the world, both individually and socially. The series "New Testament Teaching for Modern Living," and also "Focus on a Revolution" speak of a Christian faith that is individually and socially active. Here Michalson "proclaims" a surprisingly well-developed and coherent Christian ethic of responsibility, formulated a la Kierkegaard, Bultmann, and Gogarten, and implemented a la Reinhold Niebuhr. It is a contextual ethic, centered in works of love and offered as free response to God's grace, that represents an extension of preaching. As such it has implications for both individuals and society.

2. The Ethical Content of Engagement with the World

In "New Testament Teaching for Modern Living," Michalson sets forth more specifically what he means by justice as "the

---

[27]Michalson's last book, Worldly Theology, clearly portrays preaching as the impetus to engagement with the world. In fact, much of Michalson's later writings indicate an increased awareness of the gravity of social issues in the life of the church. This indicates that Michalson, had he lived, might well have gone on to speak definitively about both individual and social action as a consequence of faith. His premature death, however, precluded any major developments in this regard, and makes this opinion, though indicated, purely speculative. Just the same, Michalson must be considered a theologian/ethicist. His understanding of faith as responsible by nature and design, and his ethical formulation and implementation, justify and require this designation.

highest possible equivalent of spontaneous love."[28] He also speaks of justice in relation to other clearly defined ethical issues--among them human rights, economics, politics, and war and peace. His treatment of these issues (See above, Chapter III, pp. 124-130) indicates again his intent to see preaching engaged in responsibility for the world, and further, offers a *glimpse* of that engagement's content.

"New Testament Teaching for Modern Living" represents a serious attempt by Michalson to "broadly view" preaching as confrontation and engagement with the world. Here Michalson seeks to address the claims of the gospel to the world, in order to effect responsibility and maturity at both the individual level (lessons 1-6 of "New Testament Teaching") and the community level (lesson 7ff, "New Testament Teaching"). Here the New Testament message is "proclaimed" in order to convey personal virtues, and also to "leaven the whole lump of society with brotherliness and humanitarian kindness."[29] To these ends, Michalson preaches the need to "repossess truths in our New Testament faith" and "appropriate a kind of social intelligence."[30]

---

[28] See Michalson, "Faith Must Be Expressed in Works of Love," in *Witness of Radical Faith*, pp. 95-108.

[29] Michalson, "New Testament Teaching for Modern Living," p. 23.

[30] Ibid.

The content of Michalson's "preaching the New Testament for modern living" clearly reflects this conviction that there are two dimensions of Christian existence--the personal and the social. His delineation of justice as "the highest possible equivalent of spontaneous love" at the social level, and his speaking to the issues of human rights, economics, politics, and war and peace, illustrate a (Reinhold) Niebuhrian understanding and are calculated to avoid idealistic frustration and irrelevance. Michalson's social ethics (again, see above, Chapter III, pp. 124-130), are primarily operational and reflect his attempt to work in and through, while not succumbing to, the world's centers of power.

Michalson assumes a similar stance on the civil rights issue. In "Focus on a Revolution," he states that "when I demonstrate on behalf of civil liberties, I do it as a theologian."[31] Given his understanding of the task of theology, the inference is clear: Michalson approached the civil rights issue as a proclaimer of the word or preacher. He goes on to say, "I am sure that one cannot do theology today without involving God in just such historical causes as the. . .civil rights enterprises give us a chance to do."[32]

Here again we see the inescapable logic of Michalson's theology and ethics, and the necessity of relating the two.

---

[31]"Focus on a Revolution," Appendix A, p. 254

[32]Ibid.

Christian proclamation by design and nature is involved in eradicating evil both individually and systemically. By doing this, says Michalson, "we. . .have a sense [of] fulfilling our human responsibility [and] we. . .give God a chance to be born again."[33] For Michalson, the Christian is one who proclaims the word. And proclamation of the word cannot but be engaged with the world, seeking to change the hearts and minds of people, and seeking also to change the structures of society that deny God's word of grace and freedom in Christ.

There are those who would disagree with Michalson's adoption of Niebuhrian constructs to effect this transformation. His intent, however, is clear--to engage the world through preaching. And his means represent a legitimate option in light of Christian proclamation and that stated intent. Michalson thus not only conceived of preaching as engaging the world and promoting the Good. He also sought, through his preaching, broadly conceived, to convey and promote the Good's content, at both the personal and social levels, as Christian maturity and faithfulness.

---

[33]Ibid., p. 256.

CHAPTER SIX

The Implications of Carl Michalson's Ethics for More Recent Ethics

Carl Michalson's Christian ethics of responsibility is ethics conceived as an extension of preaching. Michalson's ethics also represent, at both the individual and social levels, a well defined and formed ethical construct, with a definite shape and content. Given its shape and content, and the extent to which Michalson developed his Christian ethics of responsibility, it has been and is my contention that Michalson's thought can make a contribution to Christian ethics today. His Christian ethics of responsibility, established, set forth, and summarized above, can address contemporary formulations, especially those associated with liberation theology, evangelical perfectionism, and the ethics of virtue and character.

To be sure, any statement of the implications of Michalson's ethics for more recent Christian ethics is largely a <u>projection</u> of what he might have said, on the basis of what he actually said. However, on the basis of what Michalson actually said, this projection is clearly implied and can be substantiated. And on the basis of what Michalson said <u>in relation to</u> the shape and content of the contemporary formulations here set forth, this projection is not only implied, but demanded!

In this chapter, I will briefly set forth these more recent and contemporary formulations by examining representatives of each.[1] I will then bring Michalson into dialogue with these newer statements of ethics, and, in this way, explore his relevance and contribution to current discussions.

A. Ethics of Responsibility and Liberation Theology as a Source of Ethics

Liberation theology is an overarching term used to describe several identifiable contemporary theological enterprises. Among these theological enterprises are Latin American liberation theology, black theology,[2] and feminist theology. Each of these movements has its own origin, vitality, distinctive features, and setting. At the same time, shared traits allow for their being examined together.

Though liberation theologies designate themselves as theologies rather than ethical systems (and thus seek to be more comprehensive in concern and scope), they each have a strong ethical agenda. Being theologies "from below," they promote the necessity of social change, the abolition of oppression, and emphasize

---

[1] Admittedly, an examination of representative views from liberation theology, evangelical perfectionism, and the ethics of character and virtue is not a comprehensive treatment of these important contemporary ethical formulations. However, in each case, these representative views are from recognized authorities, and express clearly and concisely the main tenets of the perspective in question.

[2] Though some would argue that the word "black" should be capitalized because it denotes a special group, like the word "American", this usage is not universally accepted. James Cone, quoted extensively below, does not capitalize "black," and I have chosen to be consistent with him. Cone does, however, capitalize "Black Power."

freedom of destiny and aspiration through the power of Christ.[3] Liberation theologies have little use for theories and perceptions of a transcendent God that are imposed on the world. Rather, liberation theories and perceptions of God represent "critical reflection on praxis." Theology thus "develops from what we learn and experience by seeking to transform the world as Christians work (alongside of God) on behalf of the poor."[4] Liberation theology is a different theology, developed from a different starting point. As such it also has a different interlocutor (the poor are its dialogical partners), a different set of tools (socio/political and economic analysis depicts its situation), a different analysis (injustice is its primary concern), and a different mode of engagement (action and involvement give rise to its reflection).[5]

1. **Third World Perspective**: Jose Miguez Bonino

Jose Miguez Bonino's liberation theology represents the attempt of theologians in Latin America to become involved in the

---

[3]See Long, *Survey of Recent Christian Ethics*, pp. 156-158.

[4]Robert McAfee Brown, *Theology in a New Key*. (Philadelphia: Westminster, 1978), pp. 60-70, cited by Long, *Survey of Recent Christian Ethics*, p. 159.

[5]Ibid. This description of liberation theology reflects Brown's six feature characterization of theologies "from below." Since Brown's schema underlies my characterization of liberation theology, it will serve also as a means of bringing Michalson's thought into dialogue with liberation theology. It will thus function as a common denominator for comparisons and contrasts.

struggle to abolish oppression and establish freedom in the countries south of the Rio Grande River.

> . . .The theology of liberation offers us not so much a new theme for reflection as a new way of making theology. Theology as critical reflection on historical praxis is thus a liberating theology, a theology of the liberating transformation of the history of mankind and, therefore, also of that portion of it--gathered as ecclesia--which openly confesses Christ. [It is] a theology which does not limit itself to think the world, but which attempts to place itself as a moment of the process through which the world is transformed: opening itself--in the protest against the trodden dignity of man, in the struggle against the plunder of the immense majority of men, in the love which liberates, in the constructuion of a new, just and fraternal society-- to the gift of God's Kingdom.[6]

Because his theology is a reflection on praxis rather than "ideas imposed from without" and because his concern is to effect structures of oppression, the use of socio-political analysis is crucial to Miguez Bonino's theological enterprise. Socio-political and economic theories allow him to conceptualize the situation he confronts, and the systems of injustice and bondage that control the situation. Miguez Bonino then seeks to assess and impact those systems of injustice and bondage.

Marxism plays a crucial role in Miguez Bonino's social analysis. Says Miguez Bonino,

> I have believed that certain elements of the Marxist economic and social analysis were correct. . . .
> . . .On this basis I have found it possible to work together with Marxists and others--on questions of human rights, for instance--with clarity and mutual respect.

---

[6]Jose Miguez Bonino, Doing Theology in a Revolutionary Setting. (Philadelphia: Fortress, 1979), pp. 61-83.

At the same time, he feels it necessary to clarify liberation theology's relationship to Marxism--to demythologize the Marxian question.

> . . .This socialist option. . .is the immediate context of my theological work. It is not an absolute, not an object of faith, but simply a sociopolitical decision (a lucid one, I hope) which concretely defines my Christian obedience in the world at this time. Theologically, I think it is a historical project partially and ambiguously but really and intrinsically related to God's Kingdom, and therefore to my Christian hope. The gospel does not stand or fall with the correctness of this view. But my theology does.[7]

The conclusion Miguez Bonino draws from examining his region's history, with the tools of social analysis in general and Marxism in particular, is that "life has been made finally only a function of the economic process."[8]

> . . .The human subject vanishes and only the "fetish" (capital? property? the economic laws?) remains in control. Repression, torture, disappearances, the withdrawal of social, educational and health services, the cultural or physical genocide of native Indians, the suppression of all expressions of public opinion--these are not the result of the whim or the cruelty of bloodthirsty tyrants: they are "the necessary social cost" of "freedom." It is the sacrifice that the highest god, "the economic laws," demands.[9]

These insights establish the framework for Miguez Bonino's theology, a theology that says God has chosen sides.

> . . .He has chosen to liberate the poor by delivering them from their misery and marginality, and to liberate the rich by bringing them down from their thrones. Christians and

---

[7] Jose Miguez Bonino, "For Life and Against Death: A Theology That Takes Sides," in *Theologies in Transition*, ed. James M. Wall (New York: Crossroad, 1981), p. 176. See also Miguez Bonino, *Christians and Marxists* (Grand Rapids: Eerdmanns, 1976) and *Revolutionary Theology Comes of Age*.

[8] Miguez Bonino, "For Life and Against Death," p. 171.

[9] Ibid.

churches are invited to take the side of the poor, to claim solidarity with them in their struggle. And theology comes at the rear guard, as a reflection, as a help to rethink and deepen (and thus perhaps, also, if we are faithful, to correct and enrich a commitment already undertaken as an act of obedience.[10]

In short, theology arises from and gives itself to the struggle of the poor.[11]

Miguez Bonino's theology not only enunciates correct doctrine; its overriding feature is the correction of a social-political situation. His is truly a theology where theory, though important, is subserviant to impacting the social-political situation, where orthodoxy is secondary to <u>ortho praxis</u>. His <u>is</u> a new way of theologizing that does not think about God, so much as it assists action on God's behalf and in defense of the poor.

As stated at the outset of this discussion, and glimpsed throughout, liberation theolgy, by definition and design has a strong social ethics agenda. Miguez Bonino's book, <u>Toward a</u>

---

[10] Ibid., p. 172.

[11] Miguez Bonino's belief that theology arises from and gives itself to the struggle of the poor is expressly stated in his article, "Doing Theology in the Context of the Struggles of the Poor."

"The specificity of our discipline--the demands of the Word of God and faith--within the historical context of our world converge to point out a place for the theologian: solidarity with the poor. I am not speaking of 'a theology of poverty', not even necessarily of 'a theology of the poor', but of a theology which 'thinks' the Gospel from within a conscious and lucid option for the poor." Miguez Bonino, "Doing Theology in the Context of the Struggles of the Poor," <u>Mid-stream</u> 20 (October, 1981):370.
See also Miguez Bonino, "The Struggle of the Poor and the Church," <u>The Ecumenical Review</u> 27 (January, 1975):37-43.

Christian Political Ethics, is an example of this interrelatedness.

In Toward a Christian Political Ethics Miguez Bonino seeks to develop a dialectical method that begins with praxis as history, moves to ethical theory, and concludes with praxis as strategy. To this end, Miguez Bonino sees a capitalistic transnationalism threatening to sacrifice human life for economic process in Latin America. And he opposes this with a project of liberation that moves toward a democratic socialism and open society.[12] Rejecting the Augustinian (i.e. the Constantinian) model, in which concern for order overrides concern for justice, Miguez Bonino calls for a "radical transformation inspired by the prophetic-messianic focus on the justice and peace of the kingdom of God."[13]

> The true question is not "What degree of justice (liberation of the poor) is compatible with the maintenance of the existing order?" but "What kind of order, which order is compatible with the exercise of justice (the right of the poor)?". . .
> . . .Justice is the foundation of order.[14]

The ethical strategy that results from Miguez Bonino's ethical conviction is somewhat sketchy and imprecise, but several affirmations are clear.

---

[12] See Jose Miguez Bonino, Toward a Christian Political Ethics (Philadelphia: Fortress, 1983), p. 77ff.

[13] Ibid., p. 84.

[14] Ibid., p. 86.

1. It is crucial (and within the realm of possibility) that the oppressed gain a new consciousness wherein they see themselves as responsible for their own destiny.

2. Action, especially violent action, toward attaining justice and freedom needs to be looked at in a utilitarian way. Action has its cost, but so does not acting and these need to be weighed against each other.

3. Even though suffering (and failure) may result from the struggle for liberation, the struggle itself grants meaning and fulfillment because the struggle is Love Incarnate.

> A project of liberation is freed from the danger of absolutization. . .by being related to its own inner meaning, which is love. Love is thus the inner meaning of politics, just as politics is the outward form of love. When this relation is made operative in the struggle for liberation, there is both the flexibility necessary for humanizing the struggle and the freedom necessary for humanizing the result of the struggle.[15]

Miguez Bonino's Christian political ethics firmly establishes his theology of liberation. Here he grounds his theology of liberation in political action that is based on the ideals of the Kingdom of God and defined by the gospel's dictum of love for neighbor. By so doing he seeks to actually liberate his region from oppression.

---

[15]Ibid., p. 114.

2. **Black Perspective:** James Cone

James Cone is recognized by many as the leading proponent of black theology.[16] His essay, "Christianity and Black Power," which later formed the basis of his book Black Theology and Black Power,[17] was his first consideration of and serves as an introduction to this important expression of liberation thought.[18]

Although some "consider Black Power the work of the Anti-Christ," Cone's thesis is that "It is rather Christ's central message to 20th Century America." The Church, according to Cone, "must become prophetic," fighting for the immediate and total emancipation of all people, in keeping with the message of Christ.

> The Church cannot afford to deplore the means which oppressed people use to break the chains of slavery because. . .[to do so] gives comfort and assistance to the oppressor. . . .Embracing Black Power is not only possible

---

[16]Rosemary Ruether, in reviewing Cone's A Black Theology of Liberation (The Journal of Religious Thought 28,1 [Spring-Summer, 1971]:74-77) calls him "the foremost black theologian in America. Gayraud S. Wilmore, in reviewing the same book (Union Seminary Quarterly Review 26.4 [Summer, 1971]:413-419) calls Cone's theology "the most radical and far reaching program since the publication of Reinhold Niebuhr's Moral Man and Immoral Society in 1932."
For a full autobiographical account of Cone's life and work, see James Cone, My Soul Looks Back (Nashville: Abingdon, 1982). Because Cone's theology is, by his own admission, so closely linked to his lifelong firsthand experience of white racism, My Soul Looks Back is very important to understanding his thought.

[17]See Cone, My Soul Looks Back, p. 48.

[18]See also James Cone, Black Theology and Black Power (New York: Seabury Press, 1961); A Black Theology of Liberation (New York: Lippincott, 1970); and For My People: Black Theology and the Black Church (Maryknoll, N.Y.: Orbis, 1984.)

but necessary if the Church wants to remain faithful to the traditions of Christianity. . .[19]

Black Power (which means "the full emancipation of black people from white oppression by whatever means black people deem necessary") is "irrational" in the face of reasoned appeals which "merely support the perpetuation of the ravaging of the black community." It insists that black people "say 'No!'" to all do-gooders who insist they need more time and urges black people to fight for freedom and dignity. Black Power is not, according to Cone, a call for "black supremacy."

> There is no analogy--by any stretch of definition or imagination--between the advocates of Black Power and white racists. . . .The goal of the racists is to keep black people on the bottom. . . .The goal of black self-determination and black self-identity--Black Power--is full participation in the decision-making processes affecting the lives of black people.[20]

Given his understanding of Black Power and its aim, Cone says the message of Black Power is the message of Christ.

> If the Gospel is a gospel of liberation for the oppressed, then Jesus is where the oppressed are--proclaiming release to the captives and looking askance at those Christians who silently consent to their discomfiture. If Jesus is *not* in the ghetto, . . .then the Gospel is a prevarication and Christianity is a mistake. Christianity cannot be alien to Black Power; it *is* Black Power![21]

And the church, as the people of God, must render its service to the liberation that Black Power--i.e. the Gospel--espouses.

---

[19]James Cone, "Christianity and Black Power," in *Is Anybody Listening to Black America?*, ed. Eric Lincoln (New York: Seabury Press, 1968), p. 4.

[20]Ibid., p. 6.

[21]Ibid., p. 7.

Failure to do so results in a racist church that is the antithesis of Christian faith.

Black theology, like third world liberation theology, also has tremendous consequences for Christian ethics. In *God of the Oppressed*, Cone addresses the theme of "Liberation and the Christian Ethic." Criticizing the status quo ethic of Constantine, Augustine, Aquinas, Luther, Calvin, and Wesley (not to mention Reinhold Niebuhr and James Gustafson) Cone says:

> Theologians of the Christian Church have not interpreted Christian ethics as an act for the liberation of the oppressed because their views of divine revelation were defined by philosophy and other cultural values rather than by the biblical theme of God as the Liberator of the oppressed.[22]

In response to the status quo ethic, Cone contends that:

> The black Christian ethic must start with Scripture and the black experience. We must read each in the light of the other, and then ask, "What am I to do?". . .
>
> Because the ethical question "What am I to do?" cannot be separated from its theological base, Christian ethics is. . ."koinonia ethics". . .I contend that the koinonia is limited to the victims of oppression and does not include the oppressors. The ethical behavior of Christians, therefore, is defined in and by the oppressed community whom God has called into being for freedom.[23]

Christian behavior, then, arises from the oppressed community's responding to God's call to obedience. And, in line with this, "the criteria of ethical judgment can only be hammered out

---

[22]James Cone, *God of the Oppressed* (New York: Seabury, 1975), pp. 199-200.

[23]Ibid., pp. 205-206.

in the community of the victims of injustice."[24] Concretely, this means that Christian ethics must be hammered out in the oppressed community by the victims of injustice.

> What are we to do, . . .is not decided by abstract principles but is defined by Jesus' liberating presence in our community. The oppressed community is the place where we are called to hammer out the meaning of Jesus' presence for Christian behavior. . . .We may not always agree on a common action. . . .But our common knowledge that we are enslaved by the structures of injustice binds us together and forces us to fight the good fight so that our children will have a more humane place in which to live.[25]

3. **Feminist Perspective**: Rosemary Ruether

A third version of liberation theology is feminist theology. Broadly speaking, feminist theology focuses on sexism--the historical and contemporary exclusion of women from leadership and education in the Christian tradition. In the face of the church's subjugating women under patriarchy, feminist theology seeks to recover and formulate an alternative theology of equality, that may or may not be based in the Judeo-Christian tradition.

Rosemary Ruether is a recognized and representative spokesperson of feminist theology.[26] She identifies idolatry ("the

---

[24]Ibid., p. 207.

[25]Ibid., pp. 212-213.

[26]Rosemary Ruether's credentials as a leading feminist theologian are beyond doubt. As the dust cover of one of her books says, she is recognized as "one of America's most original theologians," (Rosemary Ruether, Disputed Questions: On Being a Christian [Nashville: Abingdon, 1982]) and her book, Sexism and God Talk: Toward a Feminist Theology, has been called "the most extensive critique of Christian theology from a feminist stand-

confusion of the self-projections of ruling groups with the divine nature and will") as "the disease of theology," and encourages the reclaiming of the prophetic tradition as a means of reconceiving religion. For Ruether, the prophetic tradition is that which recognizes that "God is redeemer as creator" and identifies redemption with the historical universe. Given this "link between transcendence and the visible transformation of created reality" as central to the Biblical message, Ruether advocates a liberation theology.

> Liberation theology builds upon the discovery of transcendence as future historical possibility. . .and as critical, iconoclastic reflection. . .But it. . .rejects that division of reality into an unrealizable transcendence (Christ) and enclosed finitude (us) which gave the jeremiads of the last generation their "reassuring" hopelessness ("reassuring" because it allows the theological establishment to sound critically prophetic without believing that anything can be changed that will upset its own position). . . .
> Liberation theology comes from those who cannot be reassured by "realistic" hopelessness, because they speak as persons who have no place, no peoplehood, no hope, no possibility of a new world.[27]

And liberation theology advocates place, personhood, hope and possibility for those persons--specifically for the poor, for blacks, and for women.

Since sexism denies the truth of the prophetic tradition, it is sinful and must be opposed by liberation theology. Sexism is "the alienated oppressive relationship of the man to the

---

point." Winsome Munro, review of <u>Sexism and God Talk,</u> by Rosemary Ruether, in <u>Religious Educator</u> Fall, 1983, p. 596.)

[27]Rosemary Ruether, "What is the Task of Theology," <u>Christianity and Crisis</u> 36 (May 24, 1976):121-123.

woman. . .which translates certain initial biological advantages into a power relationship."[28] The result of sexism is the depersonalization of women.

> Women are depersonalized. . .into a body-object to be used or abused sexually, but not really encountered through sexuality as a person. Male-female relations are envisioned as a kind of social extension of mind-body relations. This implies a subject-object or I-It relation between men and women. . .
>
> Salvation can appear only as the resurrection of women. . . [which] means woman's self-definition as an autonomous person. She establishes herself as an autonomous self in any encounter. . .[29]

A liberation theology for women assists in this resurrection first by consciousness raising, and then by mediating this transformation of consciousness.

> The theological virtues which mediate this transformation of consciousness are <u>anger</u> and <u>pride</u>. . . .
> . . .Anger and pride come as grace welling up from the ground of their being, . . .springing loose the trap of their pacification. Anger and pride are the power for Exodus, for disaffiliation from the Egypt of male definition and use. . . .This exodus is a rebellion against the dead world of I-It relationship, reducing persons to things for exploitation and use by the sovereign ego of the Master, in whose image he made his God. It is the revelation of the possibility of co-humanity for the first time.[30]

Ruether's 1983 book, <u>Sexism and God-Talk: Toward a Feminist Theology</u>, is her most comprehensive statement to date. She starts with the premise that whatever promotes the full humanity

---

[28] Rosemary Ruether, "Sexism and the Theology of Liberation: Nature, Fall and Salvation as Seen from the Experience of Women." <u>Drew Gateway</u> 43 (Spring, 1973):139.

[29] Ibid., pp. 140, 142.

[30] Ibid., pp. 142-143.

of women (including parts of our pagan and gnostic heritage) reflects the divine. Whatever denies, diminishes and distorts the humanity of women is contrary to the divine. This she terms "the critical principle of feminist theology."[31]

Ruether then systematically examines Christian theology from the standpoint of women's experience, which "explodes as a critical force, exposing classical theology, . . .as based on male experience rather than on universal human experience."[32] At the heart of this discussion is Ruether's asking "Can a Male Savior Save Women?" She concludes that there can be a feminist Christology since

> Fundamentally, Jesus renews the prophetic vision whereby the Word of God does not validate the existing social and religious hierarchy but speaks on behalf of the marginalized and despised groups of society. Jesus proclaims an iconoclastic reversal of the system of religious status: The last shall be first and the first last. . . .
> [And] women play an important role in this gospel vision of the vindication of the lowly in God's new order.[33]

In the same way that she discusses Christology, Ruether treats a host of other topics (God, Mary, nature, evil, redemption, and the church). In order to deal with their implicit sexism, she jettisons ways they restrict and incorporates ways they resource an inclusive theology. Also in Sexism and God-

---

[31]See Rosemary Ruether, Sexism and God-Talk: Toward a Feminist Theology (Boston: Beacon Press, 1983), p. 18ff.

[32]Ibid., p. 13.

[33]Ibid., pp. 135-136.

Talk, Ruether again decries idolatry,[34] and utilizes the biblical "Prophetic Principle"[35] to discuss the congruence between the Gospel and "liberation from sexism."[36]

Rosemary Ruether is not as specific as Jose Miguez Bonino and James Cone in terms of Christian ethics. However, in her maintaining that liberation theology is "for the world," we glimpse ethical concerns that are common to and dealt with in the ethical agendas of Latin American and black theology.

> Liberation theology seeks to overcome the alienations and encapsulations created by Christendom and spiritualization. Ethics reestablishes its relation to social transformation, conversion to revolution. The church dissolves its sacral privatism to discover its discontinuity with Christendom and its continuity with the true human project. The split between thinking and doing, theory and practice, theology and the praxis of liberation, is overcome, transforming each term. Messianic hope is reclaimed, not just to judge the world but as hope, real hope for the enlargement of creation.[37]

4. Summary of Liberation Theology

The black theology which Cone has articulated and the feminist theology of Rosemary Ruether are very much akin to the third world liberation theology of Miguez Bonino, discussed above. Like Latin American liberation theology, black theology's starting point and feminist theology's starting point are in experience--in this instance the experience of black people and women.

---

[34] See Ibid., pp. 66-67.

[35] See Ibid., pp. 22ff.

[36] Ibid., p. 195.

[37] Ruether, "What is the Task of Theology?", p. 124.

The black and feminist experiences then influence and impact "God-talk," which, rather than intellecutal consideration and assent to propositions regarding a God "out there," has to do with God's revealing himself in solidarity with black people's and women's struggles for liberation. Like Latin American liberation theology, black theology and feminist theology have different *interlocutors*. Their dialogical partners are disenfranchised blacks and women, bearing the burden of racial and sexual oppression. Black theology and feminist theology listen to their pleas and seek to offer God's word of grace to their situations. In line with this, black theology's and feminist theology's *tools*, rather than philosophical speculation and linguistic analysis, are black history and experience and women's history and experience. Again there is commonality with Latin American liberation theology. The Bible is interpreted from the perspective of an historical community which has experienced oppression and is engaged in struggle. The Exodus becomes the central event of Scripture which, in Christ, is to be reiterated in the lives of black people and women today. Black theology and feminist theology, like Latin American liberation theology, also have a different *analysis* and a different *mode of engagement* than dominant theologies. Theological analysis is made in the struggle against white racism and male sexism, and theological engagement comes when theory is related to involvement in these same struggles.[38]

Given their common concerns and themes, it should be clear that liberation theologies do indeed represent a new way of doing theology. It should also be clear that they are theologies that seek to make the faith relevant and meaningful here and now, by a well considered commitment that confronts the church with the truth of the gospel and forces decisions for Christ, both ethical and otherwise.

5. Michalson's Contribution to Liberation Perspectives

As indicated above (See especially pp. 10-12, pp. 59-66), Theodore Runyon, in "Carl Michalson as a Wesleyan Theologian," sees Michalson as related to Latin American liberation theology. ("If the vectors. . .from Michalson's existentialist period through his last developments were extended. . .to the present they would bear surprising resemblance to. . .Latin American

---

[38]The primary difference between black theology and feminist theology on the one hand and Latin American liberation theology on the other, is the formers' reluctance, up to this point, to embrace Marxism. In the case of black theology, Cone attributes this to the fact that while Latin Americans emphasize class oppression, blacks, in America at least, emphasize racial oppression. Cone sees this as unfortunate in that "[black theologians in the U.S.] have given the impression that all we want is an equal piece of the North American capitalist pie." (Cone, My Soul Looks Back, p. 110) In line with this, he too points to "the importance of Marxism as a tool for social analysis," and implies the need for black theology to critique captialism, lest it simply advocate a more inclusive oppression. (Ibid. For a complete discussion of the differences between third world liberation theology and black theology, see Cone, My Soul Looks Back, pp. 108-113.) Ruether seems to concur with this assessment.

liberation theology.") Runyon bases his comparison on the fact that "the Latin Americans have decried the. . .Reformation views which equate salvation with personal faith," and are "calling instead for an understanding which is world transforming." This, coupled with Michalson's moving away from a (Lutheran) position centered in justification and toward Wesley's "transformationist theology" centered in holiness, leads Runyon to conclude:

> Though it may be true that on a continuum running from Luther to Marx. . .Wesley and Michalson would be only about half way, this is no reason to consign them to pietism and existentialism respectively and assume that they have little to contribute to the current theological debate.

Because Michalson sees forgiveness "as only the first step along a way that leads to [the historical realization of] the fruits of the Spirit"[39] and thus understands holiness and not forgiveness as the crux of faith, Runyon views him as related to liberation theology.

I have stated and have tried to substantiate my support for Runyon's theological analysis of Michalson. I agree with Runyon's analysis of Michalson as a Wesleyan theologian and in this study have found Michalson's emphasis on the necessity of Christian responsibility in the world in line with and evidence of his Wesleyan heritage. At the same time, I have expressed some reservations about Runyon's view.[40]

---

[39] All of the above citations are from Runyon, "Carl Michalson as a Wesleyan Theologian," pp. 10-12.

[40] See Chapter II, pp. 58ff., above.

In Michalson's shift of emphasis, from justification to sanctification, Runyon sees him making the natural world the object of salvation. I think Runyon pushes Michalson's "theological shift" too far. I see Michalson as shifting his focus from "human meaning as such," to human existence in the world, rather than to the world itself. This distinction allows for responsibility in the world without allowing the world to dominate human existence, and is in keeping with Michalson's concern that the world not become a religious object.

Runyon's portrayal of Michalson's relationship to Latin American liberation theology strikes me in much the same way as his analysis of Michalson's theology. I agree that Michalson and liberation theology share a common concern, but I see some significant differences between them as well. These differences are rooted in Michalson's understanding of Christian ethics as an extension of preaching, and directly related to Michalson's reluctance to make the world a religious object.

Without doubt, Michalson would have shared liberation theology's concern for freedom of the poor from oppression. His involvement in the Montgomery civil rights march (the "main opportunity for the expression of faith. . . today"[41]) and his likening that struggle to the first century church's contest against legalism point to precisely this concern. In "Focus on a Revolution" Michalson demonstrates his awareness that "one can't

---

[41] Michalson, "Focus on a Revolution" (Appendix A), p. 255.

be a theologian without being involved in just such causes." Michalson goes on to ask, though, "Can one remain a theologian if all he does is get involved in such causes?"[42] Thus, he *implies* some differences between himself and liberation theology.

At the outset of The Hinge of History Michalson calls his theology "a theology of correlation," where "historiography. . . is made the foundation for the relation between the divine and human concerns."[43] Despite the shifts of emphasis during his theological career noted above, Michalson began Worldly Theology in a similar fashion--i.e. with similar methodological presuppositions.

> During the last few years an unacknowledged Barth-Bultmann axis has been developing in the theological world. It expresses itself as the overcoming of the old dichotomy between theology and anthropology which had Barthians against the world for so many years.[44]

According to Michalson,

> Barth, by his exclusive preoccupation with the Christian Gospel in its own terms, has run the risk of moving parallel to modern culture, although he himself understands that the connection between God and the world is a circuit which God, not the theologian, completes. Bultmann, with his concern for the meaning of human existence, has run the risk of changing the traditional form of the gospel, although not the gospel itself. . . .
> The great merit of Barth is that he has developed in theology today a conscience about the unique source of the Christian faith in the reality of God and His revelation. The merit of Bultmann is that he has been willing to lose

---

[42] Ibid.

[43] Michalson, Hinge of History, p. 9.

[44] Michalson, Worldly Theology, pp. 5-6.

his faith in its traditional form in order to find it as a meaningful reality.[45]

Standing on this Barth-Bultmann axis, Michalson wishes to hold together, in dialectical tension, the subjective and objective aspects of the Christian faith. Standing between a revelational positivism on the one hand, and the reduction of the faith to anthropology on the other, Michalson, through preaching "broadly conceived," seeks to have the faith address the modern world.[46] Given this theological/ethical method, Michalson undoubtedly would have problems with a theology/ethics that is adamant in its starting "from below."

In his book *Theology in the Wesleyan Spirit*, Albert Outler speaks of John Wesley's eclecticism as one of the best Christian traditions.[47] Outler then speaks of the alternatives.

> . . .any theology that is content to be exclusively bibli-c<u>ist</u>, or traditional<u>ist</u>, is invalid and finally fruitless-- just as, on the other side, any theology without an evangel-

---

[45]Ibid., p. 70.

[46]See Chapter V p. 165ff., above.

[47]Albert Outler, *Theology in the Wesleyan Spirit*. (Nashville: Tidings, 1975), p. 5. Outler calls this eclecticism "plundering the Egyptians."
> "In Exodus 12:18-36 there is that strange story about the departing Israelites applying to their erstwhile Egyptian masters for 'gifts.' Moreover, says the Exodus historian, 'The Lord made the Egyptians well-disposed toward the Israelites and let them have whatever they asked. In this way, they [the Israelites] plundered the Egyptians.'. . .The thoughtful Christian who understands the live core of the gospel and who is deep-rooted in the biblical witness to God's self-revelation is. . .entitled and encouraged to exploit the full range of secular literature, science, and philosophy--always with a view to the enrichment of one's Christian wisdom and the enhancement of his effectiveness in communicating the Christian message." (pp. 4-5).

ical focus will soon drown in its surrounding secular milieu.[48]

Michalson (with his understanding of ethics as preaching engaging the world), would affirm liberation theology's concern for freedom of the poor from oppression as true to the tradition of eclecticism and, thus, positive. At the same time, he would caution liberation theology against an "of the world-ness" that could easily drown its eclecticism and faithfulness. Michalson's comments about Marxism are exemplary in this regard.

Michalson sees Marxism as a positivism and a secular counterpart to Christian eschatology.[49] Marxism replaces questions about Ultimate Reality with questions about the ultimate reality of history. It does this by "dividing time into pre-history and history beginning at the proletarian revolt."[50] Marxism thus completely secularizes Christian eschatology and materializes history. Michalson quotes Kierkegaard as to the effect of this.

> Kierkegaard's comment in his Papirer upon reading Marx's Communist Manifesto seems to have become prophetic. The Marxian revolution, he observed, appears to be a socio-economic revolution with a religious aspect. When it comes about, however, it will be found to be a religious revolution with a socio-economic aspect.[51]

---

[48] Ibid., p. 5.

[49] See Michalson, Hinge of History, p. 126, 177.

[50] Ibid., p. 177.

[51] Ibid., p. 243.

Michalson's point is this: Insofar as Marxism participates in that "phase of history in which everyone is killing everyone else's [false] gods," it is positive and applauded. ("This can only. . .result in religious health for a community whose trust is in the real presence of the God beyond all gods.")[52] Marxism, however, does not just kill false gods. Michalson states that Marxism is itself becoming a false god. Having usurped the authority of Ultimate Reality, Marxism isolates human existence in the secular. And for Michalson, "to be isolated from the be-all and end-all of one's existence [Christ] is to be more dead than alive."[53]

According to Michalson, Marxism claims to be concerned with the here and now, as opposed to Christianity's promise of "pie in the sky when you die." In reality, though, Marxism projects a materialistic "apocalyptic future whose fulfillment has not come,"[54] while it denies Christian eschatology's worldly implications and conferment of fulfillment in the present. Michalson applauds Marxism's eradication of false notions and gods. But he claims that by denying the wholeness of and usurping Christian eschatology, Marxism has itself become a false god.

Liberation theology has, to an extent, guarded against this critique by affirming Marxist analysis while repudiating Marxism

---

[52] Ibid.

[53] Ibid., p. 178.

[54] Michalson, *Rationality of Faith*, p. 141.

as a system. Still, there is clearly a danger of liberation theology's assuming a Marxist (apocalyptic) posture.[55] With regard to this danger, Michalson could be of tremendous assistance. Michalson, while affirming the validity of liberation theology's struggle against oppression, in line with his concern that Christian theology be responsible "in the world, but not of it," sees the liberation struggle eschatologically. This allows for a more wholistic struggle and, further, one that is based in the present as well as the future.

In summary, I think Michalson would affirm liberation theology's "identification with the oppressed in the struggle against injustice as the. . .way to overcome ideological blindness"[56] (its analysis). Further Michalson could affirm liberation theology's recognition of the poor as a viable interlocutor and its emphasis on praxis, as a mode of engagement, as long as the poor are not the sole interlocutors and praxis does not totally eclipse theory.[57] However, Michalson would have difficulty with

---

[55] See especially Miguez Bonino, "For Life and Against Death," pp. 175-176. See also Cone, My Soul Looks Back, pp. 123-138.

[56] Brown, Theology in a New Key, cited by Long, Survey of Recent Christian Ethics, p. 159.

[57] I am aware that liberation theology leans toward exclusivity in terms of its interlocutor and mode of engagement. At the same time, Miguez Bonino, Cone, and Ruether have all pointed to the necessity of engaging the church at large in liberation theology's struggle and thus dialoging with a wider audience. They have also affirmed the necessity of theory in relation to praxis (see esp. Miguez Bonino, "For Life and Against Death," pp. 172-175). Thus I would maintain that there is a commonality

liberation theology's starting "from below," and would point out problems inherent in liberation theology's using Marxism as an analytical tool. His theology/ethics, by standing on a Barth/ Bultmann axis, and engaging the world through preaching (broadly conceived), advocates a more comprehensive starting point that allows for being in the world but not of it. His theology also avoids apocalyptic materialism in favor of a wholistic, and, to an extent, realized eschatology. In these ways Michalson can and does provide "insight and correctives" to liberation theology.[58]

B. Ethics of Responsibility and Rejection of Accommodation to the World (Evangelical Perfectionism)

As stated at the beginning of this chapter, evangelical perfectionism describes the program of intentional Christian ethicists who "radically challenge the accommodation to principalities and powers that began when Constantine recognized the church and Augustine worked out the theory of the two cities."[59] Ethicists who subscribe to these views are included in and repre-

---

between Michalson and liberationists on these points.

[58]Runyon, "Michalson as a Wesleyan Theologian," p. 12. I realize the risk of oversimplification in terming liberation theology a theology "from below," with limited interlocution, a too exclusive mode of engagement, and insufficient analytical tools. My point is not that liberation theology always and necessarily demonstrates these characteristics. Rather, these are tendencies I detect in liberation theology that I think Michalson addresses and puts in perspective.

[59]Long, Survey of Recent Christian Ethics, p. 82.

sent a current expression of the intentional motif in Christian ethics.

> Because they assume that the dedicated Christian should manifest some shining luster, some unique spirituality by which he can be differentiated from non-Christians and even from ordinary Christians, intentionalists generally seek a heroic ethic, a demanding morality, and the satisfaction attending the performance of special duties.[60]

Will D. Campbell and William Stringfellow are examples of evangelical perfectionists who offer intentional alternatives to "the ambiguity of institutions and. . .the demonic character of the violence upon which politics depends."[61]

1. Will D. Campbell

Will D. Campbell presents his reader with an ethic of "being," as opposed to "doing," based on Paul's imperative in II Corinthians 5: "Be reconciled!" (Katallegete!). The relatedness

---

[60] Long, Survey of Christian Ethics, p. 52.

[61] Ibid. I have chosen to deal with Campbell and Stringfellow as examples of evangelical perfectionism not only because they represent intentional alternatives to Constantinianism, but because they also represent, respectively, evangelical perfectionism's tendencies toward spiritualization and futurism. To be sure, the rejection of Constantianism, is a central tenet of evangelical perfectionism, and Campbell and Stringfellow are good representatives in this regard. But evangelical perfectionism is more than simply a rejection of Constantinianism, as Campbell and Stringfellow clearly demonstrate.

Campbell and Stringfellow may not be the most prominent examples of evangelical perfectionism. That distinction probably belongs to John Howard Yoder (see especially The Politics of Jesus: Vicit Agnus Noster [Grand Rapids: Eerdmans, 1972]). However, Campbell and Stringfellow represent clearly, the central thrust of evangelical perfectionism and point also to two of its most salient traits. Thus, together, they provide a clear and comprehensive picture of this important position.

of "being" to the imperative is crucial for an understanding of Will Campbell's thought. By so delineating the Christian faith, he walks the narrow path between antinomianism and works righteousness, the path of Paul (trusting obedience), Luther (faith overflowing in love), and countless others who would see the necessity of response to God's Word without relying on one's own merit. In Will Campbell's thought, the dialectical relationship between faith and works is recalled for a generation of activists whom, he fears, has forgotten it.

> We agree with those who have reminded us in recent years that the Christian faith is <u>indicative</u>. . . .not imperative. . . .But we believe that St. Paul's imperative use of "reconcile" calls attention to a special kind of behavior by the Christian toward the world, behavior which "does" by <u>being</u>, "acts" by <u>living</u>--that is, <u>being</u> and <u>living</u> as God made us in Christ. . . .
> . . .Sharing? Yes! <u>Not</u> as a program, but as a parable, a thanksgiving, for what God has done for us in Christ![62]

In stating his case, Will Campbell speaks strongly against social action, politics and education--all institutions of Caesar. The church's interaction with and involvement in these areas is fruitless, as it cannot avoid <u>accommodation</u>, and thus fails to effect the transformation of humanity (i.e. reconciliation with God) that is possible in Christ. Likewise, he speaks of the church's error in <u>abdicating</u> to Caesar's law the responsibility called for by said transformation (reconciliation). "We must <u>be</u> what we are--what we <u>already</u> are by God's doing, not

---

[62] Will D. Campbell and James Y. Holloway, <u>Up to our Steeples in Politics</u> (New York: Paulist Press, 1970) pp. 1, 2.

ours. And what _are_ we already? We are in Christ, reconciled to God and therefore to man."[63]

Social action, contrary to reconciliation in Christ, is, for Will Campbell, an attempt at works righteousness. It is living under the law, trying to please God by accomplishment that is finally, self serving. The church's social action lends support to political systems he views as totalitarian. In its social action, the church allows the state to set its agenda, and then, hand in hand with the state, tries to "solve" humanity's problems with politics. In this ill-fated endeavor Will Campbell sees "the political messianism of contemporary totalitarianism and of Revelation 13."[64] Through its educational structures and institutions, the church effects the same union, with the same disasterous results.

> The Church has, in a word, tried to effect reconciliation where there already _is_ reconciliation, while the _only_ thing that God ever asked from the Church was to _live_ thanksgiving for others and so express thanksgiving for what he has done for us![65]

Is Campbell's ethic a retreat from responsibility, a disengagement? Not at all. The life in Christ that Will Campbell advocates--the life of thanksgiving--involves feeding the hungry, offering drink to the thirsty, clothing the naked, etc. The imperative is present for Campbell, but not as a program, rather

---

[63] Ibid., p. 3.

[64] Ibid.

[65] Ibid.

as thanksgiving. The list of our attempts to do God's work is endless. (It includes group dynamics, T-groups, political activism, counseling centers, and marriage-and-the-family instruction.) The life of the Christian, contrary to all of this, is one of evangelism[66]--an active evangelism that reflects our reconciliation with God and our fellows. In short: in the place of <u>action</u> (with Caesar) Will Campbell calls for <u>reaction</u> to God's gift of reconciliation. He seeks a rejection of social action, political activism and church-related education, and calls for evangelism to replace them. Evangelism is the church's proclamation by its Word <u>and</u> <u>deeds</u>: evangelism is the work of God, that work which is the only message the church has ever had for the world. As will be seen, for Campbell that work is personal (in an impersonal world) and it speaks to all, whether Jew or Greek, male or female, slave or free, black or white.

Put another way, for Will Campbell worldly standards cease to count. Beauty, sex, race, politics, and lack of education no longer control our lives. The reconciliation effected by God in Christ has altered our outlook, changed our priorities, and created us anew. Our "task" is to live our lives in proclamation of this truth.

---

[66]See Campbell and Holloway, <u>Up to our Steeples in Politics</u>. See also <u>Race and Renewal of the Church</u> (Philadelphia: Westminster Press, 1962) which appears to be an expansion of the article "The Role of Religious Organizations in the Desegregation Controversy" (<u>Union Seminary Quarterly Review</u> 16 [January, 1961]); and <u>Brother to a Dragonfly</u> (New York: Seabury Press, 1977.

Campbell thus calls on Christians to accept the gift of new life in Christ and then to share it, via proclamation (which includes feeding the hungry, clothing the naked, visiting the sick and imprisoned, etc.), with our fellows. In the social action heretofore taken, he sees too much accommodation to and conformity with a depersonalized world. Further, Campbell points to instances where the church has allowed the world to do it's (the church's) work. The broken relationships between people and people and between people and God will not be healed by human ministrations, regardless of whether they be in the form of social action, political involvement or education. Neither can we rely on the law to effect reconciliation for us. Rather, only by repentance, and the life of service granted by repentance, can ministry (or ethics) take place. What are we supposed to do? Nothing. We are supposed to be--reconciled by God. And only in being reconciled by God can we respond. It is, therefore, through the indicative (the fact of God's reconciliation accomplished in and through Jesus Christ), and only through the indicative, that the imperative exists. Katallegete!

For Will Campbell, the starting point for Christian concern is to get behind the symptoms and confront a sick and sinful society. Says Campbell, there has been too much said and done by and for man, and too little concern for God. The church must proclaim the sovereignty of God.

> Thus far we have said little of the Lordship of Jesus Christ, which is the way the Christian must ultimately speak of God's sovereignty in this "time between," this "era of the church." It would appear, however, that today when the

comfortable life of Americans deludes them into thinking that they have already achieved redemption one must speak more forcefully of creation, of finitude, and of sin. The doctrine of the sovereignty of God needs to fall afresh on the ears of this generation. The God who is Sovereign has made Jesus "both Lord and Christ". (Acts 2:36).[67]

2. William Stringfellow

The ethical thought of William Stringfellow is closely related to that of Will Campbell. In fact, Stringfellow enthusiastically endorses Campbell's thought. In a review of Campbell's Up to Our Steeples in Politics, Stringfellow says, Campbell's is "an insight into the revolutionary integrity of Christ's involvement in the world and a clue to the perpetual, insatiable and versitle character of social revolution for the Christian."[68]

Stringfellow, of course, makes his own statement of intentional ethics. Drawing heavily on scripture, Stringfellow, like Campbell, calls upon the church to use its freedom in Christ and proclaim life in the face of death. In his 1964 book, Free in Obedience, the Letter to the Hebrews forms the basis of an attack on the principalities and powers that proclaim a "gospel" of self-preservation. These secular attempts to escape death and claim sovereignty over human life deny God's sovereignty, and according to Stringfellow, must be exposed. In the face of them, the Church lives and proclaims Christ's resurrection.

---

[67] Campbell, Race and the Renewal of the Church, p. 60.

[68] William Stringfellow, "The Steeple in Perspective: Four Views," Christianity and Crisis 29 (March 3, 1969):40.

The Church as the Body, and Christians as members of Christ's Body, are authorized and empowered by God to live in this world, free from bondage to death and free from idolatry of the powers of death. The fruits of the ministry of Christ, the triumph of the resurrection itself, are bestowed upon the Church and those, then and thereafter, baptized into it.[69]

A similar argument is set forth in Conscience and Obedience, utilizing Romans 13 and Revelation 13. Here again, Stringfellow uses Scripture as a basis for viewing and acting within the world. Our age, as a result of the "Constantinean arrangement," is alienated from the Bible. Since Constantine, the church has had too much at stake in the political status quo.[70] Stringfellow calls this accommodation "Bombast and Blasphemy"[71] and, in line with the Barmen Declaration,[72] rebukes "the demonic reality of political authority,"[73] by the Word of God that is "active and

---

[69] William Stringfellow, Free in Obedience (New York: Seabury Press, 1964), p. 75.

[70] See William Stringfellow, Conscience and Obedience (Waco: Word Books, 1977), p. 55ff.

[71] Ibid., p. 67.

[72] The Barmen Declaration is a statement of faith prepared by the underground confessing Church in Germany, following Hitler's take-over of established German church structures for propaganda purposes. It's chief tenets, according to Stringfellow, are its audacity and Biblical authenticity." . . .It is the confession that the Word of God is sovereign here and now." (Conscience and Obedience, p. 75.)

[73] Stringfellow, Conscience and Obedience, p. 70.

efficacious in judgment of the rulers of this passing and perishing age."[74]

Although Stringfellow is primarily concerned with a criticism of American institutions and a prophetic call for national repentance, he set forth a constructive ethic in his 1973 book, An Ethic for Christians and Other Aliens in a Strange Land. Again basing his analysis on scripture, his book is an attempt to analyze contemporary American society by utilizing the Book of Revelation. In so doing, Stringfellow concludes that America, given the principalities currently in power within it, is a modern Babylon--a fallen humanity. He lifts up the book of Revelation, specifically its vision of and for Jerusalem, as a source of hope in the face of this fallenness, and points to the vigilance and consolation advocated therein as our only recourse.

In line with his call for a new Jerusalem, Stringfellow advocates a sacramental ethic.

> The ethical discernment of humans cannot anticipate and must not usurp the judgment of God, but is an existential event, an exercise of conscience--transcient and fragile. . . . Moreover, it is the dignity of this ethical posture which frees human beings, in their decisions and tactics, to summon the powers and principalities, and similar creatures, to their vocation--the enhancement of human life in society (Gen. 1:20-31; cf. Mark 10:42-43).[75]

---

[74]Ibid., p. 75. See also William Stringfellow, Dissenter in a Great Society (New York: Holt, Rinehart and Winston, 1965); "The Great Society as a Myth," Dialog V (Autumn, 1966); and "A Matter of Repentance," Christianity and Crisis (January 21, 1980):341, 342.

[75]William Stringfellow, An Ethic for Christians and Other Aliens in a Strange Land. (Waco: Word, 1973) p. 57.

Stringfellow then chronicles "Christian resistance to death" and "the efficacy of the Word of God as hope" as expressions of a sacramental ethic.

> A spontaneous, intimate, and incessant involvement in the biblical Word as such--that is, Bible study--is the most essential nurture of contemporary biblical people while they are involved, patiently and resiliently, in the common affairs of the world. Biblical living means, concretely, practicing the powers of discernment, variously perceiving and exposing the moral presence of death incarnate in the principalities and powers and otherwise.
> Biblical living discloses that the ethical is sacramental, not moralistic or pietistic or religious. . . .[76]

In what he terms "the timely coincidence of the apocalyptic and the eschatological," Stringfellow calls upon biblical people to live "in vigilance and consolation." Thus, "Biblical living means watching for and hoping for the next advent of Jesus Christ."[77] In short, Stringfellow says that Babylon will fall. Hope, therefore, is eschatological. And through Biblical living that reflects ethical concerns for the individuals and society, hope is brought to bear on the principalities and powers by a people watching for and hoping for Christ's second advent.

3. **Michalson's Contribution to the Ethics of Evangelical Perfectionism**

In many ways liberation theology and evangelical perfectionism are diametrically opposed. Liberation theology starts "from below," uses the insights of socio-political analysis, and develops its theological perceptions in praxis. Evangelical perfec-

---

[76] Ibid., p. 151.

[77] Ibid., p. 152.

tionists start "from outside" the world's fallen institution, seeking to bring the Bible and a transcendent God to bear on a reconceived, rather than a revolutionized, society. And yet, the goals of liberation theology and evangelical perfectionism are strikingly similar. Both seek to alter current forms of Christianity's accommodation to the world and its institutions, thus both oppose the Constantinian accommodation. And both want to enact the biblical ideals of love, equality, and justice in the world. In short, liberation theology and evangelical perfectionism approach common goals with almost diametrically opposed means.

Given the nature of their similarities and differences, I think Michalson's criticism of and contribution to the ethics of evangelical perfectionism would closely resemble his criticism of and contribution to the ethics of liberation theology. In much the same way that Michalson's thought broadens and centers liberation theology, it can do the same for evangelical perfectionism. But here, rather than confronting a too materialistic and "of the world" ethic with the perspective of faith, Michalson's theology and ethics confront a biblicism with the need for contextual input and correction. For Michalson, it is indeed dangerous to be completely "of the world". But it is just as dangerous not to be "in the world" enough.

In relation to evangelical perfectionism, Michalson's theology once again speaks to the question of theology's proper starting point. Michalson's theology of correlation--wherein preaching addresses the world--recognizes the intentionalist's consciousness of and concern about "the unique source of the Christian faith in the reality of God and His revelation." At the same time, Michalson avoids "moving parallel to modern culture"[78] and the danger of being cut off from the world. Says Michalson,

> It is true, as Barthians insist, that God reveals himself in history and that revelation is what properly constitutes history. It is just as true that it is in history that God reveals himself.[79]

Michalson then summarizes his position, and its attractiveness, by saying:

> A theology which exists in the service of God and draws its insight from the historical reality of Jesus of Nazareth will express itself in the constitution of a meaningful world.[80]

Michalson's thought--rooted in faithfulness, and expressed in proclamation that engages the world--is an exemplary synthesis of Word and world. The divine command, so crucial to intentionalists, is central. At the same time, Michalson gleans from the world, or context, that which can assist in bringing his ethics of responsibility to fruition.

---

[78]Michalson, Worldly Theology, p. 70. Michalson is here trying to hold to the Barthian promise without falling prey to Barth's problem. Says Michalson:
"The great merit of Barth is that he has developed in theology today a conscience about the unique source of the Christian faith in the reality of God and His revelation." (p. 70) However, ". . .by his exclusive preoccupation with the Christian Gospel in its own terms, [Barth] has run the risk of moving parallel to modern culture. . ."(p. 70)

[79]Ibid., p. 5.

[80]Ibid., p. 25.

Michalson's eschatology could also impact evangelical perfectionism. Whereas liberation theology, with its Marxist posture, runs the risk of a materialistic and futuristic eschatology that ignores spiritual reward and the present, evangelical perfectionists run the risk of a spiritual and futuristic eschatology that ignores material reward and the present.[81]

Illustrative of the risk of spiritualism is Will Campbell's castigation of the law as ethically inadequate. The law, says Campbell, is an inadequate minimal.[82] Speaking with regard to the Civil Rights movement in particular, Campbell says:

> . . .the rejections continue, the killings go on, the hostilities mount and intensify, perhaps to be set loose wholesale again on another day when the Feds and the Marchers have all gone home, or turned to stopping the war with Venus, . . .[83]

He then quotes Reinhold Niebuhr to this effect:

> The self cannot be cured by law but only by grace; and. . . the profoundest forms of the Christian faith regard . . .

_____

[81] In making these assertions about evangelical perfectionism, I realize the risk of oversimplification. A similar risk was present in analyzing liberation theology strictly from the standpoint of its being a theology "from below." In the same way I have been reluctant to stereotype liberation theology, <u>I do not mean to imply that evangelical perfectionism relies solely on a spiritualized and/or future reward</u>. Again, my point is this: <u>these are tendencies that Michalson addresses in evangelical perfectionism</u>. And by his addressing these tendencies, with a balanced perspective, he contributes to evangelical perfectionism and holds it accountable in the same way he contributes to liberation theology and holds it accountable.

[82] Will D. Campbell, "Law and Love in Lowndes," <u>Katallagete</u> (1965--II):12.

[83] Ibid., p. 12.

preoccupation [with self] as not fully curable and therefore as requiring another kind of grace: that of forgiveness.[84]

Legalism has failed, says Campbell. The milestones have turned into millstones, a source of pride rather than repentance. We have allowed the law to stand in the place of Christian witness, and it's failure confronts us--an inadequate minimal. In concluding his argument, Campbell tempers his point a bit (simple justice is important), but maintains the gross inadequacy of the law. "The Civil Rights Acts leave the ghettoes intact and the white suburbs safe."[85] The Civil Rights Act may allow a black to sit down in a restaurant next to a white, but it cannot stop the white from vomiting in his plate. Thus, "it falls far short of the reconciliation affected by a crucified God."[86]

The risk of a futuristic eschatology is illustrated more by Stringfellow than Campbell. At the conclusion of his article, "A Matter of Repentance," Stringfellow says:

> . . .At the outset of the 1980's, I say the US needs repentance. It needs to be freed of blasphemy. . . .Perhaps that will happen, somehow, in this decade. If not, it will happen in the time of the judgment of the Word of God.[87]

As stated above, Michalson's theology addresses evangelical perfectionist's <u>tendencies</u> toward spiritualism and futurism with a wholistic eschatology that is concerned about the material and

---

[84]Ibid., p. 13.

[85]Will D. Campbell, "Repentance and Politics I: Milestones into Millstones," <u>Katallagete</u> (Winter, 1966-67):4.

[86]Campbell, "Law and Love in Lowndes," p. 14.

[87]Stringfellow, "A Matter of Repentance," p. 342.

spiritual and that is both present and future oriented. The concurrent ethical formulations can thus offer the possibility of living in the world but not of it, and allow for the <u>realization</u> of Christ's benefits--spiritually in faith and materially through Christian responsibility--both now and forevermore.

In terms of Robert McAfee Brown's schema, Michalson would provide essentially the same insight and corrective for evangelical perfectionism as he would provide for liberation theology. Evangelical perfectionism's starting point should be broadened. Its interlocutor needs to be more inclusive. By being so centered in the Bible it ignores the assistance that socio-political tools can offer. It's analysis and mode of engagement are too narrowly focused.

I have sought to allow Michalson's theology and ethics to impact both liberation theology and evangelical perfectionism. In effect, Michalson's engaging the world through preaching provides a broader based mediating position that, he contends, "exists in the service of God. . .draws its insight from the historical reality of Jesus [and] will express itself in the constitution of a meaningful world."[88] Michalson, therefore, enlarges the perspectives of liberation theology and evangelical perfectionism and tempers their exclusivity.

---

[88]Michalson, <u>Worldly Theology</u>, p. 25.

One of Stringfellow's reviewers wrote that "Set in a context of academic theology, it would be fair to say that in general the book may be more provocative than it is profound."[89] Another reviewer wrote, "To put it bluntly, Bill Stringfellow is a much better prophet than he is preacher."[90] These comments reflect a widely held attitude that applies, generally, to both liberation theology and evangelical perfectionism. Michalson, as an academic and preacher (par excellence) who enlarges the perspectives of liberation theology and evangelical perfectionism, accounts for and softens the impact of these criticisms.

At the same time they are criticized for narrowness, liberation theology and evangelical perfectionism are highly regarded and reputed for their passion and their polemical nature. In short, both liberation theology and evangelical perfectionism are bona fide prophetic movements. Michalson would applaud the provocativeness of both liberation theology and evangelical perfectionism, and abhor the thought that academics or preaching might blunt the impact of their prophetic message. Just as he recognized the necessity of going to Montgomery, Michalson undoubtedly would today recognize the necessity of liberation theology's and evangelical perfectionism's "freedom to demon-

---

[89]LaVern K. Grose, review of Free in Obedience by William Stringfellow, in Lutheran World 15,1 (1968):82.

[90]John M. Pratt, review of Dissenter in a Great Society, by William Stringfellow, in Union Seminary Quarterly Review 22 (November, 1966):63.

strate" and "involvement in. . .such causes."[91] It should be clear, then, that Michalson's insight and correction to both liberation theology and evangelical perfectionism would be offered dialectically, and without pretext or pretense. Likewise, Michalson's insight and correction are offered here, in order to strengthen the message, not to soften the impact of these prophetic movements!

C. Ethics of Responsibility and Ethics of Character and Virtue

The ethics of character and virtue, as set forth by James Gustafson and Stanley Hauerwas, is concerned with "the significance of the character of the moral agent and in the question as to how the kind of person one is bears upon the kind of decisions one makes."[92] "The 'sort of person' one is"[93] shapes ethical response and thus is important to the ethical inquiry. In fact, Hauerwas claims that the ethical agent's character and virtue are prior to and more central than the norms the agent holds. According to Hauerwas, the moral agent's character is of primary importance, since character, to a large extent, shapes norms and determines action.[94]

---

[91]Michalson, "Focus on a Revolution," Appendix A, p.

[92]Long, Survey of Recent Christian Ethics, p. 101.

[93]See Gustafson, Can Ethics be Christian?, p. 25ff.

[94]Hauerwas, Character and the Christian Life, p. 89ff.

1. James Gustafson

James Gustafson's book, Can Ethics be Christian? introduces the ethics of character and virtue. Here Gustafson discusses how character type, life style, and the quality of personhood inform ethical action. Says Gustafson, "Beliefs, [and] dispositions. . . are interrelated in persons." These factors "inform. . .reflection and action. . .executed with reference to particular purposes in the sequence of events."[95] Thus "the 'sort of person' one is" is directly related to one's ethical ideas and conduct.

Having discussed how "who one is" informs "what one does" ethically, Gustafson then discusses the significance of the Christian faith in the formation of personhood, and consequently "the formation of certain widely held human and moral values." Though Gustafson will not argue that Christianity is necessary for morality and readily recognizes the fact that Christianity does not guarantee morality, he does say that:

> . . .if one experiences the reality of God, particularly in the context of Christian history and life, there are or ought to be consequences for the sort of person one becomes morally.[96]

And Gustafson goes on to say that

> If one is religious in Christian and Jewish traditional senses, there are sufficient and compelling reasons to be moral. These reasons might even color or accent the ways in which one is moral, and acts morally.[97]

___

[95]Gustafson, Can Ethics be Christian?, p. 45.

[96]Ibid., pp. 48, 60.

[97]Ibid., p. 80.

Though not currently popular, Gustafson argues that a sense of dependence on God and the awareness of finitude engender trust and confidence, and thus provide "a reason of heart and mind to be morally serious. . . . " So might a sense of gratitude to God, or a sense of repentance provide a reason for morality. "To experience God as orderer and sustainer is to have a sense of obligation, . . .for being moral."[98] Also, the faith might provide a sense of possibilities or a sense of direction, and either of these could engender morality.

Gustafson thus concludes that religious beliefs can and do influence conduct. Ethics can be Christian in the sense that morality is impacted by Christian character and virtues. "The 'sort of person' one is," one's character, has enormous consequences for morality. In fact, the sort of person one is, whether Christian or not, to a large extent determines moral norms and conduct.

2. Stanley Hauerwas

Stanley Hauerwas has been inspired by Gustafson[99] to develop an extensive ethics of character and virtue. Hauerwas believes that both principled and situational approaches err since they overemphasize the ethical *decision*. Hauerwas thus concerns

---

[98] Ibid., pp. 99, 109.

[99] See Hauerwas, *Character and the Christian Life*, p. viii.

himself with what it means to _act_ morally. The indicative supercedes and supplants the imperative.[100]

Ethics for Hauerwas is not simply a matter of _doing_; rather, _being_ ethical is prior to doing ethics. Hauerwas therefore, concentrates his energies on what it means to be ethical, and, in polemical fashion, makes the ethics of character and virtue primary. In fact, he is suspected of "driving a wedge between an ethics of duty and an ethics of virtue. . .between acts and agents."[101]

His approach is neatly summarized by Edward L. Long.

> Hauerwas proposes an approach in which the moral notions of the agent have more fundamental consequences than they have in the thinking of the situationalists. Attention is directed to the moral notions of the agent rather than to the decisions that agent should make. "The moral life is not first a life of choice--decision is not king--but is rather woven from the notions that we use to see and to form the situations we confront. Moral life involves learning to see

---

[100] Hauerwas's concern for the indicative in ethics, rather than the imperative, recalls to mind Will Campbell's thought; indeed Hauerwas cites Campbell as influential for him. (See Stanley Hauerwas and William H. Willimon, "Embarrassed by God's Presence" The Christian Century 104, 4 [January 30, 1985]) Both Campbell and Hauerwas stress the fact that God in Christ creates new beings who _consequently_ reflect their transformation. At the same time, they each have their own concerns and agendas. Campbell is primarily an intentionalist, concerned about duly recognizing the God who creates and properly locating human institutions and their efforts under Him. Hauerwas is concerned about the agent who is created anew. He thus represents a distinctive position that, though not necessarily liberal (Again, see Hauerwas and Willimon, "Embarrassed by God's Presence."), puts much more stress on the agent's capacity and self determination than does Campbell.

[101] Tom L. Beauchamp and James F. Childress, Principles of Biomedical Ethics, cited by Long, A Survey of Recent Christian Ethics, p. 106.

the world through an imaginative ordering of our basic symbols and notions."[102]

Hauerwas's emphasis on "the moral notions of the agent" implies the idea of agency--i.e. that persons are capable, responsible and have "the capacity for self determination." By speaking of humanity's "capacity for self determination," Hauerwas reemphasizes the fact that "the 'sort of person' one is" is central to the moral life, and that one's vision of reality is determinative for one's ethical decisions. Action is formed and effected because of who we are, how we see the world, and our abilities to change existing circumstances by our behavior. In short, action results from character, of which self determination is a vital part.

In line with Hauerwas's strong emphasis on agency, he recognizes that "those theologies that make the language of command central for their ethics tend to be critical of, or at best find it difficult to account for, much less imply, an ethics of character."[103] The ethics of Rudolf Bultmann and Karl Barth are cases in point. Though there are significant differences between Bultmann and Barth,[104] both are viewed by Hauerwas as thoroughly

---

[102]Long, Survey of Recent Christian Ethics, p. 107.

[103]Hauerwas, Character and the Christian Life, p. 114.

[104]Hauerwas explains the differences between Bultmann and Barth as follows:
Bultmann's ethics is an "attempt to carry through in a radical manner the Protestant principle of justification by faith. It assumes that all human activity is. . .an attempt to secure the self from the demand of God. . . .
   [Thus Bultmann states that] man's salvation is possible only as a response to the prior proclamation of the kerygma

theocentric. "The first word for both is what God has done, not what man can do."[105]

Given Bultmann's and Barth's concern that ethics be conceived as response to God, neither of them deal with the idea of character to any extent. In fact, both Bultmann and Barth see "a tension between God's activity on man's behalf and its actual significance for man," and are concerned that programs like the ethics of character and virtue emphasize human behavior at the expense of what God has done.

> Both have a tendency to associate the very concept of ethics with man's attempt to justify himself before God. Barth, for example, goes so far as to say that any "general conception of ethics coincides exactly with the conception of sin," since any such conception necessarily replaces God's command with man's.[106]

of God's saving action on our behalf. . .[that] demands radical obedience from the hearer." (Hauerwas, Character and the Christian Life, p. 133.)
". . .For Barth, . . .ethics can be done only in the context of dogmatics, for it is only within the circle of the being and activity of God that the ethical question of man's determination can be raised with proper seriousness. . . .Thus Barth's theological ethics, in contrast to Bultmann, begins in terms of the nature of God rather than the question of justification." (Ibid., pp. 137-138.)

While Bultmann's ethics start with humanity's asking "What must I do to be saved?," Barth's ethics start with the question, "What does God require of me?" Both questions are answered by the divine command, expressed and made known by Jesus Christ. And for both Bultmann and Barth, ethical action is an adherance to the divine command.

[105] Hauerwas, Character and the Christian Life, p. 140.

[106] Ibid., p. 131.

Hauerwas, while "in sympathy with Barth and Bultmann's attempt to describe the Christian life in terms of the fundamental relationship of the self to God," claims that "neither Bultmann nor Barth found a completely adequate means to suggest how the believer's actual moral self is determined in Christ."[107] His ethics of character seeks to maintain Bultmann's and Barth's theological insights, while giving growth and character their due. He does this by developing the ethics of character--i.e. treating the self's duration, growth and unity--in the context of sanctification. The doctrine of sanctification allows Hauerwas to account for, yet keep in perspective, Christian growth and development.

> . . .At the very center of the Christian's belief about what God has done for him is the affirmation of the change that makes in the believer; a change that not only reorientates his understanding of his existence, but a change that makes for a radical reorientation of his character and conduct.[108]

John Wesley's doctrine of perfection is recognized by Hauerwas as portraying Christian growth and development with the proper perspective. Wesley understands justification as what God does for us through Jesus Christ, and sanctification as what God works in us by his Spirit. Thus he accounts for both the objective and subjective changes that are wrought in persons of faith, and by holding the two in tension, avoids the suggestion that the Christian life can be understood apart from Christ's working in

---

[107]Ibid., pp. 176, 176-177.

[108]Ibid., p. 183.

the believer.[109] Utilizing this "dialectical interdependence of justification and sanctification [as] a way of indicating the real effect of Christ's work upon the believer without separating that effect from its source,"[110] Hauerwas develops his ethics of character in a similar proper perspective.

3. **Michalson's Contribution to the Ethics of Character and Virtue**

Michalson has been characterized as a situational or contextual ethicist, and closely akin to Rudolf Bultmann. It would, therefore, appear that Michalson's ethical thought is precisely what Hauerwas is writing against. However a closer examination of Hauerwas's views on contextualism and Bultmann, in relation to Michalson's, reveals that this is not the case. In fact, and as will be seen, what Hauerwas _affirms_ in contextualism and Bultmann is precisely that reflected in Michalson's contextualism and affinity with Bultmann. And, given their common emphases on Wesleyan sanctification, Hauerwas and Michalson share a concern for character and virtue as well.

The differences between Hauerwas and Michalson occur at the point where Michalson emphasizes the ethical _decision_ (the pri-

---

[109]See Albert Outler, ed. John Wesley (New York: Oxford University Press, 1964), p. 198ff. See also Colin Williams, John Wesley's Theology Today, (London: Epworth Press, 1960)pp. 98-125. See also Albert Outler, Theology in the Wesleyan Spirit, especially his discussion of the sermon "The Scriptural Way of Salvation," pp. 56-59.

[110]Hauerwas, Character and the Christian Life, p. 188.

mary concern of both contextualism and Bultmann) to the same extent that he emphasizes character and virtue. This is also the point at which Michalson makes a direct contribution to Hauerwas's ethics of character and virtue--not in the sense that Michalson opposes the ethics of character and virtue, but in the sense that he enhances it.

Hauerwas's criticism of situation ethics centers in the situationalists' theological and anthropological affirmations.

> . . .The "situation-ethics". . .debate. . .has been but an extension of the dominance of the command metaphor and its correlative understanding of the self. . .demanding only that we do the loving thing in the concrete situation.[111]

Given these understandings, Hauerwas feels the act of decision making has eclipsed the importance of the self that makes decisions.

At the same time Hauerwas is critical of contextualism, he affirms its rejection of pre-determined, standing moral norms. For Hauerwas too, ethical reflection needs to engage the indifference and ambiguity of the world. It does this, however, not simply by decision making, but by decision making grounded in God's command *and* in the self's character, virtue and vision. Hauerwas's criticism of contextualism is not that it is contextual, but that it is an ethics of individual fulfillment. Says Hauerwas,

> If the objectivity of [God's] command is lost, as it has been in situation ethics, the language of judgment and forgiveness has no meaning. Rather the moral life is direc-

---

[111]Ibid., p. 5.

ted toward fulfillment of the self through individual decisions.[112]

Further, Hauerwas claims that by ignoring the role of character and virtue as formative for decision making, contextualism is truncated.

Bultmann, according to Hauerwas, assumes that the divine command is ethically operative, standing over against the self in judgment and forgiveness. But he too has a truncated model for ethical behavior.

> For Bultmann. . .to be a Christian is to find oneself in a discontinuous relation to our past as the "necessities" of the moment always stand in a negative relation to the preceding "moments" or our life.
> . . . Bultmann's stress on the [existentialist] moment as that which alone is graced seems finally to be a way of . . .denying the human side of God's grace. In other words, the man that Bultmann sees involved in God's justifying work is not a real man with a real history, but an abstraction.
> . . .Bultmann. . .has failed to see that man's actual agency must be determined through his past.
>
> This. . .does not mean that Bultmann has not made some important points to which any attempt to develop the significance of character for the Christian life must pay attention. His insistence on the open nature of the Christian life is crucial. . . .
> . . .[And] Bultmann provides a valuable check on any suggestion that the Christian is concerned with the acquisition of character as an end in and of itself.[113]

Michalson, like Bultmann, takes very seriously the divine command.[114] As stated in Chapter four, ethical guidance, for

---

[112]Ibid., pp. 177-178.

[113]Ibid., pp. 163-164, 167.

[114]As stated in Chapter IV, pp. 145-148, above, Michalson's understanding of divine command, like Bultmann's, is set in a relational context. Thus, divine command is better expressed as divine initiative. Michalson, again like Bultmann, understands the divine initiative as "commanding" (in the sense of inviting)

Michalson, comes from God's command to "Love thy neighbor as thyself," _and_ from the context of the ethical dilemma. Since Michalson reduces the law to the formulation "Love thy neighbor as thyself," his ethic is less prescriptive than Brunner's, Barth's, or Bonhoeffer's, but, nonetheless, ethics for Michalson is conceived as response to the divine command. Michalson adopts Bultmann's concept of "radical obedience" as response to the dawning of the Kingdom of God, and believes that in Jesus Christ, the Kingdom of God has broken into human existence. Because of this, humanity lives eschatologically, in radical obedience to God. In Michalson's terms, preaching, broadly conceived, engages the world.

Given his affinity to Bultmann, Carl Michalson simply cannot be accused of an ethics of individual fulfillment. But to what extent does Michalson fall prey to the truncated understanding of moral reflection that ignores the role of self determination in decision making, and that plagues both contextualism and Bultmann?

Insofar as Michalson's ethic is one of response to the divine initiative, his ethical thought clearly falls into the category of ethics based on command and obedience, where decision is of paramount importance. However, Michalson, like Hauerwas, also adopts and uses Wesley's doctrine of sanctification to point

---

a response that entails a (crucial) decision on humanity's part.

to the conclusiveness of God's turning to humanity in Christ. The preaching that engages the world does so by <u>changing self understandings</u> (which <u>in turn</u> are redirected toward other individuals and society). This allows Michalson to speak of the Christian--i.e. the ethical actor--as mature in the world, as "man come of age,"[115] and, to this extent, sanctified and holy, and "elevated to the faith of a son."[116] Michalson thus demonstrates a concern for the indicative as well as the imperative, sees the self as significantly changed by the faith, and could affirm Hauerwas's being "concerned with explicating and analyzing how the self acquires unity and duration in relation to the Christian's conviction that Christ is the bringer of God's Kingdom."[117]

For Carl Michalson, Christian ethics is preaching engagng the world, through changed self understandings. Michalson's ethics, then, demonstrates a concern for both ethical decision (as response to God) and the ethical actor (as having been endowed with the character and virtue). Therefore, Michalson cannot be accused of a truncated ethic that ignores the role of self determination in decision making. Hauerwas, on the other hand, might be accused by Michalson--as he has, in fact, been

---

[115] Michalson, Rationality of Faith, p. 131.

[116] Ibid., p. 151.

[117] Hauerwas, Character and the Christian Life, p. 2.

criticized by others[118]--of truncating ethics by neglecting to discuss ethical decision and action. His ethics of character and virtue might well benefit from Michalson's ethics of divine command, character, and virtue. Michalson's schema allows for action and actor to be kept in proper relation since, by stressing that God commands decision as well as changes the deciding agent, Michalson avoids giving the deciding agent too much autonomy.[119]

Without doubt, the ethical actor's character and virtue forms an important part of Michalson's ethics. At the same time, a nagging feeling remains that Michalson would have some difficulties with Hauerwas's ethics of character and virtue. Hauerwas's concern for self determination and his concern that the ethical self "bring from his past" in order to "enliven the present and give direction to the future"[120] could be construed as softening the effect of God's transforming humanity in Christ.

---

[118] See Tom L. Beauchamp and James F. Childress, Principles of Biomedical Ethics, cited by Long, Survey of Recent Christian Ethics, p. 106.

[119] I personally suspect that Hauerwas's neglecting to discuss ethical decision is more polemical than substantive. (See especially Hauerwas, Character and the Christian Life, pp. 130-131.) If this is true, Michalson and Hauerwas may be kindred spirits with simply different emphases. Michalson, as a theologian doing ethics, would naturally be less concerned about self determination, while Hauerwas, as an ethicist whose thought is grounded in theology, would concentrate on the ethical ramifications of similar theological insight. Still, Hauerwas's position could benefit from Michalson's insight and correction.

[120] See Hauerwas, Character and the Christian Life, pp. 163-167.

To be sure, Hauerwas understands character as a gift of God, and in this respect "maintains the otherness of God's justifying action in relation to man."[121] But Hauerwas's strong emphasis on the self would probably offend Michalson's theological sensibilities and could/can be called into question.

Therefore, I would lift up Michalson's ethics as a <u>theological</u> ethic of character and virtue, that, because of its stress on ethical decision as response, keeps action and actor in proper perspective and, more importantly, keeps the ethical actor and his or her action, in continued proper relationship to God. These emphases, coupled with the genuine engagement with the world through preaching that characterizes Michalson's ethics as "in the world but not of it," make for a strong and balanced ethical stance.

Michalson's is an ethic of decision and response; it is also an ethic of character and virtue. And because these emphases are in the context of a preached ethic that engages the world (individually and socially), Michalson stands on a firm foundation indeed. He avoids the criticism of "decision without character," and he avoids the criticism of "virtue without response." He also avoids the criticisms of "excessive worldliness" and "excessive individual piety."

---

[121]Ibid., p. 163.

Michalson's Christian ethics of responsibility has shown itself to be a balanced, wholistic perspective. In terms of the ethical decision, Michalson's thought has consistently demonstrated that it is open to both command and context, and at the same time, enslaved to neither. This is true of Michalson's expressing his ethics as "preaching enagaged with the world." It is true too of his ethic in relation to the formulations of liberation theology and evangelical perfectionism.

Michalson is also able to relate to Hauerwas's ethics of character and virtue. The ethical decision that is preaching engaged with the world comes about through a changed self understanding. Michalson's thought thus effects a new synthesis that is truly dialectical, and gives added depth to both its component parts. Michalson's Christian ethics of character and virtue is, to borrow Robert McAfee Brown's metaphor, ethics in a new key,[122] which can indeed draw its insight from the historical reality of

---

[122] Brown uses the musical example of a diminished seventh chord in characterizing liberation theology as theology in a new key.
"In writing music,. . .composers sometimes introduce a chord called a diminished seventh, which enables them to shift quite abruptly to a different key. By means of this device they can move in unexpected directions and take their listeners by surprise." (Robert McAfee Brown, "Starting Over: New Beginning Points for Theology," in Theologians in Transition, p. 196.
I find this image an apt way to characterize Michalson's ethics, since his utilizing Wesleyan sanctification to characterize worldly responsibility allows for a new ethical synthesis of decision, and character and virtue. (My use of Brown's image, however, does not imply an identification of Michalson's ethics with liberation theology.) See also Godsey, "The Legacy of Carl Michalson," p. 76.

Jesus of Nazareth, exist in the service of God, and express itself in the constitution of a meaningful world.[123] And it does so as ethical decision _and_ ethical character and virtue.

---

[123]See Michalson, <u>Worldly Theology</u>, p. 25.

CHAPTER SEVEN

Conclusion

I introduced this study by saying that the salient features of Michalson's theology are his attempt to make the faith viable, his recognition of the faith's communal nature, and his conviction that Christianity enables and demands responsibility in/for the world. I have sought to demonstrate that Michalson's conception of the faith as responsible represents a significant Christian ethic, in theory, substance, and application. I have presented a Michalsonian model of theological ethics, and I have sought to bring Michalson's formulations into dialogue with three more recent ethical statements. It remains for me to, briefly, state some conclusions about Michalson's Christian ethics of responsibility and state his contribution to the field.

A. Michalson's Concept of Responsibility: The Influence of H. Richard Niebuhr and Friedrich Gogarten

It has been said, here and elsewhere[1] that H. Richard Niebuhr's thought was tremendously important to, and reflected by Carl Michalson. The theologies of Niebuhr and Michalson both seek to reconcile the relativities of history with the absoluteness of God. Both recognize God's revelation as the means

---

[1] See p. 33ff, above. See also Ivey, "The Concept of the Holy Spirit," p. 49; and Godsey, "The Legacy of Carl Michalson," p. 78.

whereby reconciliation is effected, and both posit a social existentialism as a means of conceptualizing that reconciliation.[2] Also, both see history as the context of theology and utilize history in a similar way.

In addition to a common conception of the theological problem and a shared theological method, both Niebuhr and Michalson understood Christian ethics in terms of responsibility, and can be characterized as relational ethicists. Michalson, in fact, quotes Niebuhr's The Responsible Self as a source for his most extensive formal statement on ethics, i.e. his discussion of existential ethics.[3] Here Niebuhr is "recognized as one of those ethicists who has accomplished the movement away from legalism,"[4] which is central to Michalson's understanding of human responsibility that defines and transvaluates the ethical.

Michalson's understanding of responsibility as transvaluating the ethical, though closely related to and influenced by

---

[2] To call Michalson's theology a "social existentialism" is, admittedly, hazardous. But insofar as he subtitled The Hinge of History "An Existentialist Approach to the Christian Faith" and thus posited his theological inquiry in the subjective rather than the objective, I think it safe to dub him an existentialist. Granted, Michalson sees Christianity as eschatological, and felt that, as such, it supercedes existentialism (the discipline of thirst). Therefore, he considered the term "Christian Existentialism" to be a contradiction. But broadly speaking, and in terms of his philosophical and theological orientation, Michalson adopted an existential posture (from Kierkegaard, primarily) to elucidate the truth of the Christian faith.

[3] See Michalson, "Existential Ethics," Dictionary of Christian Ethics, p. 124. This statement is also found in Worldly Theology, pp. 32-33 and has been discussed above, pp. 107-110.

[4] Ibid.

Kierkegaard's "teleological suspension of the ethical,"[5] is also traceable to H. Richard Niebuhr. In The Meaning of Revelation Niebuhr describes revelation as the means whereby God makes himself known historically, and thus effects the reconciliation of the relativities of history and His absoluteness. Niebuhr then discusses the moral implications of God's revelation for the reconciled person of faith.

> Revelation is not a development of our religious ideas but their continuous conversion. God's self-disclosure is that permanent revolution in our religious life by which all religious truths are painfully transformed and all religious behavior transfigured by repentance and new faith.
>
> Our thoughts also about the goods which deity sustains are caught up in the great turmoil of a transvaluation. The self we loved is not the self God loves, the neighbors we did not prize are his treasures, the truth we ignored is the truth he maintains, the justice which we sought because it was our own is not the justice that his love desires. The righteousness he demands and gives is not our righteousness but greater and different.[6]

This, Edward L. Long has rightly recognized,[7] is the epitome of transvaluation. It is also essential to Michalson's concept of responsibility.

In addition to reflecting the influence of H. Richard Niebuhr, Michalson's concept of human responsibility also reflects the thought of Friedrich Gogarten. Gogarten, like Michalson appro-

---

[5]See Michalson, "Existential Ethics," for Michalson's references to Kierkegaard's "teleological suspension of the ethical."

[6]Niebuhr, The Meaning of Revelation, p. 133.

[7]Long, Survey of Christian Ethics, p. 33.

priating Niebuhr, understood God's calling humanity not only to existence, but to responsibility. Paul's understanding of Sonship (Galatians 4) is the paradigm for this. Sonship implies not only responsibility though. It also implies maturity.

According to Gogarten, God has delivered the principalities and powers into the hands of his mature sons and daughters, and given them dominion over the world. Runyon has summarized Gogarten's position in this regard:

> A son is distinguished from a child in that, whereas the child is completely dependent upon the parent for his continued existence, the son--who has come of age and received an inheritance which is his to manage--has the ability to stand on his own, to be independent, no longer bound to the father by the necessities of his physical survival. The inheritance bestowed upon man is the world; he is given dominion over it and charged with the responsibility to "till it and keep it." His position with regard to the world thus frees him for a mature and noncompulsive relationship with the Father, while his filial relation to the Father frees him for a mature and noncompulsive attitude toward the world.[8]

Michalson adopts this understanding of responsibility wholeheartedly.

> To be a "child of God" is. . .the possibility in history which Jesus. . .commences. To be "a child of God" is to be set within an historical framework in which one begins to assume his responsibility for a world which God has turned over to him.
>
> Jesus of Nazareth is the open door by which the whole of history may live a history of wholeness. . . .Not the end of dependence upon God, but the beginning of an existence in which everything is received from God, hence under responsibility to him. Therefore, not the end of God in the world but the end of God as the explanation of the

---

[8]Runyon, "Friedrich Gogarten," p. 434.

world and the beginning of God as the source of the world's meaning.[9]

B. Michalson's Ethics: Preaching Engaging the World

The parameters of responsibility that Michalson learned from Niebuhr and Gogarten are reflected in the ethical thought that grows out of his thinking about responsibility. Responsibility, for Michalson, implies the relation of sonship, wherein humanity is related to God, yet mature. Ethics, as preaching engaging the world, brings these ideas of responsibility and sonship to life. In short, Michalson's ethics, wherein preaching engages the world, makes his theory of responsibility a practical reality.

As has been shown above (Chapter V, pp. 163-177), preaching, broadly conceived, is at the heart of Michalson's ethics. In fact, for Michalson, preaching, broadly conceived, is ethics. Through the church's preaching, her sonship is born out. The church's preaching is the Christian faith's being engaged with the world, prophetically and redemptively. It is the faith's actually liberating the world and energizing and motivating people for a new world in the sight of God. Preaching engenders freedom and maturity by attacking both individual and systemic evil, and by effecting the right way of being in the world. Preaching as ethics, and ethics as preaching, thus makes concrete Michalson's theory of responsibility in that preaching as ethics, and ethics as preaching is the point at which responsibility is born out and the Good is <u>actually</u> realized.

---

[9]Michalson, <u>Rationality of Faith</u>, pp. 132, 134-135.

C. Michalson's Ethics:
Command[10] and Context; Character and Virtue

The parameters of responsibility that Michalson learned from Niebuhr and Gogarten are also reflected in Michalson's ethics, by the dialectical nature of his ethical thought. As just stated, responsibility, for Michalson, implies the relation of sonship, wherein humanity is related to God, yet mature. Similarly, his Christian ethics of responsibility, wherein preaching engages the world, recognizes the reality of God's command and the necessity of obedience to that command (Bultmann), while at the same time recognizing the importance of the self who responds to that command (Wesley).

As stated above (Chapter VI, p.227), Michalson's ethics, in many respects, closely resembles Bultmann's. The language of decision, with emphasis on both divine command and context as formative of action, is central. In Jesus Christ the possibility of experiencing the Kingdom of God is opened to humanity, giving life an eschatological dimension and diminishing the importance of all else. Thus, radical obedience to God is thrust upon humanity as a crucial choice and becomes all important, to the extent that radical obedience defines Christian life. The language of decision is also reflected in Michalson's ethics by his contextualism. Hand in hand with his conceiving ethical action as command (to "Love thy Neighbor"), Michalson feels that context dictates the content of love.

---

[10]See again Chapter VI, p. 229, note 114, above.

Just as Michalson's Christian ethics of responsibility reflects the language of decision, his thought also reflects the language of character and virtue. In this regard, Michalson adopts Wesley's concept of holiness and perfection to express what he considers the Bible's ultimate intention: the transformation of the world. Holiness is seen by Michalson as augmenting humanity's being addressed by God, and providing a "newer and higher stage of the Christian life."[11] Thus Michalson incorporates into his ethics a genuine concern for sanctification, and an awareness of, to use Hauerwas's phrase, "the self's acquiring unity and duration[12] in relation to Christ's bringing God's kingdom. Clearly, Michalson could and would affirm Hauerwas's saying:

> Even though the action of God is the first word for any Christian ethic, it is not the only word. . . .[and] while the basis of the Christian life is what God has done his action also includes the reality of human behavior. What God has willed to do for man is not done in such a way that man is excluded from his activity.[13]

D. Michalson's Contribution: The Possibility of Ethics in a New Key

1. **Michalson's Synthesis of World and Word** (Worldly Theology

Michalson's contribution to the field of Christian ethics is twofold. His Christian ethics of responsibility first provides a means whereby the Christian can take seriously the injunction to live in the world, but not of it. By Michalson's recognizing the

---

[11] Michalson, *Worldly Theology*, p. 147.

[12] Hauerwas, *Character and the Christian Life*, p. 2.

[13] Ibid., p. 136.

need for, and treating, the reconciliation of the relativities of history with the absoluteness of God (Niebuhr), he provides an apologetic theology (in the best sense of the word[14]) that gives necessary and proper perspective on the claims of the world. At the same time, his understanding that God's revelation calls humanity to responsibility demands that the Christian live maturely in the world. In this, Michalson has effected a dialectical tension between God and world that cannot, and should not, be dissipated. He has guarded against too much worldliness on the one hand and too much "theo-logia" on the other. In short, for Michalson, the world must be engaged by preaching, and it is only by preaching that the world can rightly be engaged!

The importance of Michalson's conception of Christian ethics, as the _world_ engaged by _preaching_, cannot be overstated. His Christian ethics of responsibility stands as a continual reminder of what the gospel considers a necessary, but tenuous relationship between the Word and the world. Michalson's Christian ethics of responsibility also serves as an exemplary means of keeping this necessary but tenuous relationship intact. This is seen, especially, when his worldly theology/ethics is compared with the political ethics of liberation theology and the other worldly ethics of evangelical perfectionism.

---

[14]Michalson, Worldly Theology, p. 66.

As discussed above (See Chapter VI, pp. 196-204 and pp. 212-220), Michalson's Christian ethics of responsibility, based as it is in a theology of correlation, is more comprehensive and wholistic than either the ethics of liberation theology or the ethics of evangelical perfectionism. Michalson's ethical thought has a broader starting point, a more inclusive interlocutor, a more comprehensive set of tools, and a more widely focused analysis and mode of engagement than either liberation theology's ethics or evangelical perfectionism's ethics. Further, Michalson adheres to an eschatology that avoids apocalyptic materialism on the one hand and excessive spiritualism and futurism on the other. Thus, Michalson's Christian ethics of responsibility provides "insight and corrective" to both the ethics of liberation theology and the ethics of evangelical perfectionism. In fact, Michalson's ethics represents a mediating position that, because it "exists in tbe service of God. . .will express itself in the constitution of a meaningful world."[15]

Michalson's Christian ethics of responsibility represents an inclusiveness sorely needed in an age of caucus Christianity and political ethics that, though noble and virtuous, ofttimes falls short of the Gospel's message of reconciliation for all. The inclusiveness of Michalson's ethics is hinted at in the dialectic spelled out above, but is clearly seen in relationship to the political ethics of liberation tbeology.

---

[15]Ibid., p. 25.

The inclusiveness of Michalson's Christian ethics of responsibility is the result of several factors. His concern for preaching and the expression of his ethics as preaching that engages the world, coupled with his conception of ethics as "integral to theology," dictated an <u>overtly</u> theological ethic, with the gospel's dictums and theological concerns saliently expressed. Thus, as has been pointed out, Michalson's is a distinctly Christian ethic that transvaluates the moral.

The implications of Michalson's distinctly Christian ethics are enormous. In Michalson's ethics, there is very little, if any, place for the "simply ethical" solution. Rather, his decidedly Christian ethic continually harkens to and seeks to express the gospel's command to love.[16] Michalson's transvaluated ethic therefore, speaks to the political ethics flourishing today, in much the

---

[16]To be sure, Michalson recognized the necessity of (Reinhold) Niebuhr's realism at the social and political levels. His adaptation of Niebuhr's understanding of justice as "the closest approximation of love" is an example of his ability to be realistic and to compromise. Michalson's realism, though, must be seen in the context of his eschatology and his ultimate aim of "love for neighbor." It is never intended to reduce the Gospel's demand! The sermon "Faith Must be Expressed in Works of Love" demonstrates clearly that the gospel's dictum of love for neighbor is always first on his ethical agenda, even though it assumes different forms in different situations.

same way that the gospel speaks to prophecy.[17]

Without doubt, the high moral vision of liberation theology's political ethics is noble and just, and our world is in dire need of precisely this vision. However, if this vision is to become a reality, it must be something more than moral idealism from below, that continues to hearken to notions of right and wrong more reminiscent of Old Testament prophecy than the gospel's understanding of reconciliation. As Edward L. Long, Jr. has stated in "The Particularism of Morality and the Universalism of Love," with regard to the vision of peace in Micah 4:1-5:

> . . .Such an idealism has never been made real. It has nurtured the hope but never achieved. . .reality. . .and never has become a description of an historical achievement. It remains a moral ideal--a vision that is always "not yet"; a statement of what ought to be rather than a proclamation of what has become.
> . . .We must remain loyal to the mind-set of [Micah]. To deny or betray the demand implicit in the passage would be to be unfaithful to the Bible--verily heretical and even apostate. . . .Moral idealism remains the only viable prolegomena to the search for peace, though that search will never be culminated on the moral level alone and must lead on to a self-giving and compassionate love that transcends the particularity of moralism by the power of grace.[18]

---

[17] I am indebted to Edward L. Long, Jr. for this distinction. His unpublished sermon, "The Particularism of Morality and the Universalism of Love" compares Micah 4:1-5 and John 10:11-18, and thus distinguishes between the prophetic (moral) vision and the gospel's vision of love. Dr. Long's distinction figures prominently in my distinguishing between Michalson's ethics and liberation theology's ethics, since they consciously ground themselves in the gospel's "Love thy Neighbor," and the prophetic tradition, respectively.

[18] Edward L. Long, Jr., "The Particularism of Morality and the Universalism of Love" (Unpublished sermon) pp. 2-3.

Michalson's ethics, with its synthesis of Word and world into a worldly theology/ethics can assist political ethics in defining its vision, and bringing it to reality. Michalson's ethics, with its more inclusive starting point, interlocutor, set of tools, analysis, and mode of engagement, seeks to transform the moral vision, where achievement and judgment are the operative words, into a vision of grace and love. Again, Long is instructive.

Contrasting the vision of peace in Micah 4 with the vision in John 10:11-18, Long writes as follows about John's vision.

> . . .The terminology in John is the terminology of care and nurture. . . .Where the concept of nurture governs there can be no permanent exclusion. Love never lets go of the object of its care--even if that love is not responded to. Morality judges; . . .Judgmentalism, even in a quest for virtue, can engage in rancor and the condemnation of others. That is why wars are generally fought only when people on both sides come to regard themselves as sufficiently righteous to legitimate their destruction of others.
> A redemptive love, in contrast, that constantly seeks to include others in community, even until all are embraced, becomes a source of renewal.[19]

Because Michalson's ethics infuses political ethics with grace and love, it can and should offer "insight and correctives" to these acknowledged views from below.

Evangelical perfectionism is well aware of the dangers of a "strictly moral" ethical program. Will D. Campbell--himself a onetime liberal who had fallen prey to a "we/they" mindset dependent on who was and who was not, according to liberal views, doing

---

[19] Ibid., pp. 4-5.

God's work--is personally acquainted with the folly of ethical action that neglects reconciliation. As Campbell puts it, the indicative must come prior to the imperative.

> The Christian faith is <u>indicative</u>. . .not <u>imperative</u>. . . But we believe that St. Paul's imperative use of "reconcile" calls attention to a special kind of behavior by the Christian toward the world, behavior which "does" by <u>being</u> and <u>living</u> as God made us in Christ.[20]

The problem with evangelical perfectionism is not that the world's understandings are exalted. Instead, there is a danger that they are trivialized and neglected. Campbell's counseling people not to vote, for example[21] is so violent a reaction to the affairs of the world that living in the world is unimportant. Once again, Michalson's understanding of the <u>necessary</u> but tenuous relationship of Word and world can and should offer insight and correctives.

Michalson's first contribution to the field of Christian ethics then, is in his synthesis of Word and world, into a worldly theology that avoids excessive worldliness on the one hand and other worldliness on the other. His conception of the world as engaged by preaching keeps in perspective and dialectical tension that necessary but tenuous relationship between Word and world that the Christian life demands.

---

[20] Campbell and Holloway, <u>Up to Our Steeples in Politics</u>, p. 1.

[21] See Ibid., p. 127.

2. Michalson's Synthesis of Decision and Character

Secondly, Carl Michalson has contributed to the field of Christian ethics by developing, in his Christian ethics of responsibility, a dialectic that recognizes <u>God's</u> dealing with humanity, while at the same time recognizing that God deals with <u>humanity</u>. In this regard, his contribution to the field lies in his effecting a Wesleyan-like synthesis in his ethical thought. He takes seriously the fact that it is God in Christ who stands behind and enables responsibility for the world, while taking just as seriously the fact that God's dealings with humanity effect very real transformations in human beings. Thus Michalson's Christian ethics of responsibility does indeed proclaim that "In Christ God delivers up his rule to men, but he continues to reign,"[22] and his is an ethics "which exists in the service of God and draws its insight from the historical reality of Jesus of Nazareth. . ." while at the same time expressing itself in "the constitution of a meaningful world"[23]

Michalson's ethic takes seriously humanity's continual need for God's guidance and direction, while at the same time recognizing that God's turning to humanity in Christ is transforming. Therefore, Michalson's Christian ethic of responsibility allows for the importance of both ethical decision and the virtue and character of the ethical actor. Michalson's ethic then, in addition to trans-

---

[22]Michalson, <u>Worldly Theology</u>, p. 215.

[23]Ibid., p. 25.

cending the dichotomy between God and world, also transcends the dichotomy between action and actor. This is indeed ethics in a new key.

Michalson's ethics takes seriously the fact that God has turned to humanity, while taking just as seriously the fact that humanity must continue to live in the world. His ethics also recognizes that God in Christ transforms humanity while recognizing that, as humanity, we need to continually be attuned to God's initiative, and respond to God's initiative ever anew. By affirming the dialectical nature of the God/person relationship at these two levels, Michalson's theology/ethics stands in a long traditon of Christian thought that stretches back through neo-orthodoxy to the Reformation, and to Paul. Given this illustrious history, it might be better to say that Michalson's ethics, rather than ethics in a new key, is ethics in a very, very old key, that, though ofttimes neglected, should always be voiced. His ethics of Christian responsibility does indeed stand as a reminder and example--a reminder and example of how the Christian faith can and should be related to human action.

APPENDIX A

FOCUS ON A REVOLUTION

by Carl Michalson[1]

I have about three very small questions I'd like to raise, though I have no expectation of answering them, save possibly one. And I must say also that I'm greatly embarrassed about my involvement in this particular situation, because, as Barney Anderson hinted, I enjoyed the whole thing so much. I think I'd much rather face the southern whites than the Drew theologians, in [my] classes. So I left my tape recorder and went off to Montgomery, but I had to confront myself with three questions: One, "Why did I go?" and another, "Would I do it again?" and a third, "What will we all do when we have further occasions like this?" (I assume this third is a big open question which I know I'm not going to be able to answer, but which ought to occupy some discussion.)

I think I went, not because I expected to integrate Alabama--although I take pride in the fact that Dean Anderson and I did integrate a latrine. I couldn't have gone to integrate Alabama, because that is a work of Sisyphus, and furthermore, it's something we haven't even completed in my own community of Morristown. So

---

[1] Early in 1965, Bernhard Anderson, Carl Michalson, and Howard Clark Kee represented the Drew Theological faculty at a civil rights march in Montgomery, Alabama. Upon returning to Drew, they addressed a Theological School assembly that attempted to "Focus on a Revolution." Presented here is Michalson's address on that occasion. (Carl Michalson, "Focus on a Revolution," as transcribed and edited by Samuel R. Roberts, III. has also appeared in The Drew Gateway, 56, No.3 [Spring, 1986]:48-50.)

I might rather have stayed at home if that had been my motive. I think I went mainly to demonstrate on behalf of the freedom to demonstrate. I think that was the occasion that really called us there. And it's an important thing, because the hope of civil liberties everywhere will depend upon our continued freedom to demonstrate on behalf of just causes.

Then I ask myself, "Why a theologian in a situation like that?" "Why not better at home with my books?" And that's even harder for me to answer. One might say, "I didn't go as a theologian, I went as a man." But that's a bifurcation I don't accept. I pat my neighbor's dog as a theologian. I kiss my wife as a theologian. (That's why theology is so crucial.) And when I demonstrate on behalf of civil liberties, I do it as a theologian.

As a matter of fact, I understand that the very existence of God is at stake in what men do in history. And I got a little advance clue to that last night when reading a poem by Robert Frost:

> I turned to speak to God about the world's despair,
> But to make bad matters worse, I found that God wasn't there.
> God turned to speak to me--Don't anybody laugh.
> God found I wasn't there, at least not over half.

I'm sure that one cannot do theology today without involving [God] in just such historical causes, as the present civil rights enterprises give us a chance to do.

But then, "Would I do it again?" That all depends on whether what we did there was like a baptism, which is unrepeatable, because so indelible, or like pastoral calling, which is infinite in its demands upon us. And it seems quite obvious that many aspects of this experience were like a baptism. (We just will never be able to shake the memory of it from us. I have been baptized! We will say that over and over again, because of this experience.) At the same time we know that it was not just something that happened once, but it was an invitation to repeated acts of responsibility.

So that leads me to my third question, "What will we do when we have these repeated opportunities to leave our immediate responsibilities and go off in this way?" I just don't know. (Here's where I don't think I have any answer at all, but I'll be very eager to participate in discussion about it.) You see, one can't be a theologian without being involved in just such causes, but can one remain a theologian if all he does is get involved in such causes? That's the difficulty I face.

As I understand the situation in the first century church, as reported by the apostle Paul, there was mainly one big opportunity for the expression of faith--the contest against legalism. And why couldn't it be just as true today, that there's one main opportunity for the expression of faith--the contest against racial injustice? That could be the case. It could be so much the case that we'd rewrite our curriculum. We'd have a core curriculum in which everything we discussed would be built around the question of racial inequity. We would have civil rights as an epoch in Heilsgeschichte. And we'd have field work in which we would not just do everything in general under District Superintendents, but we would do one thing in particular. We would train ourselves for efficiency in seeing to it that in every one of our communities, civil liberties were increasingly respected. And we'd have a varsity team to go off to these remote places like Selma and Montgomery to carry on [these] contests on our behalf, on the front lines. But in doing it all, we would have a sense that in fulfilling our human responsibiity, we were giving God a chance to be born again.

A SELECTED BIBLIOGRAPHY

Utilizing the bibliography "The Writings of Carl Michalson"
Compiled by Lawrence O. Kline[1]
and Updated and Enlarged by Edward J. Wynne, Jr.[2]

I. Writings, Editions, and Selections by Carl Michalson

A. Books

Christianity and the Existentialists. Edited by Carl Michalson. New York: Charles Scribner's Sons, 1956.

Faith for Personal Crises. New York: Charles Scribner's Sons, 1958.

The Hinge of History: An Existential Approach to the Christian Faith. New York: Charles Scribner's Sons, 1959.

Japanese Contributions to Christian Theology. Philadelphia: Westminster Press, 1960.

Prayer for Today's People. Edited by Edward J. Wynne, Jr. and Henry O. Thompson. Washington, D.C.: University Press of America, 1982.

The Rationality of Faith: An Historical Critique of the Theological Reason. New York: Charles Scribner's Sons, 1963.

The Witness of Kierkegaard: Selected Writings on How to Become a Christian. New York: Association Press, 1960. A Reflection Book.

The Witness of Radical Faith. Edited by Gordon E. Michalson and Olin M. Ivey. Nashville: Tidings, 1974.

Worldly Theology: The Hermeneutical Focus of an Historical Faith. New York: Charles Scribner's Sons, 1967.

---

[1] Lawrence O. Kline, "The Writings of Carl Michalson," Drew Gateway XXXVI, 3 (Spring-Summer, 1966)

[2] Edward J. Wynne, Jr., The Implications of Carl Michalson's Theological Method for Christian Education. (Lanham, Md.: University Press of America, 1983) pp. 13-35.

B. Parts of Books

"Authority," in *A Handbook of Christian Theology*, pp. 24-28. Edited by Marvin Halverson and Arthur A. Cohen. Cleveland and New York: World Publishing Co., 1958.

"Bultmann Against Marcion," in *The Old Testament and Christian Faith*, pp. 49-63. Edited by Bernhard W. Anderson. New York: Harper & Row, 1963.

"Christian Interpretation and Y.M.C.A. Practice," in *Christian Education in Y.M.C.A. Youth Program*, pp. 18-25. New York: National Council of Young Men's Christian Associations, 1953.

"The Finality of Christ in an Eschatological Perspective," in *The Finality of Christ*, pp. 155-174. Edited by Dow Kirkpatrick. Nashville: Abingdon Press, 1966.

"The Hermeneutics of Holiness in Wesley," in *The Heritage of Christian Thought: Essays in Honor of Robert Lowry Calhoun*, pp. 127-141. Edited by Robert E. Cushman and Egil Grisles. New York: Harper & Row, 1965.

"Irrationalism," in *Twentieth Century Encyclopedia of Religious Knowledge*. An Extension of the New Schaff-Herzog Enclyclopedia of Religious Knowledge. Vol I, pp. 573-575. Edited by Lefferts A. Loetscher, et.al. Grand Rapids: Baker Book House, 1955.

"The Issue: Ultimate Meaning in History" in *Christian Mission in Theological Perspective: An Inquiry by Methodists*, pp. 77-88. Edited by Gerald H. Anderson. Nashville: Abingdon Press, 1967.

"Karl Heim," in *A Handbook of Christian Theologians*, pp. 273-294. Edited by Deane P. Peerman and Martin E. Marty. Cleveland and New York: World Publishing Co., 1965.

"The Real Presence of the Hidden God," in *Faith and Ethics: The Theology of H. Richard Niebuhr*, pp. 245-267. Edited by Paul Ramsey. New York: Harper & Row, 1957.

"Rudolf Bultmann," in *Ten Makers of Modern Protestant Thought*, pp. 102-113. Edited by George L. Hunt. New York: Association Press, 1958.

"Theology as Ontology and as History," in *New Frontiers in Theology: Discussions Among German and American Theologians*. Vol. I: *The Later Heidegger and Theology*, pp. 136-156. Edited by James M. Robinson and John B. Cobb, Jr. New York: Harper & Row, 1963.

"What is Existentialism?," in <u>Christianity and the Existentialists</u>, pp. 1-22. Edited by Carl Michalson. New York: Charles Scribner's Sons, 1956.

C. Articles

"Barthianism and Evangelism," <u>The Drew Gateway</u> XVII, No. 4 (Summer, 1946):57.

"Between Nature and God," <u>The Journal of Religion</u> XXXV, No. 4 (October, 1955):229-241.

"The Bible in Japanese Church Life," <u>Bible Society Record</u> 107, No. 5 (June, 1962):68-69.

"The Boundary Between Faith and Reason: A Study of Hegel's <u>Glauben und Wissen</u>," (The Drew University Studies, No. 3), The Drew University Bulletin 39, No. 4 (December, 1951), separate pagination.

"Christian Faith and Existential Freedom," <u>Religion in Life</u> XXI, No. 4 (Autumn, 1952):513-526.

"Coexistence," <u>The Journal of Pastoral Care</u> XI, No. 2 (Summer, 1957):110-111.

"Communicating the Gospel," <u>Theology Today</u> XIV, No. 3 (October, 1957):321-334.

"Continental Theology Today Through the Eyes of Drew Fellowship Students in Europe," <u>Drew Gateway</u> XXV, No. 1 (Autumn, 1954):20-26.

"The Crisis of Vocation," <u>The Christian Scholar</u> XLI, No. 2 (June, 1958):89-100.

"Dr. Michalson Answers Questions About Your Faith," <u>Together</u> 1, No. 13 (Oct. 15, 1957):33; 1, No. 14 (Nov. 15, 1957): 34; 1, No. 15 (Dec. 15, 1957):21; 2, No. 1 (Jan. 15, 1958):57; 2, No. 2 (Feb. 15, 1958):57; 2, No. 3 (Mar. 15, 1958):56; 2, No. 4 (Apr. 15, 1958):44.

"The Ecumenical 'Sic et Non'," <u>Drew Gateway</u> XXIII, No. 2 (Winter, 1953):64-73.

"The Edwin Lewis Myth," <u>Drew Gateway</u> XXX, No. 2 (Winter, 1960): 102-107.

"Existentialist Ethics," in <u>The Dictionary of Christian Ethics</u>. Edited by John Mcquarrie. Philadelphia: Westminster, 1967.

"Existentialism and Radical Faith," "Demythologizing and Meaningful Faith," "Language and the Event of Faith." Edited by Ann Drake. Notes from the Garage Door, 2nd issue (January, 1966):10-29.

"Existentialism in Theology Today," The Chaplain 16, No. 5 (October, 1955):355-368.

"Faith for Personal Crises," The Pastor. 1. Theology for Crucial Situations, 15, No. 7 (March, 1952):13-14; 2. The Crisis of Anxiety, 15, No. 8 (April, 1952):17-19; 3. The Crisis of Suffering and Death, 15, No. 9 (May, 1952):10-12; 4. The Crisis of Vocation, 15, No. 11 (July, 1952):11-12; 5. The Crisis of Marriage, 16, No. 1 (September, 1952):14-15; 6. The Crisis of Doubt, 16, No. 2 (October, 1952):11-12.

"Faith for the Crisis of Marriage," The Journal of Pastoral Care XI, No. 4 (Winter, 1957):193-206.

"Faith for the Crisis of Suffering," Religion in Life XXVII, No. 3 (Summer, 1958):401-413.

"Fifty Years of Theology in Retrospect: An Evaluation," The Journal of Bible and Religion XXVIII, No. 2 (April, 1960): 215-221.

"The Ghost of Logical Positivism," The Christian Scholar XLIII, No. 3 (Fall, 1960):223-230.

"The Gospel as Invocation and Benediction," Theology Today XXIII, No. 2 (July, 1966):167-175.

"The Hinge of History," Religion in Life XXV, No. 2 (Spring, 1956):259-270.

"History and Hermeneutics," Christian Advocate VI, No. 20 (September 27, 1963):7-8.

"History, Hermeneutics and Systematic Theology," Drew Gateway XXXIII, No. 3 (Spring, 1963):154-162.

"The Holy Spirit and the Church," Theology Today VIII, No. 1 (April, 1951):41-54.

"How our Lives Carry Christ's Death and Manifest His Resurrection: Atonement, Redemption, and Ethics," Encounter 20, No. 4 (Autumn, 1959):410-425.

"In the Beginning, the Word," Workers with Youth. I. Interpreting the Bible, 18, No. 11 (July, 1965):2-4; II. The Biblical Meaning of the Word, 18, No. 12 (August, 1965):2-4; III. The Meaning of Incarnation, 19, No. 1 (September,

1965):14-16; IV. The Meaning of Resurrection, 19, No. 2 (October, 1965):2-4.

"Is American Theology Coming of Age?" Drew Gateway XXXVI, No. 3 (Spring-Summer, 1966):65-75.

"The Issue: Ultimate Meaning in History," Religion in Life XXVIII, No. 3 (Summer, 1959):376-384.

"Jesus Christ as Word Become Flesh," The Christian Century LXXVIII, No. 18 (May 3, 1961):552-553.

"Karl Heim's Dimension of Faith," Drew Gateway XVII, No. 1 (Autumn, 1945):14.

"Kierkegaard's Theology of Faith," Religion in Life XXXII, No. 2 (Spring, 1963):225-237.

"The Koehler Library at Drew," Drew Gateway XXI, No. 4 (Summer, 1951):17-19.

"Language, History, and Meaning," Theology Today XIX, No 1 (April, 1962):1-8.

"Maturity of Sonship," Concern 7, No. 20 (November 15, 1965):10-12.

"The Meaning of Easter," Studies in Christian Living 3, No. 2 (Spring, 1955):3-12.

"The Meaning of Preaching as Communication," Christian Thought 2, No. 7 (July, 1958):34-43.

"Neo-Orthodox Theology," Drew Gateway XXI, No. 1 (Autumn, 1950): 3-9.

"New Testament Teaching for Modern Living," Christian Action 10, No. 4 (October-December, 1955):1-48.

"Protestant Missionary Obligation at the End of Our Time," Occasional Bulletin (Missionary Research Library) XIV, No. 6 (June, 1963).

"The Reality of the Resurrection," Drew Gateway XXIV, No. 3 (Spring, 1959):178-189.

"Reason in Nature and in History." Prepared for the Spring, 1962 meeting of The Society for Theological Discussion. Mimeographed.

"The Task of Apologetics in the Future: Karl Heim's Theology After Fifty Years," Scottish Journal of Theology 6, No. 4 (December, 1953):362-378.

"The Task of Systematic Theology Today," The Centennial Review VIII, No. 2 (Spring, 1964):189-199.

"The Ten Books Which Have Had the Greatest Influence in Shaping My Life." (Mimeographed) Included in the Drew University Theological School Alumni Association Booklet for the Class of 1962.

"The Theology of Luther in Japan," The Lutheran Quarterly XIV, No. 1 (February, 1962):68-71.

"We Gather Together," Christian Advocate VII, No. 8 (April 11, 1963):14.

"What Doth the Lord Require of Us?," The International Review of Missions XLV, No. 178 (April, 1956):145-154.

"What Existentialism is About," Union Seminary Quarterly Review XIII, No. 2 (January, 1958):3-11.

"Why Methodists Baptize," The New Christian Advocate II, No. 6 (June, 1958):3-11.

D. Reviews

Barth, Karl. Against the Stream. New York: Philosophical Library, 1954. Drew Gateway XXV, No. 1 (Autumn, 1954):41-42.

_____, Karl. Die Kirchliche Dogmatik III, 4. Die Lehre von der Schopfung. Zurich: Evangelischer Verlag/A. G. Zollikon, 1951, in "Athiesm and Ethics," Drew Gateway XXII, No. 1 (Autumn, 1951):34-36.

Bonhoeffer, Dietrich. Act and Being. Translated by Bernard Noble. New York: Harper & Row, 1962. Christian Advocate VI, No. 13 (21 June, 1962):17.

Brown, James. Subject and Object in Modern Theology. New York: Macmillan Co., 1955, in "Biblical Christianity and Philosophy," Drew Gateway XXVI, No. 3 (Spring, 1956):128-131.

Brunner, Emil. The Christian Doctrine of Creation and Redemption. Dogmatics II. Translated by Olive Wyon. London: Lutterworth Press, 1952, in "Recent Studies in Protestant Doctrine," The Ecumenical Review VII, No. 2 (January, 1955):192-196.

Cochrane, Arthur C. The Existentialists and God. Philadelphia: Westminster Press, 1960. Theology Today XVIII, No 3 (October, 1956):419-421.

Elem, Paul. The Restoration of Meaning to Contemporary Life. New York: Doubleday & Co., 1958. Religious Education LIV, No. 3 (May-June, 1959):312-313.

Heim, Karl. The World: Its Creation and Consummation. Philadelphia: Muhlenberg Press, 1962. Theology Today XIX, No. 4 (January, 1963):556-557.

Hofmann, Hans. The Theology of Reinhold Niebuhr. New York: Charles Scribner's Sons, 1956. Drew Gateway XXVII, No. 3 (Spring, 1957):165.

Hough, Lynn Harold. Living Democracy. New York: Fleming H. Revell Co., 1943. Drew Gateway XIV, No. 4 and XV, No. 1 (Autumn, 1943):10-11.

Lavelle, Louis. The Meaning of Holiness. Translated by Dorthea O'Sullivan. New York: Pantheon Books, Inc., 1954, in "Mysticism and Catholicism," Drew Gateway XXVI, Nos. 1-2 (Autumn-Winter, 1955-56):49-50.

Lewis, C. S. The Abolition of Man. New York: The Macmillan Co., 1947. Drew Gateway XIX, No. 1 (Autumn, 1947):13.

Marcel, Gabriel. The Philosophy of Existence. New York: The Philosophical Library, 1949, in "Existentialism and Modern Theology." Drew Gateway XX, No. 4 (Summer, 1950):32-33.

_____. Man Against Mass Society. Chicago: Henry Regnery Co., 1952. Religion and Life XXII, No. 4 (Autumn, 1953):628-630.

Munby, Denys L. The Idea of a Secular Society. New York: Oxford University Press, 1963. The Journal of Pastoral Care XIX, No. 3 (Fall, 1965):174.

Outler, Albert C. The Christian Tradition and the Unity We Seek. New York: Oxford University Press, 1957. Drew Gateway XXVIII, No. 1 (Autumn, 1957):51-52.

Peters, John L. Christian Perfection and American Methodism. New York: Abingdon Press, 1956. Theology Today XIV, No. 2 (July, 1957):298-300.

Skard, Bjarne. The Incarnation. Translated by Herman E. Jorgensen. Minneapolis: Augsburg Publishing House, 1960. The Christian Century LXXVII, No. 38 (September 21, 1960):1090.

Soper, David Wesley, ed. Room for Improvement. Chicago: Wilcox & Follett Co., 1951. Drew Gateway XXII, No. 4 (Summer, 1952):163.

Trueblood, D. Elton. Foundations for Reconstruction. New York: Harper & Brothers, 1946. Drew Gateway XIX, No. 1 (Autumn, 1947):71.

Wild, John Daniel. Human Freedom and Social Order: An Essay in Christian Philosophy. Durham: Duke University Press, 1959. Theology Today XVII, No. 2 (July, 1960):242-244.

E. Academia

Human Responsibility in the Republic of Plato and in the Synoptic Gospels. M.A. thesis, Drew University, 1940.

The Doctrine of Reason and Revelation in the Theology of Karl Heim. Ph.D. dissertation, Yale University, 1945.

II. Secondary Sources Pertaining to Michalson

A. Books

Courtney, Charles; Ivey, Olin M.; Michalson, Gordon E., eds. Hermeneutics and the Worldliness of Faith: A Festschrift in Memory of Carl Michalson. Drew Gateway, Nos. 1-3 (1974-5).

Langford, Thomas A. Practical Divinity: Theology in the Wesleyan Tradition. Nashville: Abingdon Press, 1983.

Wynne, Edward J. Jr. The Implications of Carl Michalson's Theological Method for Christian Education. Edited by Henry O. Thompson. Lanham, MD.: University Press of America, 1983.

B. Articles About Carl Michalson

1. Memorial Articles

Anderson, Bernhard W. "Carl Michalson's Vision: The Power of the Interpreted Word." Christian Advocate X, No. 12 (June 16, 1966):7-8.

Godsey, John D. "Thinking the Faith Historically: The Legacy of Carl Michalson," Drew Gateway XXXVI, No. 3 (Spring-Summer, 1966):76-88.

Herberg, Will. "Some Comments on the Theological Scene at Drew." Drew Gateway XXXI, No. 2 (Winter, 1961):82.

Hopper, Stanley Romaine. "Meditation Delivered at a Service of Worship Occasioned by the Death of Dr. Carl Michalson," Drew Gateway XXXVI, No. 3 (Spring-Summer, 1966):114-121.

Kirkpatrick, Dow. "Carl D. Michalson '39: 1915-1965." Alumni Notes, Theological School and Graduate School, Drew University Magazine (Winter, 1966).

Maddox, J. Edward. "Carl Michalson, Author, Teacher, Churchman," Methodist History VIII, No. 4 (July, 1970):30-40.

"Minutes of the Faculty Meeting, The Theological Shcool, Drew University, Madison, N.J., Dec. 10, 1965. (Mimeographed).

Osborn, Robert T. "Carl Michalson as Teacher." Drew Gateway XXXVI, No. 3 (Spring-Summer, 1966):101-108.

Pennington, Chester A. "Carl Michalson as Churchman," Drew Gateway XXXVI, No. 3 (Spring-Summer, 1966):109-113.

Runyon, Theodore Jr. "Carl Michalson as Radical Theologian," Drew Gateway XXXVI, No. 3 (Spring-Summer, 1966):89-100.

Shiner, Larry. "Carl Michalson's Contribution to Theology," Religion in Life XXXVI, No. 2 (Spring, 1967):80-91.

2. Addresses to the Carl Michalson Society

28 April, 1978: John D. Godsey, "The Maturity of Faith in Carl Michalson's Theology," Drew Gateway XLIX, No. 3 (Spring, 1979):1-9.

27 April, 1979: Theodore Runyon, Jr., "Carl Michalson as a Wesleyan Theologian," Drew Gateway LI, No. 2 (Winter, 1980):1-13.

5 May, 1981: Lawrence E. Toombs, "The Foolishness of Preaching," Drew Gateway LII, No. 1 (Fall, 1981):14-20.

3. Academia

D'Angelo, James J. "The Historical and Hermeneutical Focus of Theology: Carl Michalson's Contributions to the Problem of Theological Language." Master's thesis, Princeton Theological School, 1968.

Eslinger, Richard Laurence. "Historicity and Historicality: A Comparison of Carl Michalson and Oscar Cullmann." Ph.D. dissertation, Boston University, 1970.

Ivey, Olin Marion. "The Concept of the Holy Spirit in the Thought of Carl Michalson." Ph.D. dissertation, Claremont Graduate School, Claremont, California, 1974.

Johnson, Ellis Blane. "Carl Michalson's Concept of History as a Theological Method." Ph.D. dissertation, Boston University, 1969.

Wynne, Edward James Jr. "The Implications of Carl Michalson's Theological Method for Christian Education." Ph.D. dissertation, New York University, 1971.

4. Obituaries

Asono, Janichi. Journal of Christian Studies 12 (May, 1966)

Ann S. Boyd, Circuit Rider--Drew University Theological School (Nov. 18, 1965), 3.

Christian Century LXXXII (Nov. 24, 1965), 1435.

Kempel, Ben. American Philosophical Association XL (October, 1967)

Memoir, 1966 Journal of the Minnesota Annual Conference of The United Methodist Church, p. 214.

Minutes of the Faculty Meeting, Drew University Theological School, Dec. 10, 1965.

Noro, Yoshio. The Journal of Pastoral Care XX, No. 1 (March, 1966)

Publishers' World 188 (Dec. 13, 1965), 37.

Dean Charles W. Ranson's Announcement to the Drew Community, Nov. 11, 1965.

Stewart, Charles. The Journal of Pastoral Care XX, No. 1 (March, 1966)

*Note: Also important to this study were Michalson's course lectures, letters, and papers that are accessible through Drew University's library. Too, I have examined reviews of Michalson's books and those sources used by Michalson in his published works (especially sources written by his teachers, and thinkers directly influencing him). A complete listing of those reviews and sources is available in Edward James Wynne, Jr., The Implications of Carl Michalson's Theological Method for Christian Education. Lanham Md.: University Press of America. See Appendix A, VIII, p. 341ff and Appendix B, p. 355ff.

III. Secondary Sources Pertinent to Michalson Study

Baillie, J., ed. Natural Theology: Comprising "Nature and Grace" by Professor Dr. Emil Brunner and the Reply "NO!" by Dr. Karl Barth. London: The Centenary Press, 1946.

Brunner, Emil. Man in Revolt. Philadelphia: Westminster Press, 1939.

Brown, Arlo. "Lynn Howard Hough--Student and Dean." Drew Gateway XVIII, No. 3 (Spring, 1947).

Buber, Martin. I and Thou. New York: Charles Scribner's Sons, 1963.

Bultmann, Rudolf. Jesus and the Word. 2nd ed. New York: Charles Scribner's Sons, 1958.

Cauthen, Kenneth. "An Introduction to the Theology of H. Richard Niebuhr." Canadian Journal of Theology X, No. 1 (1964).

Davis, George W. Existentialism and Theology. New York: Philosophical Library, Inc. 1957.

Ebeling, Gerhard. Introduction to a Theological Theory of Language. Philadelphia: Fortress Press, 1971.

_____. Theology and Proclamation. Philadelphia: Fortress Press, 1961.

_____. Word and Faith. Philadelphia: Fortress Press, 1963.

Frei, Hans. "In Memory of Robert L. Calhoun." Reflection 82, 1 (November, 1984).

Gilkey, Langdon. Reaping the Whirlwind: A Christian Interpretation of History. New York: Seabury Press, 1981.

Gogarten, Friedrich. Christ the Crisis. Richmond: John Knox Press, 1970.

_____. Despair and Hope for Our Time. Philadelphia: Pilgrim Press, 1970.

_____. The Reality of Faith. Philadelphia: Westminster Press, 1957.

Green, Marvin. "Contemporary Theories of Evil." Ph.D. dissertation, Drew University, 1945.

Hardwick, Charley. "Edwin Lewis, Introduction and Critical Remarks." Drew Gateway XXXIII (Winter, 1963).

Harvey, Van. A Handbook of Theological Terms. New York: Macmillan Company, 1964.

Hopper, Stanley. "Memorial Meditation." Drew Gateway XXXVI, No. 3 (Spring-Summer, 1966).

Hough, Lynn Harold. The Christian Criticism of Life. Nashville: Abingdon Press, 1941.

_____. Evangelical Humanism. New York: Abingdon Press, 1925.

_____. The Meaning of Human Experience. New York: Abingdon Press, 1945.

_____. "Then and Now." Drew Gateway XXVIII, No. 1 (Autumn, 1957).

Kierkegaard, Soren. Concluding Unscientific Postscript. Princeton: University Press, 1941.

_____. Either/Or. 2 vols. Princeton: University Press, 1944. Paperback edition, 1971.

_____. Fear and Trembling and The Sickness Unto Death. Translated by Walter Lowrie. Princeton: Princeton University Press, 1941.

_____. Journals of Kierkegaard. Edited by Alexander Dru. New York: Harper & Row, 1959.

_____. Philosophical Fragments. Princeton: Princeton University Press, 1936. Paperback edition, 1967.

Lewis, Edwin. A Christian Manifesto. New York: Abingdom Press, 1934.

_____. The Creator and the Adversary. New York: Abindgdon Press, 1948.

_____. Jesus Christ and the Human Quest. New York: Abingdon Press, 1924.

_____. "From Philosophy to Revelation." The Christian Century LVI, No. 24 (June 14, 1939).

_____. A Philosophy of the Christian Revelation. New York: Harper & Brothers, 1940.

_____. The Practice of the Christian Life. Philadelphia: Westminster Press, 1942.

Macquarrie, John, ed. Dictionary of Christian Ethics. Philadelphia: Westminster Press, 1967.

Niebuhr, H. Richard. Christ and Culture. New York: Harper & Brothers, 1951.

_____. The Kingdom of God in America. New York: Harper & Brothers, 1937.

_____. The Meaning of Revelation. New York: MacMillan & Co., 1960.

_____. The Responsible Self. New York: Harper & Row, 1963.

_____. Radical Monotheism in Western Culture. New York: Harper & Brothers, 1960.

_____. The Social Sources of Denominationalism. New York: Henry Holt & Co., 1929.

Niebuhr, Reinhold. "Lynn Harold Hough in Detroit." Drew Gateway XVIII, No. 3 (Spring, 1947).

Oden, Thomas. Radical Obedience: The Ethics of Rudolph Bultmann. Philadelphia: Westminster Press, 1964.

Ogden, Schubert M. Review of The Rationality of Faith by Carl Michalson. Perkins School of Theology Review XVII, 2,3 (Winter-Spring, 1964).

Outler, Albert. Theology in the Wesleyan Spirit. Nashville: Tidings, 1975.

_____. John Wesley. New York: Oxford University Press, 1964.

Robinson, James M. and Cobb, John B. Jr. New Frontiers in Theology. Vol. II: The New Hermeneutic. New York: Harper & Row, 1964.

Robinson, James M. A New Quest of the Historical Jesus. London: SCM Press, 1959. Reprint edition, 1971.

Runyon, Theodore, "Friedrich Gogarten." A Handbook of Christian Theologians. Edited by Martin Marty and Dean Peerman. Nashville: Abingdon, 1965.

Seamands, Stephen Arnett. "The Christology of Edwin Lewis: A Study in Transition." Ph.D. dissertation, Drew University, 1983.

Shiner, Larry. The Secularization of History. Nashville: Abingdon Press, 1966.

Slaatte, Howard, The Pertinence of the Paradox. Washington D.C.: University Press of America, 1982

Smart, James M. The Divided Mind of Modern Theology. Philadelphia: Westminster Press, 1967.

Thomas, George F. Review of The Meaning of Revelation by H. Richard Niebuhr. Journal of Religion 21 (October, 1941).

Williams, Colin. John Wesley's Theology Today. London: Epworth Press, 1960.

IV. Ethics Sources

A. General Works Pertinent to this Study

Beach, Waldo and Niebuhr, H. Richard, eds. Christian Ethics: Sources of the Living Tradition. 2nd ed. New York: John Wiley & Sons, 1973.

Barth, Karl. Community, State and Church. New York: Doubleday Anchor, 1960.

de Beauvoir, Simon. Ethics of Ambiguity. Translated by B. Frechtman. New York: Citadel Press, 1962.

Bonhoeffer, Dietrich. The Cost of Discipleship. New York: The Macmillan Co., 1958.

_____. Ethics. New York: The Macmillan Co., 1955.

_____. Life Together. New York: Harper & Brothers, 1954.

Brunner, Emil. The Divine-Human Encounter. Philadelphia: Westminster Press, 1943.

_____. The Divine Imperative. Philadelphia: Westminster Press, 1947.

Cox, Harvey, ed. *The Situation Ethics Debate*. Philadelphia: Westminster Press, 1968.

Dewey, John. *Human Nature and Conduct: An Introduction to Social Psychology*. New York: Henry Holt and Co., 1922.

Fletcher, Joseph. *Moral Responsibility: Situation Ethics at Work*. Philadelphia: Westminster Press, 1967.

_____. *Situation Ethics: The New Morality*. Philadelphia: Westminster Press, 1966.

Gogarten, Friedrich. *Die Kirche in der Welt*. Heidelberg: Lambert Schneider, 1948.

_____. *Der Mensch Zwischen God und Welt: Eine Untersluchung uber Gesetz und Evangelium*. Heidelberg: Lambert Schneider, 1952.

Kierkegaard, Soren. *Works of Love*. Translated by D. F. and L. M. Swenson. Princeton: Princeton University Press, 1946.

Long, Edward Leroy Jr. "The Particularism of Morality and the Universality of Love." Unpublished Sermon.

_____. *A Survey of Christian Ethics*. New York: Oxford University Press, 1967.

_____. *A Survey of Recent Christian Ethics*. New York: Oxford University Press, 1982.

Niebuhr, Reinhold. *An Interpretation of Christian Ethics*. New York: Merican, 1956.

_____. *Moral Man and Immoral Society*. New York: Charles Scribner's Sons, 1932.

Ramsey, Paul. *Basic Christian Ethics*. New York: Charles Scribner's Sons, 1950.

_____, ed. *Faith and Ethics: The Theology of H. Richard Niebuhr*. New York: Harper & Row, 1957.

Tucker, Rexford. "H. Richard Niebuhr and the Ethics of Responsibility." Ph.D. dissertation, Drew University, 1970.

Wilder, Amos H. *Eschatology and Ethics in the Teachings of Jesus*. New York: Harper & Brothers, 1950.

B. Liberation Theology, All Sources

1. Books

Bennett, John C. The Radical Imperative. Philadelphia: Westminster Press, 1975.

Boesak, Allan Aubrey. Black Theology and Black Power. London: A. R. Mowbray & Co., 1976.

_____. Farewell to Innocence: A Socio-Ethical Study on Black Theology and Black Power. Maryknoll: Orbis, 1977.

Brown, Robert McAfee. Making People in the Global Village. Philadelphia: Westminster, 1981.

_____. Theology in a New Key: Responding to Liberation Themes. Philadelphia: Seabury Press, 1978.

Carmichael, Stokely; and Hamilton, Charles V. The Politics of Liberation in America. New York: Random House, 1967.

Cone, James; and Wilmore, Gayraud, S., ed. Black Theology: A Documentary History, 1966-1979. Maryknoll, N.Y.: Orbis, 1979.

Cone, James H. Black Theology and Black Power. New York: Seabury Press, 1969.

_____. A Black Theology of Liberation. New York: Lippincott, 1970.

_____. God of the Oppressed. New York: Seabury Press, 1975.

_____. My Soul Looks Back. Journeys in Faith Series. Edited by Robert A. Raines. Nashville: Abingdon, 1982.

Dussel, Enrique D. Ethics and the Theology of Liberation. Maryknoll, N.Y.: Orbis Books, 1978.

Goulet, Denis. A New Moral Order: Studies in Development Ethics and Liberation Theology. Maryknoll, N.Y.: Orbis Books, 1974.

Hodgson, Peter C. New Birth of Freedom: A Theology of Bondage and Liberation. Philadelphia: Fortress Press, 1976.

Jones, Major J. Christian Ethics for Black Theology. Nashville: Abingdon Press, 1974.

Jones, William. Is God a White Racist?" Preamble to Black Theology. New York: Doubleday, 1973.

Lincoln, C. Eric. *The Black Experience in Religion: A Book of Readings*. Garden City, N.Y.: Anchor Press/Doubleday, 1974.

_____, ed. *Is Anybody Listening to Black America?* New York: Seabury Press, 1968.

McFadden, Thomas. *Liberation, Revolution and Freedom: Theological Perspectives*. New York: Seabury Press, 1975.

Miguez Bonino, Jose. *Bonhoeffer*. Buenos Aires: Federation Mundial Christiana de Estudiantes, 1965.

_____. *Christ and the Younger Churches: Theological Contributions from Asia, Africa and Latin America*. London: SPCK, 1972.

_____. *Christians and Marxists: The Mutual Challenge to Revolution*. Grand Rapids: Eerdmans, 1976.

_____. *Doing Theology in a Revolutionary Situation*. Philadelphia: Fortress Press, 1975.

_____. *Faces of Jesus: Latin American Christologies*. Maryknoll, N. Y.: Orbis Books, 1983.

_____. *La fe in Busca de Eficacia: Una Interpretacion de la Reflexion Teologia Latina Americana de Liberacion*. Salamania, Edicones Siqueme, 1977.

_____. *The Historical Spectrum of Protestantism in Latin America: Historical Expressions*. Davenport: Latin American Bureau Program Office, 1967.

_____. *Polemica, Dialogo y Mision: Catholicismo Romano y Protestantisms en la America Latino*. Montevideo: Centro de Estudios Cristianos, 1966.

_____. *Room to be People: An Interpretation of the Bible for Today's World*. Geneva: World Council of Churches, 1979.

_____. *Toward a Christian Political Ethics*. Philadelphia: Fortress Press, 1983.

Ruether, Rosemary Radford. *Disputed Questions on Being a Christian*. Nashville: Abingdon, 1982.

_____. *Religion and Sexism: Images of Women in the Jewish and Christian Tradition*. New York: Simon & Schuster, 1974.

_____. *Sexism and God Talk: Toward a Feminist Theology*. Boston: Beacon Press, 1983.

_____. To Change the World: Christology and Cultural Criticism. New York: Crossroad, 1981.

_____ and Keller, Rosemary Skinner, eds. Women and Religion in America. San Francisco: Harper & Row, 1981.

Russell, Letty M. Becoming Human. Library of Christian Faith. Philadelphia: Westminster Press, 1982.

_____. Human Liberation in a Feminist Perspective: A Theology. Philadelphia: Westminster Press, 1974.

Segundo, Juan Luis. Liberation of Theology. Mary Knoll, N. Y.: Orbis Books, 1978.

Swomley, John M. Jr. Liberation Ethics. New York: Macmillan, 1972.

Wall, James M., ed. Theologians in Transition. New York: Crossroad, 1981.

West, Cornel; Cookley, Margaret; and Guidote, Coridad, eds. Theology in the Americas: Detroit II Conference Papers. Maryknoll, N.Y.: Orbis Books, 1982.

2. Articles

Cone, James H. "Biblical Revelation and Social Existence." Interpretation 28 (October, 1974):422-440.

_____. "Black Theology and Ideology: A Response to My Respondents." Union Seminary Quarterly Review 31 (Fall, 1975):71-86.

_____. "Black Theology on Revolution, Violence and Reconciliation." Union Seminary Quarterly Review 31 (Fall, 1975):5-14.

_____. "Content and Method of Black Theology." Journal of Religious Thought 32 (Fall/Winter, 1975):90-103.

_____. "Sanctification, Liberation and Black Worship." Theology Today 35 (July, 1978):139-152.

_____. "Social Context of Theology: Freedom, History and Hope." Risk 9, No. 2 (1973):13-24.

Jones, William. "Theodicy and Methodology in Black Theology: A Critique of Washington, Cone and Cleage." Harvard Theological Review 64 (October, 1971):541-557.

Miguez Bonino, Jose. "Christian Unity in Search of Locality." Journal of Ecumenical Studies 6 (Spring, 1969):185-199.

_____. "The Church and the Latin American Social Revolution." Perspective 9 (Fall, 1968):213-232.

_____. "Doing Theology in the Context of the Struggles of the Poor." Mid Stream 20 (October, 1981):369-373.

_____. "Protestantism's Contribution to Latin America." The Lutheran Quarterly 22 (February, 1970):92-98.

_____. "Struggle of the Poor and the Church." The Ecumenical Review 27 (January, 1975):36-43.

_____. "Violence and Liberation." Christianity and Crisis 32 (July 10, 1972):169-172.

_____. "Vocacion y Mision de la Christianos in America Latina en la Decada de los Ochentos." Christianisims Soc 20, No. 3 (1982):7-14.

Munro, Winsome. Review of Sexism and God Talk: Toward A Feminist Theology, by Rosemary Ruether. Religious Educator (Fall, 1983).

O'Connor, June. "Process Theology and Liberation Theology: Theological and Ethical Reflection." Horizons 7 (Fall, 1980):231-247.

Oglesby, E. H. "Ethical and Educational Implications of Black Theology in America." Religious Education 69 (July-August, 1974):403-412.

Ruether, Rosemary Radford. "Augustine and Christian Political Theology." Interpretation 29 (July, 1975):252-265.

_____. "Crisis in Sex and Race: Black Theology vs. Feminist Theology." Christianity and Crisis 34 (April 15, 1974):67-73. (Replies by C. Anderson and others, and Rejoiner in 34 (June 24, 1974):139-143.

_____. "Monks and Marxists: A Look at the Catholic Left." Christianity and Crisis 33 (April 30, 1973):75-79.

_____. "Outlines for a Theology of Liberation." Dialog 11 (Autumn, 1972):252-257.

_____. Review of A Black Theology of Liberation, by James Cone. The Journal of Religious Thought 28, No. 1 (Spring-Summer, 1971).

_____. "Sexism and the Theology of Liberation: Nature, Fall and Salvation as Seen from the Experience of Women." *Drew Gateway* XLIII (Spring, 1973):138-148.

_____. "What is the Task of Theology?" *Christianity and Crisis* 36 (May 24, 1976):121-125.

Ryan, Michael D. "Liberation Theology: Implications for Christian-Jewish Relations." Drew University, Madison, N.J., February, 1981 (Mimeographed).

Williams, P. N. "James Cone and the Problem of a Black Ethic." *Harvard Theological Review* 65 (October, 1972):493-494.

Wilmore, Gayraud S. Review of *A Black Theology of Liberation* by James Cone. *Union Seminary Quarterly Review* 26, No. 4 (Summer, 1971).

C. Ethics That Reject Accommodation to the World (Evangelical Perfectionism)

1. Books

Campbell, Will D. *Brother to a Dragonfly*. New York: Seabury Press, 1977.

_____. *Cecilia's Sin*. With an historical introduction by Eric Gritsch. Macon: Mercer University Press, 1983.

_____. *The Failure and the Hope: Essays of Southern Churchmen*. Grand Rapids: Eerdmans, 1972.

_____. *Forty Acres and a Goat*. San Francisco: Harper & Row, 1986.

_____. *The Glad River*. New York: Holt, Rinehart & Winston, 1982.

_____. *Race and Renewal of the Church*. Philadelphia: Westminster Press, 1962.

_____; Leonard, Walter; and Eaker, Robert. *Retrospect: Twenty-Five Years of School Desegregation*. Murfreesboro: Middle Tenn. State University, 1979.

_____ and Holloway, James Y. *Up to Our Steeples in Politics*. New York: Paulist Press, 1970.

Connelly, Thomas Lawrence. *Will Campbell and the Soul of the South*. New York: Continuum, 1982.

Stringfellow, William. Conscience and Obedience: The Politics of Romans 13 and Revelation 13 in Light of the Second Coming. Waco: Word, 1977.

_____. Count it all Joy: Reflections on Faith, Doubt and Temptation Seen Through the Letter of James. Grand Rapids: Eerdmans, 1967.

_____. Dissenter in a Great Society: A Christian View of America in Crisis. New York: Holt, Rinehart & Winston, 1966.

_____. An Ethic for Christians and Other Aliens in a Strange Land. Waco: Word, 1976.

_____. Free in Obedience. New York: Seabury Press, 1964.

_____. Imposters of God: Inquiries into Favorite Idols. Dayton: G. A. Pflaum, 1969.

_____. My People is the Enemy. An Autobiographical Polemic. New York: Holt, Rinehart & Winston, 1964.

_____. A Private and Public Faith. Grand Rapids: Eerdmans, 1965.

Wallis, Jim. The Call to Conversion: Recovering the Gospel for These Times. New York: Harper & Row, 1981.

Yoder, John H. The Politics of Jesus: Vicit Agnus Noster. Grand Rapids: Eerdmans, 1972.

2. Articles

Campbell, Will D. and Holloway, James Y. "Can There be a Crusade for Christ?" Katallagete (Summer, 1973):2-6.

_____ and Holloway, James Y. "The Good News from God in Jesus is Freedom to the Prisoners." Katallegete (Winter/Spring, 1972):2-5.

_____. "Law and Love in Lowndes." Katallegete (1965-II):11-14.

_____. "Repentance and Politics I: Milestones Into Millstones." Katallegete (Winter, 1966-67):2-4.

_____. "The Role of Religious Organizations in the Desegregation Controversy." Union Seminary Quarterly Review 16 (January, 1961):187-96.

_____. "The Sit-Ins: Passive Resistance or Civil Disobedience?" Social Action 27 (January, 1961):14-18.

_____. "Vocation as Grace." Katallegete (Fall-Winter, 1972): 80-86.

_____. "The World of the Redneck." Katallegete V (Spring, 1974):34-40.

Grose, Lavern K. Review of Free in Obedience by William Stringfellow. Lutheran World 15, No. 1 (1968).

Knudsen, J. "Mr. Stringfellow and the Great Society." Dialog 6 (Winter, 1967):59-60.

Praft, John M. Review of Dissenter in a Great Society by William Stringfellow. Union Seminary Quarterly Review 22 (November, 1966).

Stringfellow, William. "Bible and Ideology: The Vitality of the Word of God in the World." Sojourners 5 (September, 1976): 6-7.

_____. "The Great Society as a Myth." Dialog 5 (Autumn, 1966): 252-257.

_____. "Justification, The Consumption Ethic and Vocational Poverty." Christianity and Crisis 36 (April 12, 1976):74-79.

_____. "A Matter of Repentance (The United States in 1980)." Christianity and Crisis 39 (July 21, 1980):341-342.

_____; Moore, Arthur J.; Young, Pete; and Stiles, B.J. "The Steeple in Perspective: Four Views." Christianity and Crisis 27 (July 10, 1967):165-166.

*Note: The journals Sojourners and Katallegete have been utilized extensively, as they are both dedicated to "Ethics Opposing Accomodation to the World" (Evangelical Perfectionism).

D. Ethics of Character and Virtue

1. Books

Beauchamp, Tom L. and Childress, James. Principles of Biomedical Ethics. New York: Oxford University Press, 1979.

Gustafson, James. Can Ethics be Christian? Chicago: University of Chicago Press, 1975.

_____. *Christ and the Moral Life*. New York: Harper & Row, 1968.

_____. *Christian Ethics and the Community*. Philadelphia: Pilgrim Press, 1971.

_____. *The Church as Moral Decision Maker*. Philadelphia: Pilgrim Press, 1970.

_____. *Ethics from a Theocentric Perspective*. Vol. I: *Theology and Ethics*. Chicago: University of Chicago Press, 1981. Vol. II: *Ethics and Theology*. Chicago: University of Chicago Press, 1984.

_____. *On Being Responsible: Issues in Personal Ethics*. New York: Harper & Row, 1968.

_____. *Theology and Christian Ethics*. Philadelphia: Pilgrim Press, 1974.

_____. *Theology and Ethics*. Oxford: Oxford University Press, 1981.

_____. *Treasure in Earthen Vessels: The Church as a Human Community*. Chicago: University of Chicago Press, 1976. Midway Reprint.

Hauerwas, Stanley. *Character and the Christian Life: A Study in Theological Ethics*. San Antonio: Trinity University Press, 1975.

_____. *A Community of Character: Toward a Constructive Social Ethic*. Notre Dame: University of Notre Dame Press, 1981.

_____. *Revisions, Changing Perspectives in Moral Philosophy*. Notre Dame: University of Notre Dame Press, 1983.

_____. *Vision and Virtue: Essays in Christian Ethical Reflection*. Notre Dame: University of Notre Dame Press, 1974.

2. Articles

Gustafson, James M. "A Theocentric Interpretation of Life: How My Mind Has Changed." *Christian Century* 97 (July 30-August 5, 1980).

Hauerwas, Stanley and Willimon, William H. "Embarassed by God's Presence." *The Christian Century* 104, No. 4 (January 30, 1985).

_____. "Self as Story: Religion and Morality from the Agent's Perspective." *Journal of Religious Ethics* 1 (Fall, 1973): 73-85.

CONTEMPORARY EXISTENTIALISM

This new series is to consist of specialized studies of alternative extrapolations of existential thought — extensions of basic principles of existentialism relative to epistemological, scientific, phenomenological, ethical, and religious applications. The studies will present contemporary findings relative to broader regions of philosophy, showing that existentialism has implications relevant to a notable variety of issues in contemporary thinking.

The series editor is:
Howard A. Slaatte
Department of Philosophy
Marshall University
Huntington, WV 25701

Slaatte, Howard A.

TIME, EXISTENCE AND DESTINY
Nicholas Berdyaev's Philosophy of Time

New York, Bern, Frankfurt/M., Paris, 1988. Contemporary Existentialism. Vol. 1
General Editor: Prof. Dr. Howard A. Slaatte
ISBN 0-8204-0655-4   201 pages   hardback US $ 38.50/sFr. 54.00

Recommended prices – alterations reserved

This book explicates a Christian existentialist and personalistic philosophy of time, its meaning and implications for human destiny. Chronos or common time is given a qualitative intensity in kairos or time confronted by eternity in the present moment. This gives special meaning to destiny, for it gives a special dimension to eschaton or the end-time, which is somewhat futuristic but also destiny-making as fulfilled time. Both personal life and history are charged with special depths of significance thru kairos and eschaton.

Contents: Whereas most books based on the philosophy of Nicholas Berdyaev dwell on his strong ethical theories and spiritual metaphysics this book dwells on the undergirding views of time and eschatology, a basic framework.
«He treats the basic questions with insight and forceful defense, and few writers provide a better introduction to the thought of the great thinkers such as Berdyaev, Kierkegaard, and Tillich.» (Joseph B. Mow, West Virginia Wesleyan College)
«A book by Dr. Slaatte is always a *very important event.* In this rapid, fast changing world where superficial books are produced wholesale, his books are always as important as they are challenging. In this he reminds us of Toynbee. The secret of his amazing creativity actually involves two significant factors. While, on the one hand, he aims at truth by means of that synoptic method which tries to see all the relevant facts and their relationships, on the other hand, he maintains that same sense of balance which is so necessary in our fast changing world.» (Arthur W. Munk, Professor Emeritus, Albion College)

PETER LANG PUBLISHING, INC.
62 West 45th Street
USA – New York, NY 10036